We'd Like to do a Number Now

TED TAYLER

CEPIA BOOKS

Published by Cepia Books, Bath.

ISBN 978-1-908016-09-6

Typeset in Bell MT by Cepia Books, Bath.

Printed and bound in the UK by Imprint digital, Exeter.

Cepia Books
19 Garstons
Bathford
Bath
BA1 7TE

www.cepiabooks.co.uk

Acknowledgements

The Granary Club. The Rock Years 1969 to 1988 by Al Read. Broadcast Books 2003 (after so many years it was difficult to remember where & when we played here and who with, so thanks Al for filling in the gaps – Ted)

My late father, for one pearl of wisdom:- 'Drink and women don't mix, son'

My mother, for saying 'Goodnight' every single time I climbed the stairs after getting home from a gig, no matter what time it was.

For the most important people in my life, my family.

1. Seasons in the Sun

Where did this journey begin?

It was the early 1950s and our little crescent of sixteen council houses had the usual mix of working class and aspiring lower middle class families. Nearly all of them had kids of varying gender and ages and we played together all the time.

My childhood was mostly spent outdoors in the sunshine, or in the wind and rain depending on the season. Indoors was only allowed if Dad was working the day shift at the Avon India Rubber Company, known locally as 'The Avon'.

We played football and cricket on the large green, then later doctors and nurses in the long grass on the other side of the road which circled the playing area. Future generations were denied the latter as the council built garages when the number of families with cars increased. Of course now the present generation, obese and square eyed, are denied any activity on the grass, definitely no ball games. There are vandalised trees on the small patch of grass that remains and parking spaces for people too lazy to walk four hundred yards into town from the neighbouring estates, who drive in and park up free for an hour or two while they pootle into town to those shops that haven't closed down. Happy days.

We played football matches with boys from six to twenty six years, using jumpers as goal posts and parents watching from their front doorsteps. Couples walked past into town, the chap kicking the ball back if required

1

and ribald comments being passed between the older lads. We didn't always understand what was being said but we laughed anyway. It was a camaraderie that was innocent and okay then – and it was also okay for the ball to be hoofed way off the pitch towards the top of the road leading into the crescent as a pretty girl or, Praise the Lord, two or three girls, came into view.

It was usually one of the more mature lads that managed to do this and the youngest boy who was sent to fetch the ball. While they were scampering away to do their duty the poor girl or girls had to walk past a variety of heavily breathing youths (only partly from the exertions on the football pitch) listening to wolf whistles and lots of other appreciative noises. When I was the youngest, the girls were in white high heeled shoes, stockings with black seams that went who knew where and dresses that were either pencil slim, which made them teeter along with their rear ends moving quite alarmingly, or flouncy with lots of colour and petticoats. Either way the older lads didn't seem to mind.

When I was providing the breather with the big kick up the road it was mini skirts. Then we realised that all too often the dresses had been the better option because far too many of the local girls had tree trunks where their legs should have been. Perhaps we were just unlucky to get a below par batch or more likely, now the garages were built, the really good looking ones were picked up by their boyfriends in their Ford Anglias. Bastards.

The cricket season was always interesting. With a tennis ball the older lads could whack the balls bloody miles. Those parents whose windows were clattered and flowers mangled by retrieving fielders (the youngest again) became disenchanted and retired indoors muttering. Someone came up with the bright idea of using a proper cricket ball in order to limit the distances.

It did that. Also as wicket keeper (aka long stop) I found to my cost, when trying to catch a top edge rather than let it crash into my face, that it was bloody hard! The little finger on my left hand took the brunt of it and broke, curtailing my playing days for a short while and my wicket keeping days, with or without gloves, for eternity.

The first time I remember being able to hold a tune was when I was about eight years old. A couple of lads my age disappeared on Friday evenings to Cub Scouts. But I wasn't keen on the old Scoutmaster, he was the real deal, not one of the ones you read about in the Sunday papers, but he scared me to death.

Then one Tuesday evening several of my friends went off somewhere leaving me on my own again so I went home. Dad was asleep in the chair. We had no telly in those days and the Home Service (now Radio 4) and Mum combined had been enough to send him to sleep, plus the twelve hour shift he'd just finished. Mum asked why I was back so early and when I told her she said she thought my friends had probably gone to choir practice at St Michael's. She checked with the neighbours and, sure enough, Tuesday and Thursday evenings were choir practice nights. The following week I was scrubbed up and told to mind my manners and off I went with my pals at half past six on the Thursday to be put through my paces by the choirmaster.

Mr Taylor, the choirmaster, worked for a local solicitor until he was well into his late 70s and was still about in sheltered accommodation last time I heard. But back in 1953 he was a dapper little man not much taller than us lads. He sat on a cushion to play the organ which also helped him slide from end to end of his seat to reach the various pedals and stops. It was quite a performance, but the choir and the screen behind the stalls meant not many were privy to it every Sunday like we were.

3

After a few tentative notes on the tonic solfa, he pronounced me adequate for the trebles and so I joined up. I stayed throughout the rest of my childhood, surviving the awkward transitional stage with the squawking and embarrassing odd bum note, developing into an amusing little bass wine of reasonable vintage.

The choir was Mr Taylor's pride and joy. We sang in Salisbury Cathedral at Evensong when the Cathedral School choristers were on summer holiday and I was given the odd solo at Christmas in St Michael's both as a treble and a bass. After my confirmation I became a server at Holy Communion and even contemplated entering the Church while I was in my A level year at High School. This was not due to any real fire in my belly for religion, more that everyone else seemed to be getting their leg over but me. I had fallen head over heels for a girl called Megan, who was not in the slightest bit interested in me, so I was resigned to being the only one of my circle of friends to die a virgin. Hence throwing myself into the service of our Lord seemed the only option.

While at school I met Phil, who became our bass player. He was about two years younger than me and we travelled to school on the same bus every day. I was bus 'prefect' and we played cards on the back seat with a couple of lads from his year. Brag was our weapon of choice and we cleaned up, somehow contriving a dubious method of winning significantly more hands than they did, although forty years on I can't remember how for the life of me. If I could then Poker Million would be occupying my time and not this storytelling lark.

Both of these lads became 'hard cases' around the age of seventeen, always in scuffles on a weekend night, with or without the aid of alcohol. Whether this was a reaction to the lessons they had learned from us, or maybe it was just in their genes, we'll never know I

4

guess, I was just thankful they never came looking for retribution.

Phil was an enigma in many ways. He was fairly tall, not conventionally good looking, slightly plump and tended to suffer from 'duck's disease' when he walked. But he had more women than you've had hot dinners. I sometimes went out with them first but that's another story. He was surprisingly quick on his feet too for his build - on the school photo for 1962 he appeared twice. Often done I know, but it wasn't spotted until some time after everyone had taken their copies home. As the camera panned round he leapt down from the gym benches used to elevate the back row and legged it to the far end where he was helped up into a new position, ever so slightly blurred three from the end of the top row of grinning fifth years.

We became firm friends, although the musical side never surfaced initially. We met in the lunch hour and chatted in a corridor midway between his classroom and my sixth form study. There was a large radiator with a metal cover which meant it was a warm spot to hang out by during the winter months. As our interest in the same type of music was uncovered it became a regular meeting place to reprise some song or other from Radio Luxembourg with me singing the lyrics and Phil playing 'air guitar' with accompanying sound effects. The drums were readily available of course, the radiator taking a hammering with the only drawback being the Staff Room, which was about ten yards away. When we heard the door opening, and approaching feet, we legged it along the corridor and down the stairs into the playground. That's if we heard anything above the din we were making, when we didn't, we got a bollocking or a detention.

Still, the seeds were sown. Out of school and into the summer holidays in 1962 we started to meet up at Phil's with a couple of other local lads. Just friends from the youth club really. Phil and his parents lived in a prefab about a quarter of a mile from my house. If I tell you his Dad was called 'Jumbo' and his Mum was built in similar fashion it tells you all you need to know. The house was like an oven in the summer and a freezer in the winter.

Jumbo was an unforgettable character. He had a dry sense of humour. He never saw us play and was a tad dismissive regarding any successes we had, yet I sensed he was chuffed to bits really when our efforts paid off. He was working at the Avon too, although because of his wife's health he was on permanent days.

One summer evening I went round looking for Phil when the band was in its formative stage and Jumbo was working in his garden.

'Good evening Mr Wheeler, is Phil in?'

Jumbo leant on his fork and searched for the answer.

'No. He's gone to Trowbridge.'

'Oh, gone to Trowbridge has he?' I said not aware he was going anywhere, having left him only a couple of hours before.

'I don't know where he's gone, how would I know, he never tells me where he's going'.

I gave up and went to walk home.

'Off you go then Teddy' he called, 'that's OK I'll just do this weeding on my own as usual.'

Jumbo never did anything in a hurry. He walked to work, with his bag over his shoulder, the strap across his ample chest. A couple of years after the garden incident I was updating our 'roadie' who worked in the same department as Jumbo, on the latest gigs our agency had phoned through. Jumbo strolled in at eight minutes past two, clearly late back from lunch. The foreman spotted him and as Jumbo continued to amble slowly across the shop to his work place, moved to intercept. He said,

'Jumbo. You're late. What kept you?'

Jumbo never broke stride and, as he passed the bewildered supervisor, he said,

'Strong headwind.'

Chris, our roadie and I fell about laughing, it was Jumbo to a T. The foreman recovered his composure and shook his head with a smile. I doubt very much if Jumbo was docked a quarter of an hour's pay for bad timekeeping that day. He was worth his weight in gold.

Just to show you what a creature of habit he was. He got up every morning at five a.m. and took his wife a pot of tea before he got his lunch box ready and washed and went to work for six. When he died suddenly one day in the late 1960s Phil said the doctor was flummoxed. The autopsy reckoned the time of death was no later than four a.m. Phil had got up when his Mum called out at about six fifteen. She had not had her pot of tea in bed. She had drifted back to sleep and hadn't heard Jumbo in the bathroom or heard him come in to get dressed.

Phil found his Dad dead on the kitchen floor. The teapot was on the tray. The tea was inside. The sandwiches were in the lunchbox and his thermos was filled with hot sweet tea for his morning shift.

The doctor said to Phil,

'We don't know everything about the human body and mind Philip. Perhaps he did indeed suffer a massive heart attack at four a.m. but he got up at five to do what he always did. I haven't got a logical explanation for it.'

Spooky - or maybe just one more instance of Jumbo's special character.

2. Absolute Beginners

Phil and I passed many a lunchtime drumming on the radiator cover and singing popular songs from the charts. Meanwhile back in Melksham, there were our mates, Ian, little Roger and Brian who attended the youth club, all dead keen but by and large, as we found out during that summer of '62, with no talent for playing an instrument whatsoever.

We bought a drum kit off retired band leader Tom Silk for a fiver. He was about seventy at the time and had played with the Silkworms. His kit had seen better days and had probably been in his shed since the end of the war. He had an oversized bass drum, a high hat and a snare drum. What attracted us to the kit wasn't the single crash cymbal which sat jauntily to one side, but what looked like four shrunken heads attached to the bass drum, which when struck with sticks (which we had to purchase ourselves as Tom didn't have any) turned out to be made of wood - major disappointment, as was the sound really. The first practice session we had in the youth club ended up with the snare drum being knackered and, despite painting them up in garish colours one Sunday afternoon, the skulls were ditched in my Dad's shed, in preparation for the next war. So all in all we appeared to be doomed to failure.

Phil had got his brand spanking new bass guitar from a music shop in Bath and was working his way through Bert Weedon's 'Teach Yourself How To Play' book.

However he was on the quiet side with no amplification at this stage. In the early days this was a blessing.

At least he was prepared to save up his pennies and buy a guitar in the proper manner. The shop in question was Duck Son and Pinker's and as the Sixties wore on, all sorts of people gravitated there on Saturdays. A lot of local groups sprang up as the Beatles and Stones etcetera achieved lift off. Most of them dropped in and swapped 'war stories' about gigs, agencies, the pros and cons of various bits of kit and all the usual. Some of it was bullshit, of course, it had to be or about fifty Bath bands would have been on the verge of signing a mega recording contract that autumn.

We knew a lad called Chris from town who was a bit of a loner but hung around with us from time to time. He came along to some of our early practices, mainly because he lived just over the road and could hear the racket from the youth club. He had a fairly expensive guitar and was a passable rhythm guitarist and offered his services to add a little 'pudding' as he called it to our sound. Phil asked him where he had bought his guitar. Chris grinned.

'I never bought it, couldn't afford it matey. I bought a guitar case in there about a month ago, then went back in with it last Saturday morning. It was packed with lads nattering and jamming and the staff were all tied up with customers as usual, so I got this one off the wall. Plugged into an amp and joined in with the rest, picking up a few tips from a couple of Bath lads who were far better than me. When they had got fed up they put their guitars back on the wall and I put this in my case.'

'I got another one down and played with that for a while, then one of the staff came over and asked if he could be of assistance. I said I was just looking really, what I had come in for was to get someone to check the pick-ups on my guitar but as it was so busy I had to catch

10

my bus back to Melksham. Not to worry I'd be back in next Saturday. Then I picked up my case and walked out.'

As I said he was a strange lad and we weren't in the market for a rhythm guitarist anyway so we gave him a miss.

About three months later we heard a rumour that someone had gone into the same shop on a Saturday morning with a Vox amplifier and asked if it could be repaired. They never did anything on the premises, so it was labelled up and he walked out with a similar item as he said he needed it to continue gigging. When it was looked at in the workshop they found an empty cabinet with some weights added to compensate for the innards. Needless to say the staff were given a bollocking, casual Saturday staff were given training and systems were put in place to prevent further incidents. Who was the guy looking to get his amp repaired I hear you ask? I've got a pretty good idea, haven't you?

As that summer of '62 drew to a close we had seen a couple of 'likely lads' fall by the wayside. As I said they were mates but not musical mates. Rumours were mooted at the youth club that there was a lad at the local Secondary Modern who could play the piano. He was the same age as Phil, so we went round to his house to see him.

Merv was close on six foot and today might be classed as potentially 'clinically obese' but he was deceptive. In the summer of '63 Phil and I went to see him run in the school sports - he was entered in the two hundred yards. From the waist down he was an athlete and his long legs went into action at the gun and his upper body weight became irrelevant as he powered round that bend in the lead. I can't remember if he won or not but he impressed the hell out of me,

If you want a comparison, he was built like John Regis, except for the obvious difference in colour they could have been twins.

Merv was another one like Phil as far as the women were concerned. He was not good looking (sorry mate!) but he had a way with words and if he could just get past that first hurdle and get talking to them he was in.

Anyway I'm way ahead of myself. Merv lived with his Mum and Dad and an elder brother 'Our Derek'. I never heard him called anything else in all the years I knew him, nor 'Our Mervyn' of course. His parents were wonderful, a laugh a minute although not always intentionally. But true to the rumours, he could play - boy could he play. He had a piano in the dining room and that was where we worked on our first few numbers.

'We ought to do some jazz numbers' says Merv.

'Fuck off' says Phil, 'Chuck Berry and Bo Diddley.'

'Alright' says Merv. 'Do you have any equipment? What about a drummer? How would we get any bookings? How do you intend to get there? They'd need to have a piano or we'd be stuffed.'

Naturally we hadn't thought this through in any detail. In fact we hadn't thought this through at all. It was the early Sixties, groups were springing up all over the place and we probably imagined we only needed to get four or five of us together and Brian Epstein, Andrew Loog Oldham or Mickie Most would be in touch.

Clearly we needed to find the right people.

Merv says. 'Are you in the church choir?'

'Yes' I said defensively. I didn't broadcast it too much in case people thought I couldn't hack it as a rhythm and blues singer if I was chanting the Te Deum in my mellifluous bass tones on a Sunday.

'Malcolm and Glyn Phillips are in the choir aren't they?' said Merv, 'their dad runs the garage and Glyn does rally driving. Surely we can get the transport sorted if they come on board.'

The twins had been in the choir for the past couple of years and the family lived in a large house close to the church. The garage their father co-owned had been just across the road until very recently but was now out of town on the Chippenham road.

As I was bound to see them at choir practice, or on the Sunday, I was to see if they were interested in joining us. Malcolm was the sportier of the two brothers and played a lot of football while Glyn was basically a petrol-head and once he hit seventeen he got a souped up Ford Anglia and took to driving like a madman. As far as being in a band was concerned, Malcolm had always fancied playing the drums but never tried and Glyn was not fussy one way or the other.

Despite the unpromising start we got Malcolm along to the youth club for a practice session. Brian and Roger were still in attendance and they gave Malcolm a few of the basics - where to sit, how to hold the sticks, not much more than that because they didn't have a clue either - they were resigned to being backing singers. Sadly we were not in the market for such luxuries and not long after that they stopped coming.

Malcolm was not a natural. He tried hard though and gradually he could hold the beat together long enough for us to get through a number without crashing and burning. Another box ticked. Four confirmed members.

We spent a lot of our spare time watching other bands at gigs in the youth clubs around town and trying to pick up hints on how best to get ourselves started. One band in Westbury, Dave and the Druids, had been going for a while. I can't remember now whether they were splitting up or just buying new kit but Dave (the singer) had an amplifier and mike for sale for about fifteen quid so we all chipped in and the deal was done.

13

We were now the proud owners of an old Vox AC30 amp, one mike and one crappy drum kit! Phil had his bass guitar so he and I shared the amp for bass and vocals. We also had a piano - well it was the one on the stage at the youth club, not ours, except when we were practising there. We were a little light in the kit department it has to be said, but things were to change pretty rapidly.

Enter Martin Ricketts. He was the bloke who told us about Dave Smith having some kit for sale. He was maybe thirty, worked in one of the local factories, unmarried and lived at home with his Mum. Not obvious pop impresario background admittedly. Martin spent a lot of his spare time driving around watching groups play in youth clubs, working men's clubs and village halls – in fact anywhere and everywhere. He knew everybody.

After the success on the amplifier front we asked him to come along and have a listen to us and assess our progress.

'You need a guitarist, plus a mike for your piano and you need to do something about that drum kit.' All constructive stuff so far ... 'You're crap at the minute. Why don't you learn some stuff out of the Top Ten?'

Everyone's a critic! We went to Duck Son and Pinker's on the Saturday morning and bought another mike. Another seven pounds well spent we thought. Malcolm had his eyes on a drum kit but no way were we going to shell out fifty quid and anyway he had to get back as he was playing football for Melksham in the afternoon.

Martin found us a guitar player in a local village. We all piled into Glyn's car, rally type bucket seats and room in the back for a small toddler. Once we had performed contortions getting out of the back of the car, Phil and I followed Merv up the path to the side door of the house. After a brief conversation with an elderly gentleman,

14

who turned out not to be the rhythm guitarist we were seeking but his father, we were introduced to Gerry. He was slight, with rather long and unkempt sandy hair and had a laid back country boy personality. As teenagers from Broughton Gifford went he was about as good as we were going to get.

He was not in a group at present, but had his own kit and was up for trying out with us at our next scheduled practice at the youth club. All things being equal we were five and ready to rock and roll. I had reservations about someone wearing a Beatle jacket with a velvet collar but I was fed up with waiting for that first live gig.

The next few practices saw a steady increase in the number of completed songs for our repertoire. Gerry gave an extra dimension to our sound, filling it out and also providing some raucous supporting vocals. He wanted a solo of his own and, hey presto, into our song list went 'Boys' from the early Beatles' collection. Merv's skill on the piano persuaded us to add 'Whole Lotta Shakin' by Jerry Lee Lewis and he shared vocals with me on that number. Gradually the set took shape. The last two mentioned plus a load of Chuck and Bo meant that with a following wind we could play for about forty five minutes at a push.

We carried on playing through our set in what Martin thought was the optimum order, continually testing how long it would last and whether any really weak songs needed knocking on the head. He came to us one Saturday afternoon in September '63 to say we were booked to support a local band at the youth club on a Friday night in two weeks time.

'Does this mean you are our manager now then?' I asked.

As nobody could see Messrs Epstein, Oldham or Most in the vicinity Martin was clearly going to have to do.

Malcolm had persevered with the clapped out drum kit but enough was enough. We had to bite the bullet and find a way to finance the new one he had had his eye on in Duck Son and Pinker's all those weeks ago. How we did it now I can't for the life of me remember, it must have been legal but heaven knows who signed the hire purchase agreement, or stumped up the deposit. At any rate he had his kit and it put the rest of us to shame.

He took a while to get used to having a decent set of drums and cymbals, particularly the side drum, because he had had nothing on the right hand side of him for the past four or five months and it took ages for us to persuade him to actually hit the bloody thing. This period of adjustment was longer than the two weeks before our first gigs.

Did I say gigs? Yes indeed, Martin was on a roll. The local cinema had closed down a couple of years before. A familiar story it has to be said. The local worthies had decreed that kids needed entertaining on Saturday mornings at least and the Assembly Hall was opened for a couple of hours for a staple diet of cartoons, main feature and a local pop group to close the morning's fun with about half an hour's music. We were booked in for the Saturday around lunchtime immediately following our world premiere at the youth club on Friday night.

Were we nervous in the days prior to that first live performance in front of real punters instead of our manager, and mates who had not survived the savage vetting programme? You bet we were. I knew the lyrics to all the songs we were going to do backwards. As the day loomed ever closer it was the only way I could remember them!

The only thing that remained was to decide on a name for the band. Martin came up with some real duffers - so bad I can't remember many of them. I had just finished school and my A Level History had taught me about some bloke called Earl Jellacic and the Croats in the nineteenth century. You look him up, I can't be arsed. As a last resort, after discarding 'Brown Mouth' or 'Through A Glass Darkly' which were suggested by some older mates who spent a lot of time drinking in the local hostelries, in exasperation I suggested the Croats.

Martin was not over enthusiastic. He argued that people would struggle to pronounce it properly. The 'oa' was likely to be confused with 'throat' or 'boat' sounds and if we didn't go down well we might find we became known as The Scrotes. If we'd ignored him and gone for that from the start we might have been the first punk band in the world - sadly I was persuaded 'The Croats' was too ambiguous and the practice session ended with us no further forward on the identity front.

How wrong can you be? Martin had acquired an old Bedford van, in a fetching cream colour, which he parked in a lot at the rear of Malcolm and Glyn's dads' garage. This transport was going to be essential for our out of town bookings, not that we had any when Martin snapped up the bargain but our local impresario planned ahead!

I was walking through the Market Place on the following Monday evening when I saw the van. It came around the roundabout from the direction of the youth club, coughing and spluttering as usual, making its way down the main drag through town. As it passed by I made to wave at Martin, who was driving, but I lowered my hand and pretended I hadn't seen him as the van's side view presented itself and I, and several others either waiting at the bus stop, or passing by saw the band's name for the first time. Martin had drilled a series of holes in the ceiling of the van and attached a wooden frame which had four light bulbs inside. These illuminated the perspex side panels on which, in flowing script, he had painted "The Krowats".

17

At last the fateful day arrived - our first live performance in front of paying customers, sharing the stage with another group of young hopefuls. Whoa! Stop there. The first job we were faced with when we got to the youth club, bright and early, was to help lug the piano off the stage and onto the floor to the front and right hand side. This blocked off the doorway to a side room that was to serve as changing room for the two bands, which could also be accessed from the stage. The other group were only a four piece, three guitars and a drummer and no longer young hopefuls. They were a group we had seen several times in venues around the town and surrounding villages playing covers of 'The Shadows' and 'The Ventures' plus the usual rock and roll standards.

Undaunted, we fetched our kit from the store cupboard and set up. When the sound check was completed we bought bottles of Coca Cola and sat in the changing room to await our fate. We had no real feeling for what was going on in the main hall as we were shut away in splendid isolation. The realisation that there were a lot of people in to watch our debut came when John, the youth leader, came into the room to confirm playing times. He was smiling. Normally a rather dour Yorkshireman, he was pleased with the number of tickets being sold on the door and couldn't contain his glee —and the noise behind John as he framed the doorway was unusually loud.

'You must be better than I thought" he said "if all this lot want to hear you.'

Martin had already warned him not to expect too long a set as our play list was still in the embryonic stage. John was happy enough for us to play for forty five to fifty minutes to 'warm the audience up' as he put it. He had a record deck to fill in for a quarter of an hour while the other band got themselves prepared, then they would cover the rest of the evening with another record break somewhere in the middle.

Nervously we made our way into the hall and took our places. I had borrowed a pair of dark glasses to help portray a cool image, they also prevented the audience from seeing the fear in my eyes. It was just as well, John had turned the spotlight over the dartboard round to face our corner and it was shining straight in my face.

The reception was mixed, all our mates were in and we could hear their encouraging noises, but several non-believers were also about and despite my efforts to block them out I could hear them jeering and running us down even before we struck the first chord.

Somewhere in the mists of time there floats a play list, however I don't have much recollection of its content or order. 'Memphis Tennessee', 'Walking The Dog', 'Johnny B Goode', 'Pretty Thing', 'You Can't Judge A Book' plus of course, 'Boys' with Gerry singing and 'Whole Lotta Shaking' with Merv on vocals and frantic keyboard skills. That must have been about half of the songs we played. What else? Fuck knows, I don't remember.

What do I remember of the reaction? Our mates, Ian, Brian and Roger were amazed at the transformation since the early days. The dissenting voices were silenced, although truth be told they may have already walked out if they truly believed we were crap and beyond salvation. One gig down, many hundreds to go.

3. Around and Around

In those early days we were using the youth club for practically everything. As most of us were under eighteen we didn't pay for the hall when we used it for practice so on weekends and holidays we dropped in as often as we needed to. There was a caretaker up the road somewhere but we hardly ever bothered him. We would be in attendance on Friday nights and contrive to slip onto the stage under some pretext or other. Then the back window furthest from the road was left off the latch so we could get in as and when we chose.

We were still rather light on the equipment front so a store cupboard was sufficient as a safe place to stash our kit. Martin was a bit nervous about leaving it in the van. Whether he ever insured it for contents I don't know.

We did borrow the hall keys on occasion to make an official visit, particularly if we were out of town on a Friday and Saturday night. This became more frequent as Martin clocked up the road miles around the West Country adding more and more venues that we could tick off on our 'wish list'.

In those days most youth clubs or working men's clubs closed by half past ten, maybe eleven o'clock at the latest. We were still gigging within a twenty mile radius so we were back to base pretty early. Once we had stacked the kit in the cupboard we risked one light in the main hall, over the football table. Then we stuffed a couple of scarves we had tucked away in the cupboard into the goal mouths. One coin and we were set for a round robin tournament!

I can't remember how many weekends we got away with it. A patrol car pulled up outside on the road one week, not two minutes into the first game, and two boys in blue tapped on the door and invited themselves in.

'Hello lads. What's going on?'

We explained we had keys to get in and drop off our kit. We even opened the store cupboard to confirm to them that we were a group and had indeed been playing in Samuel Salter's Social Club, Trowbridge, that very evening.

'Bit of a dump isn't it?' one of the officers remarked.

'Hardly "Ready Steady Go". You'll be going off home now I expect?'

We agreed! Fortunately, they didn't seem to find it strange that two of us were wearing scarves in late August when we trailed out behind them. They got into the car and with a cheery wave, set off towards the town centre.

We sauntered home and had an early night for a change. A couple of times the patrol car would turn up, although the occupants never came in again. They sat by the kerbside for five or ten minutes, probably having a crafty fag. We took the hint and wrapped up that weekend's tournament without reaching the knockout stages. As the winter months began to draw in the hall got pretty nippy of a Saturday night or early Sunday morning so we knocked it on the head anyway.

All good things come to an end. As the months rolled on and more and more gigs came our way, we splashed out on bigger and better equipment - far too much for the store cupboard and far too loud for the neighbours!

As that first year came to a close we had grown up a lot too and the attractions of the youth club were beginning to fade. It was time to move on to pastures new.

It didn't matter where we went while Martin was our manager. We played at some posh girl's twenty first birthday in a village five miles out of town - in the hallway of her house. It was a big house mind you, the walk from the large front door to the oak panelled staircase would be enough to cause some of the teenagers today to be out of puff. Neither the group nor the couple of dozen guests were allowed upstairs. Mummy and Daddy were quite adamant about that. I must say it spoilt a good party.

We had bags of room in the corner by the stairs and the grub laid on in the drawing room was spiffing, or at least that's what the young chaps told us when they chatted to us in the interval. The young ladies were rather keen on Malcolm.

Phil and Merv put on their best telephone voices but were less successful. Gerry and I knew our place. Posh totty in Wiltshire were not into 'rough trade' in the early Sixties.

We did eventually sample the food - after everyone had devoured the best bits we were allowed a few dry curled up sarnies. After everyone had gone home and we were packing our kit into the van, Daddy took Martin back into the hallway to pay him for our services. He had omitted to tell us we were only getting a lousy two quid, no wonder the money changed hands in secret!

The following Friday a brief report of the celebrations appeared in the Wiltshire Times and Mummy and Daddy provided us with our first review in print. Martin was chuffed to bits until he picked the paper up and found that all it said was 'Music was provided by a new group from Melksham called the Krow Hats!'

'They couldn't even read the sign on the bloody van.' he said, 'We won't do one of those again in a hurry.'

For that money we were inclined to agree with him!

The Dolphin Hall in Tetbury was another place we played, thanks to Martins' trips around the district in his car. It was the venue for a Saturday night hop and we played there a few times, sometimes on our own and a couple of times as the support band. The bloke who was caretaker was a Mr Cooper and he and his wife opened up the hall, sold the tickets, manned the cloakroom, sold soft drinks etcetera. You get the picture. These places wouldn't have existed without people like them. They weren't in it for the money, they just wanted kids to have a good time. The problem was that there were a handful of yobs who wanted to cause trouble. A fight would break out during the evening and Mr Cooper was in there splitting up the protagonists. Out of the door they would go, not to be allowed back in that night at least. He was in his forties and tall and rangy and didn't give the impression of being a particularly strong man but he got the job done.

He was a character too. He had banned drum solos by about the third or fourth time we played there because he reckoned it was this that sparked the fights.

'It's the drums I blame,' he told us, 'it must be something in our past, when we were cavemen like. When some of these young thugs hear the drumming going on and on for five minutes see, it gets them all worked up. And I know for a fact they come here after drinking cider they buy down the offy. The cider plus the drums is a powerful mixture and they just kick off.'

He was convincing enough so we dropped the drum solo – it spared Malcolm the embarrassment anyway. But Mr Cooper wasn't finished. When we were getting ready to go home he came out for a final chat by the van.

'Here,' he said, 'we had some trouble last week look. I had a group in from Bristol and they were good. We had a lot of new kids here too. They must have come from out of town and that upset our lads. They were chatting up their girls and ... you know?'

We knew, Phil was off with one of them now and we began to hope she was of the unattached variety because we had to get the van and ourselves out of Tetbury yet. Mrs Cooper had now joined us, having locked up the hall and continued,

'We thought we were going to need to get the police up here. There were fights all over the place. He couldn't cope with it all.'

Her husband then told us of the final straw, when he thought about packing it all in. He said,

'I got a few of them out. But there was this one lad, he was built like an outhouse and had hands the size of I dunno what and he hit me round the ear. Do you know, he hit me so hard I thought his fist was coming right through the other side of me head!'

Images like that stay with you for ever. A couple with more community spirit than you find in a whole small town today and he was prepared to risk a thumping every Saturday night into the bargain. They don't make them like him anymore, more's the pity.

We were by no means the only group in the town. There were also a couple of small dance bands, but more of how we were involved with them later. The best group by far, not just in town but possibly in the region, was 'Jason and The Argonauts'.

Jason, or Bernie as he was properly known, was either a youth worker, or the oldest teenager who attended the youth club. He had tried to recruit me as lead singer for his former group, based in Westbury. They were called 'Norman and the Invaders'. He'd graduated from the Norman Conquest to Greek Mythology but try as I might I just couldn't cope with being known as Norman, so I had politely declined the offer..

The Argonauts had a fairly standard line up of lead, rhythm, bass guitar and drums. Pat and Ken were on drums and rhythm guitar and they were good looking bastards. Dave was ace on lead guitar and Ivan was very good on bass and had a dry sense of humour when presenting their act. Bernie was a competent lead vocalist who will probably not speak to me again. If you think of Freddie Garrity of 'Freddie and the Dreamers' fame, that is balding with glasses but good with it, then Bernie was your man. They were a pop group but us being rhythm and blues aficionados, we hated them.

They were far far better than we were. Musically, they tended to cover anything from the Top Twenty plus a load of standards. Dave and Ivan were old hands already, having evolved from 'The Footbeats' who had covered all the old rock and roll standards. As with many groups in those days, the time came for a stint in the clubs and US bases in Germany. They had a farewell concert at the youth club and they were off. Professionals all.

This left the home front free and clear for us to exploit. Martin went to work and bookings started pouring in. Again, this is a story I've told friends and family until they're bored shitless, but we played Devizes one week in the summer of sixty five - literally. We played the Rooster Club at the back of the Crown on Sunday, Monday night was the Corn Exchange, Tuesday the 1419 youth club and on Wednesday we were back at the Corn Exchange for a second stint. Thursday was a strange one, it was at a mental institution called Roundway Hospital. No patients were allowed to attend but they had quite a few Irish nurses working there then and a few locals turned up on the door. It boasted a vast dance hall and stage and despite the low turnout we had a great night. Phil had a grin on his face for days. In actual fact we were lucky to get off the premises that night as the night watchman thought we had an inmate in the van with us. Friday night was a posh do at the Town Hall supporting the 'Avon Cities Jazz Band' and Saturday was tucked up in the corner of the Royal Oak, probably the smallest pub in town. So we were up and down Caen Hill in the van all week and Bob's your uncle. I guess it was Carnival week which explained why there were so many gigs going, but Martin got us involved in all of them! Over exposed? You bet, but the money was useful to make our hire purchase payments.

After a three month stint away 'The Argonauts' returned for a brief holiday. We were playing in the youth club on a Saturday afternoon as usual, probably learning a few more numbers. With Gerry in the band we seemed to cover virtually every Kinks' number ever released and the Rolling Stones were good for a new disc every two months or so. We still weren't selling out completely because we didn't do Beatles, Hollies or bands of that ilk.

Our 'heroes' arrived to watch us practice and, as they were no longer falling about laughing, we presumed they could see we had improved somewhat since they had seen us last. We took a break after a while and had a chat about their experiences overseas. They told the usual war stories, loads of travelling, pretty lousy digs and lots of spare time with little money to spend. Nothing changes, with management and agents holding on to the cash for as long as possible in order to keep the 'inmates' on their toes.

Ivan was supportive of our attempts to follow in their footsteps, remarking how much better we sounded. He also had an interesting philosophy, regarding why lads like us should form a group in the first place. He said,

'There's one thing you're never short of in a group, and that's that!'

The last three words were embellished with a swift movement where he bent his left elbow immediately after he had placed his right hand on his left bicep. This was very reassuring for Malcolm and Mervyn and me, who were all some way behind Phil in the 'groupie' stakes. Gerry was a country boy and we had to explain what the visual aid had been about.

'Oh, good oh!' he muttered.

Dave was chatting to Phil and Gerry about guitars and amplifiers. Pat and Bernie didn't really offer very much to the conversation except to wish us all the best and then they made to leave, but good old Ken had to have the last word. He was good looking and he knew it, always a bit of a poser, and he wanted to make sure we knew how well they were doing now they were professional.

'I bought a new motorbike this morning,' he said as he was leaving the hall.

'How much?' asked Phil.

'A hundred and fifty notes.' Ken said then, just as he passed through the doorway, 'Cash.'

It was that more than anything that determined I was going to be a Mod.

4. Blue Moon

Only a very small percentage make the transition from young hopefuls into superstars. This was true in the Sixties and it's still true today, although when you watch the 'talent' shows on television you get the feeling that the vast majority of the contestants believe it's their God given right to have a hit record. Back when we first put ourselves in the firing line of the world and his wife (viz. the critics) there were loads of bands starting up following in the footsteps of The Beatles and The Stones. We knew the odds were stacked against us.

Some people though are beyond help. Others don't even realise they have an untapped goldmine of talent. If this is confusing, let me give you a couple of examples. On several occasions Martin got us gigs in and around Cam and Dursley, in Gloucestershire. One of the earliest was in a youth club in Cam on a Friday night. I guess it was the summer of '64. We were banging away with the rhythm and blues, both US original and British derivative via The Stones, The Animals etcetera and our support act were from the same mould. We were new on the scene and still pretty wet behind the ears but the support band were still in their baby-grows, it was only their third or fourth gig.

They were a local band and got an enthusiastic reception as they rattled through some Jimmy Reed number and good old Rufus Thomas's 'Walking the Dog'. We were watching one of the guitarists, who was throwing himself around the stage like a man possessed, collapsing to his knees each time the lead guitar played a solo, and generally getting the crowd to focus their attention on him and his one man stage act. Phil was puzzled as to why they appeared to have two bass players in this five piece line-up. Merv dug me in the ribs and pointed to the guitar lead on matey's bass. "They've only gone and tied his lead around the leg of that chair that the amp is stood on," chuckled Merv. "I wonder if he'll realise he isn't plugged in?"

After their set we were due on but first we had to tell them of their oversight.

'Fuck me, don't tell him!' said the singer to Phil and me, 'he can't play for toffee. We don't plug him in. He's desperate to be in a group, so we let him up on stage to do his thing and then we can concentrate on playing.'

Poor lad, plenty of ambition and energy, but not a snowball in hell's chance really.

On the other hand, in that same summer, I heard a voice that sent chills down my spine. I was working in Bath at the time. A mate picked me up in the mornings and drove to Bath via Bradford on Avon, picking up his fiancée and a rather attractive young lady who worked with us. She was a flirty piece and although she was virtually engaged herself, she seemed overly interested in yours truly. I was smitten it has to be said. We did a couple of gigs in Corsham and Bath where she appeared without as much as a by your leave. She cycled over with a younger brother and left before anything too substantial happened, but I got the impression that if I played my cards right she was more than interested.

One night, after a busy day in the office stretched into overtime, we all four drove back towards Bradford. My mate suggested a cold beer. After visiting a couple of pubs on the way back, we had to do a slight detour to drop this young girl off. Because my mate wanted to be left alone for a session in his Mini with his good lady, it was suggested they dropped us off and I walk her home. Game on! After about a mile flogging down this lane we eventually arrived at the sprawling, slightly dilapidated mansion she called home. I had this horrible thought that her boyfriend would walk out of the front door and proceed to fill me in, but he wasn't around.

Every step we had taken along this lane seemed to be taking us further and further down and indeed we were at the bottom of a valley. I was at last finding out what it was she had in store for me. Namely, her tongue doing battle with mine for supremacy in a brief struggle that I was perfectly prepared to lose, so that we could move on to better things. Suddenly a male voice carried on the summer night air, interrupting our romantic idyll. No, it wasn't her boyfriend. It was a fantastic voice, identity unknown, singing 'Moon River'. The acoustic quality of the valley made it all the more magical. He was some distance away from us in the fields on the valley floor. Perhaps he was a farm hand walking home after a long day's toil. My companion didn't know. As the singing continued, she rested her head on my chest and we both listened, lost in the moment. The snogging stopped. It would have been sacrilege to do anything so base to sully his virtuoso performance.

The voice was getting closer now and then we picked up some girlish giggles and it was clear our troubadour was not alone. At least one other lad was in the party because he shouted "Piss off John! Leave it out." And so he stopped. Did he ever sing again? He would have been a wow on a karaoke night. Would have won prizes. Unfortunately for him, karaoke was decades away. (Wish it still was - don't you?) If you think the guys who win television contests are the bees' knees, this bloke was better. Unaccompanied. Every note spot on. Perfect pitch. You had to be there to know how good he was.

He's probably gone through the last forty years, never realising the potential of that talent he'd been given.

As for the young lady. I said she was flirty. She got engaged and she still snogged me in the basement store room. When she dumped me it hurt like hell. I got over it eventually but I still don't like listening to 'Moon River' much though.

We played in all sorts of places for all types or age groups and clubs and organisations. Particularly while we were under Martin's wing. He got us a gig at a church service once, unpaid of course, in fact it cost us a few bob as we had to put something in the collection plate when it was passed round. It was in the early Sixties and a time when the Church of England was trying all sorts to get younger people to go to church. One of the nearby village churches got us, and a guitarist from a local dance band, to turn up to a choir practice and tried us out on an Easter hymn set to a modern tune. They provided the sheet music. The guitar player could read it and so could Merv which left Phil doing what Merv told him to play (but very quietly) and Malc using brushes on the drums so as to avoid the roof collapsing in on us.

Gerry and I were surplus to requirements, but somehow we went along anyway with Martin and Glyn in tow. Although I thought the practice was a shambles, the choirmaster and vicar were overjoyed and on Easter Sunday we arrived in the van, unloaded the gear and set up in front of the chancel steps. The congregation filed in and the lads who were to perform joined us in the pews, plus a couple of assorted girlfriends who decided to tag along for some reason or other. Perhaps it was getting whichever of us they were going out with used to the idea of being on the inside of a church. Who knows?

The hymn in question was introduced about two thirds of the way through the service and the guitarist, plus our three lads, trooped off to their respective instruments and prepared to play. The organist played the introduction and off they went. What a racket! The choir were only ten strong, maximum, nobody in the congregation had a clue how the tune went, although as it was a well known hymn, they knew the words, but that didn't help. They should have come to the practice. Mercifully it was all over in about five minutes. The vicar was chuffed to bits though and he was all for getting us back at Christmas. Martin looked at us and saw the reaction and said,

'I think Robin's free (the guitarist) why don't you have a chat with him?' Well played Martin, now let's get the hell out of here.

5.Boogie Nights

There used to be a place called The George Hotel in Trowbridge, slap bang in the middle. An old coaching inn I think, which probably means it saw its best times in the eighteenth century. By the time we played there it was on its last legs. We did several gigs there for various organisations and had to get the kit in through a back door which was at the top of a fire escape. This brought you onto a long narrow corridor, off which there was a bathroom at the left hand end, plus several bedrooms, then at the right hand end a corridor led to other rooms. Down a short flight of stairs, a small door led into a large ballroom. This was one of the more inaccessible places we had to play in, but it gave us some great nights, plus one of the best comedy moments we ever had.

The George still had its delusions of grandeur so it was not about to let a mere group of musicians hump their gear through the front door, across the foyer and upstairs to the ballroom, which would have taken no more than two minutes. Oh no, the tradesmen's entrance it was on each occasion. The ballroom had a stage and a couple of trestle tables at the opposite end, where the management condescendingly allowed an outside bar to come in and provide refreshments. It was beneath them to cater for non residents themselves. So the Rotary Club, The Buffs and The Young Farmers all got in touch with Martin and over we went to do our stuff at various times.

On that first gig we were shown the tortuous route by the hotel manager, having mistakenly pulled the van up by the front door. He ushered us along the narrow corridors, warning us that here and there they had people staying and could we keep the noise to a minimum. When everything was in we had a lot of boxes, amp covers, guitar cases and stage gear littering the front of the stage.

'You can put that,' he said pointedly, 'in the bathroom at the far end of the corridor. Just by the fire door. It's not in use.'

Fair enough. We used it as our dressing room and when we had a break, while the Rotarians had their finger buffet, we trotted along the corridor with our pints from the bar and sat around having a fag and a chat. Someone bagged the khazi, a couple on the edge of the bath, the rest of us sat on the floor. It was a big bathroom by my standards, probably two and a half times bigger than ours at home.

The night with the Buffs was pretty similar except for the beer on sale at the bar. Now you may have gathered by the frequency at which I mention the occasions when we 'popped out for a beer' that we enjoyed a pint. Having said that I was not a big drinker in those early days. I had a couple before we played, to lubricate my throat for one thing and a little Dutch courage for another, maybe a couple in the interval and one at the end of the night if the bar was still open, but that was about it, honest. The night of the Buffs' do was in mid-summer and it was very warm outside, let alone inside the George Hotel's ballroom.

The floor was packed and I needed more liquid intake to face them for some reason. So I started early on the bitter that the temporary bar had to offer. I had four before we did our first set and as I was sweating like a pig at the end of our first half, needed to top up again in the break. It was going down so smoothly I managed another four in the half hour before we were back on stage. By all accounts I should have been legless, but although I felt heady during the first set it seemed to wear off by midway through the second half, so I got Martin to get me a couple to keep me going through to the end.

Ten pints and I was still standing? Something tells me the buggers on the bar had watered it down a bit. All in all it was a good night and the Buffs were happy enough and paid the money over without a whimper. We got the gear down and lugged it out the same way we came in, clearing our stuff out of the old bathroom just as before.

The Young Farmers gig was some time later, perhaps a twelve month. We were looking forward to it as we had done several before and stories about the people we met and became friendly with appear elsewhere in these pages of fading memories. So we pitched up at The George Hotel on a Friday evening, went in the front to the desk, asked for the fire door to be opened and so on. A new young lad was in Reception, but he seemed au fait with the procedure. We got the gear up the fire escape, along the corridors into the ballroom, set up, had a sound check, then cleared the rubbish away into the old bathroom. The bar was not open yet, so we went for a pint or two to a small pub on the road behind the Hotel car park. When we returned it was time to start playing. The ballroom was packed with Young Farmers doing what they do best - having a good time. The beer flowed, but not the same brand as last time, the food was excellent and the evening looked set to be a great success. They looked after us at the break, gave us paper plates loaded up with grub and we took it with a beer along the corridor to our temporary dressing room.

We had at least three girlfriends with us, plus five band members and Glyn and we settled down to while away the half hour or so we had before we were due back on stage. Once you add in all the other paraphernalia we generally stored away in there, you can imagine there wasn't much room to spare. After only a few minutes, while it was reasonably quiet and we were munching away on our free food, the door flew open. In the doorway was a middle aged man, in his dressing gown, with a towel over his arm and his wash kit in a smart drawstring bag. He looked as if his blood pressure was getting the better of him.

'What are you doing in my bathroom?' he shouted.

'Sorry,' said Phil, 'this is our dressing room pal. You've got the wrong door.' The chap was going even redder in the face now.

'Get out now, or I'll call the manager. This is my bathroom. I'm paying three shillings a week for this!'

Realisation dawned that maybe he was telling the truth. A new lad in reception; no familiar face of Mr Manager to let us in at the top of the staircase. All change at the George Hotel then. It had been nearly a year, but we assumed nothing would ever change. So with our new roommate standing with his hand on the door handle, ready to shut the door firmly behind us, we enlisted the help of the giggling girlfriends and carried the offending items along the corridor, around the corner, down the steps and into the ballroom. Much consternation on the faces of the Young Farmer's committee who thought we were about to do a runner, but once we explained what had happened everything was cool. Mind you, explain is a bit strong. We tried to explain, but somehow they seemed to think we were making it up. You couldn't though could you?

6. Summer Holiday

We took a week off in August '65 to go on holiday to Bournemouth. Phil and Nick couldn't get the time off, but Glyn, Malcolm, Merv and myself bombed down to Bournemouth in the van, plus the kit, because we'd got a gig on the Wednesday in Bognor Regis, supporting The Ivy League in some club right on the front.

This was as far afield as we had been at this stage and the holiday wasn't going to get in the way. We parked up at the guest house the twins had found in some brochure or other. As you can imagine the landlady was a tad worried when she saw our old van spluttering its way across her driveway to a corner as far away from the road as we could get. Glyn reckoned we needed to keep the kit as far away from prying eyes as possible. As you will recall we also rather drew attention to the fact that it was a bandwagon by the fetching illuminated sign on the roof.

The landlady's humour was not improved when we arrived for our first evening meal. The four of us stuck out like rugby forwards in a chorus line. She was obviously used to a more genteel type of guest, either elderly couples or middle aged parents with teenage children. No kids. No pets. No shit.

Glyn had a way with words. His verbal mishaps were a source of amusement on many a trip around the West Country. He never could avoid saying Chipping Salisbury rather than Sodbury for one. He never got the punch line right on any joke he tried to tell either. So when he tried a witty retort to something Merv had said you almost knew he was going to crash and burn. You know the old chestnut when you want to suggest to someone that they're stating the bleeding obvious. They say, for example 'Are we going into town later for a bevy?' You reply 'Is grass green?'

Merv posed that very question thirty seconds after we had all four sat down at our designated table in the swish dining room. We were studying the menus, frantically trying to find something with chips, when Glyn waved his arms about and replied,

'What colour's grass?'

That was it, the three of us just fell about laughing and Glyn got the hump of course. The landlady had been about to approach us to take our orders, but beat a hasty retreat. By this time my sides were hurting so much from trying to stifle the laughter and the other guests were looking over, probably wondering whether 'The Laurels' had been a mistake. Her husband came over and asked us to try and 'tone it down a bit lads' and trotted back with our orders to the boss who was hidden away in the safety of the kitchen.

The first few days were uneventful enough. Usual lads on holiday fare. Down to the beach by ten, a game of footy before too many families pitched their windbreaks and associated detritus. Read the papers while lounging on a towel watching the young birds trying to get into their cozzies under a towel that is, fortunately for us, one size smaller than the one required for the job. A liquid lunch and then more footy and sod the people on the beach, keeping the ball away from the families as far as possible, but as close to the girls soaking up the rays as not to make it obvious. Okay it was bloody blatant, but it had a reasonable success rate.

Merv and I spent most afternoons chatting on the beach, mostly about music. Glyn was still in a strop. He

40

wasn't into lazing the day away on the beach. He wanted to DO something.

'Like what?' said Malcolm. Glyn waved his arms about again,

'I don't know!' he said, "Just something."

After the evening meal we walked into town, which was quite a hike, and visited a few pubs. If there was a gig on at the Winter Gardens we went there. One night we saw a young Tony Blackburn DJ-ing and I'm sure he sang too. There were plenty of young girls, either on holiday or locals, and Phil would have been in his element. In his absence, Merv and I did our best to get past first base, which was, in this instance, to get to talk to them. Our progress was slow and Malc and Glyn as twins had more luck for some reason or other - until Glyn started to get his own back for the piss taking. Anytime Malc got some girl talking and looked like getting off with her his brother would walk over and look at her mates and suggest we went on somewhere else as he was bored. As my Mum used to say, 'it'll end in tears'.

Sure enough on the Tuesday afternoon when the weather had taken a turn for the worse for an hour or two, we decided to move away from the beach and go tenpin bowling. This meant moving the van, which we had brought into town that day as the forecast hadn't been too special and we didn't fancy getting soaked on the long walk back to our digs.

Glyn drove as far as the nearest car park. One of those new fangled multi storey jobbies, not something we were used to around our neck of the woods. We all got out on the slip road on the way in, leaving him to park up the van. We told him we would go on into the bowling alley and get a lane sorted and we would see him in a couple of minutes. He started waving his arms about again, moaning about who was going to pay for the car park so, when his twin brother told him to stop whingeing and get the bloody van parked, Glyn crunched the old bus into gear and slammed his foot down on the accelerator. The van shot up the ramp into the car park at an impressive speed.

You will recall Martin's handiwork the week before we played our first date at the youth club? Halfway up the ramp to the first level was a sign which clearly stated 'Warning!' followed by the clearance in feet and inches. Sadly none of us read the sign until a couple of minutes after the incident!

Now it wasn't the van's fault, or Martin's, who couldn't possibly have known that multi storey car parks would be all the rage within a year or so of his advertising gimmick being put in situ. We were on our way towards the bowling alley when we heard the crash. The sounds of splintering wood and breaking glass assaulted our ears. We ran back to find Glyn walking towards us still waving his arms and very red faced. Not embarrassed, just bloody fuming.

'Now look what you've done! That's it I quit! You can drive the bloody van.'

This left us with a small problem. The insurance on the van was 'named drivers', and they were Martin and Glyn and Bognor Regis was definitely too far to carry the kit over our shoulders and thumb a lift. Merv and I looked at one another and as we were desperately thinking what we could do, Malcolm suddenly stepped forward and grabbed his nearest and dearest by the throat. Well to be absolutely accurate he grabbed hold of Glyn's shirt and lifted him off his feet so his balled fists were indeed right under his chin.

'For Christ's sake, grow up Glyn.' he shouted, 'I'll do the driving for the rest of today. If we get stopped you can pay the bloody fine. But you're driving tomorrow.'

Decisive action and Glyn was rather taken aback, however he couldn't let it lie immediately, he was used to getting the last word so he pulled himself away from his brother's clutches saying,

'We'll see about that mate!'

Sadly, the handiwork of the little ladies that worked for the shirt manufacturers was not used to such sudden movements and the buttons parted company with the shirt, flying in all directions. This upset Glyn even more as he had only just bought it in some trendy shop in Bournemouth, so off he went on one again.

'Why don't we carry on and go bowling as we had arranged?' asked Merv.

Glyn glowered in his direction and although we did indeed end up spending the afternoon bowling, it was not the happiest experience I've ever had but it passed a couple of hours at least and the weather had brightened up by the time we emerged.

Glyn was somewhat calmer, although relations with his brother were still a little strained. When we got back to the multi storey and Malc asked Glyn for the keys he handed them over without a word and we all piled into the van and Malcolm drove us back to 'The Laurels'. We had a less eventful evening meal than we had on our arrival and went to our rooms to wash and change ready to hit the town yet again.

Whether any of us pulled that night I can't remember. Probably not, it's not important. Building bridges was the order of the day. Merv did his best to jolly up Glyn and convince him we really needed him to drive us to Bognor the following lunchtime. Malc and I paired up and tried to drink our pints with our fingers crossed, not easy I can tell you! When we made our weary way back to our digs much later that night Glyn was in a far better mood. He had decided he was going to drive us tomorrow after all, but not before he had taken his shirt back to the shop and ask for his money back.

'You'll be lucky,' said Merv.

'I've got the receipt,' said Glyn, 'I'll tell them the buttons fell off the first time I got on the dance floor.'

And he did. And he got a full refund into the bargain!

On the Wednesday morning we awoke to clear blue skies and a warmer sun than on any day so far on our holiday but not the most comfortable weather for travelling along the south coast in a van. We stopped off for a pint and a pie at a pub an hour or so into our journey and when we came back out the van decided to play up. It wouldn't start and we were reduced to pushing it and bump starting it. With the mid afternoon sun panning down and the beer and the stodgy grub starting to take effect, we could have done without that for sure.

We arrived in Bognor Regis about six in the evening and Phil and Nick were parked up near the club. They had started to wonder where we were as our plan the previous Friday, when we made our arrangements for the gig, had been to arrive between four and five - Phil's usual thinking, that we could get into the hall, set up the gear, have a practice for an hour, then trawl the seafront pubs for crumpet.

With Plan A out the window we got into the club, set up our gear and found a pub to have a couple of beers before we were due on stage. It was bloody warm work that night I remember. It was the usual set up, support band on first for an hour or so, the place half full (or half empty if you were the promoter) but we had a reasonable reception. Of course the place filled up towards the end of our set and when The Ivy League went on the club was rammed. They did what they did well and were very professional. Lots of falsetto and close harmonies. Ho hum. After they had finished and the crowd thinned out again we went back on and played through to about half past ten and then it was time to pack up and go home. Well, not home for us, of course, we had to drive back to Bournemouth for the last couple of days of our holiday.

Phil and Nick got into Phil's 'frog-eyed sprite' and bombed off back to Melksham in no time flat, while we got the kit into the van, persuaded it to start up again, and limped back into 'The Laurels' car park in the wee small hours. We had a key for the front door, but in those days the wee small hours were off the agenda for the landlady and her hubby, so the door was firmly bolted. We were outside in the van trying to get some sleep as the sun came up on the Thursday morning. Breakfast was taken by the four of us, looking dishevelled but with a healthy enough appetite. As usual there was nowhere to get a bite to eat on the roads back to Bournemouth from Bognor so we were starving.

Our appearance was not welcomed by our hosts, who were a bit sniffy as they delivered our bacon and eggs, although that may have been the after effects of the hot van, the even hotter club and our exertions on stage, followed by half a night in the van with the four of us in close proximity after a few beers. Anyway, after we got into our rooms, washed up and changed into some fresh clothes, we felt almost normal again and headed down into town to the beach. The idea was to have a quiet read of the papers and then catch up on our sleep during the afternoon before making up for lost time looking for that elusive leg over in the evening.

Fat chance of any rest. Malcolm decided he was suffering withdrawal symptoms having not kicked a football for all of thirty six hours and reckoned a game of footy was the order of the day. We had got our papers on the way in as usual and Glyn had seen some homemade wine in a shop window and asked us to chip in a few coppers each so he could buy a couple of bottles.

We started kicking the ball about aimlessly to start with then, as the sun got higher in the sky it was clearly warmer than yesterday so the lads stripped down to the mid-Sixties equivalent of Speedos and made their way out to the water. I hated the water at the best of times and, still knackered from the day before, I just flopped down on a towel and read my paper. As I watched them in the sea, pratting about trying to look cool and scanning the beach for totty, I casually wondered what this wine Glyn had bought was like. It was in dark green bottles with the cork only jammed in the top part way, so it was not too much of a struggle to free it and even less of a struggle to tip some of the contents down my throat. It tasted sweet and quite heavy. What it was made from I never found out, there were no labels.

Well, afterwards I blamed them for staying in the water so long. I read Malcolm's paper, then Merv's and, with some regularity, returned to the bottle for a swift nip, like you do. Eventually they came back and the football was resurrected. This time it was a proper game. Malcolm would take on Merv and Glyn and they would try to score past the goalkeeper. That was me. I never professed to be a goalie; I had played left wing for various school and youth teams, despite being right footed and no athlete. I was basically a 'goal-hanger'.

And so it came to pass that the only competition for Gordon Banks in the summer of '66 was on a beach in Bournemouth in August '65 and sadly there were no agents around to snap him up and make that phone call to Alf Ramsey. The frequent swigs of wine were now in control. I have few memories of that early afternoon on the beach but a significant number of people stopped to watch as Malcolm ran rings round Merv and Glyn, but no matter what power he got behind his shot, or which angle it came at me, he was frustrated by my ability to block his goal bound efforts with some part of my body. I never felt a thing. Normally diving full length into a pile of sand was something I wouldn't be caught dead doing, but I kept it up for over an hour.

Malcolm was becoming more frustrated and was sweating like a pig. Merv and Glyn nicked the ball off him at fairly regular intervals and, as their shooting wasn't even Wiltshire Senior League standard, they troubled me even less. With all the wine on board and the unexpected exercise, my head was thumping like hell. All I wanted to do was have a lie down somewhere, possibly in a darkened room and preferably for twelve hours minimum. Eventually Malcolm gave up and flopped down on the sand.

'Fuck me Ted, where did that come from? Let's have a taste of that wine we bought, I'm gagging!'

Whoops, the truth about my secret drinking was out. The other three took the unopened bottle and finished it between them, leaving me in disgrace with the dregs of the first. Whatever it was in the bottle they had was clearly not the same as mine, since the effect was nowhere near as drastic. Their thirsts quenched, they were ready to pick up our odds and sods and stroll along the beach. Once more in pursuit of totty.

Reluctantly I picked up my towel, paper et al, and followed at a distance. I found it difficult to catch them up as by now the wine was heading south. My head still throbbed, but my legs kept buckling under me and my forward progress was slow. I blamed the depth of the sand which seemed to be clinging onto my ankles and refusing to accept that England's number two was going to leave the scene of his triumph. They had gone about fifty yards when all of a sudden they stopped, turned back and sat down with two girls. This was new. We generally sat down near girls, who either got up and moved away or stayed and rather pointedly ignored us. It seemed, from the distance I was away from the happy throng, that the girls had actually called out to them!

I lurched across the sand, covering the remaining yards with as much decorum as possible, threw my towel down onto a space just in front of one of the girls and dropped onto it.

'Hi' she said, 'you're Ted aren't you'.

It was a statement, not a question. Bloody hell I thought, these three work quickly when they get a chance, Phil would be impressed. Hang on a minute, Merv knows her already, she's a mate of his girlfriend from back home. He's out of the picture then. No playing away, it's bound to get back. The conversation carried on as I took in the curves under the one piece costume of the girl with the long dark hair. She noticed of course. It would have been difficult to miss a bloke sitting about six feet in front of her with his tongue hanging out.

My head was spinning, my legs were asleep and not long after, I succumbed to the wine, the football and the heat of the sun. Bugger me, when I woke up about an hour or so later, they were still there. Merv was making small talk - nothing that might be described flirtatious, just in case it got back. Malcolm and Glyn were homing in on 'The Body' and her fair haired mate. As I opened my eyes, wondering where the nearest bog was, I thought my chances had well and truly been blown. I wandered off up the beach to the loo and then stuck my head under a tap to clear away some of the sand and the dryness I was experiencing in my mouth.

When I returned the dark haired girl looked up and said,

'Do you know why we like to follow you around to gigs?'

I replied that I hadn't realised that they had followed us around. I wanted venues, dates so I could hit myself over the nuts with a sock full of rocks for not spotting her before. Thank God Phil hadn't clocked her, I would have had no chance! After establishing that they had seen us about seven or eight times in the past few months I tentatively asked,

'Why do you like coming to our gigs?'

It was my voice, she said. Most singers had high voices and mine was deep and therefore, more sexy. Bloody hell! Thank you Mr Taylor for all those hours of choir practice, moulding my mellifluous bass into a pulling machine. Who would have thought it? She went on to say that since Nick had joined and we had added more and more soul music into our act it was even better suited. This was a girl who knew her stuff. I could be in here and no mistake.

'What are you doing tonight girls?'

Disaster.

'When my Dad comes back from the supplier he's visiting down here today, he's picking us up over there by the clock, then we're going back to Trowbridge. We're only here for the day.'

Bollocks. Big ones. So near and yet so far. If I've told you before I'm sorry, but it's worth repeating. No matter how many gigs we did, almost without exception, if you pulled a bird on the night, the next time you went back there hoping for more of the same, they were never there. And so the Body went home to Trowbridge. We did loads of gigs in the town and all the towns around and I never saw her again. Heard a rumour from Merv's girlfriend that she already had a boyfriend back home but that was it. Vanished off the face of the earth. Bollocks again. Even bigger ones!

Of course, Merv, Malc and Glyn thought it was hilarious. Still feeling a bit delicate I trudged back to our digs with them. Starving hungry I polished off the evening meal that night and was well up for a night in town. We were back into the usual haunts, on the prowl, but dipping out as per usual. In the end we settled for a fish and chip supper and an early night.

Friday proved relatively uneventful as we had the first indications that the fine weather was coming to an end. It was very overcast and drizzly, so we mooched about from late morning to mid afternoon and ended up going ten pin bowling again, this time without the histrionics. As with most holidays you're on your way home before you know it and an hour into your first morning at work it's as if you've never been away. Forty years on I can't tell you what that last evening was all about. No leg overs between us as far as I can recall. A few beers and futile attempts at getting some girls to dance, but that was about it. Par for the bloody course!

The following morning it was very warm and sultry. A storm was brewing but it wasn't Glyn this time. We packed our bags and piled into the van ready to pull away from 'The Laurels' for the final time. The landlady's husband was wandering around the garden, pretending to give it a bit of a tidy up before the next batch of guests came through the gates.

'Cheerio lads. Hope you enjoyed your stay. Don't suppose you'll remember us when you hit the big time?'

No mention of 'we hope you come back again soon' I noticed, but far better than I had expected.

The trip to Bognor Regis, as well as the accumulated mileage both prior to us getting the van and in the time since we had been gigging, finally took its toll. The van got us about halfway home and, right out of the blue, cut out. We let it cool down for a while, pushed it a distance until we got a small slope in our favour, then bump started it. That got us a few more miles. Then the heavens opened and we sat in the middle of Salisbury Plain listening to the thunder rolling round us while an unknown drummer performed an impressive solo on the roof of our stricken van. What a great end to a holiday!

We weren't able to summon assistance of course. No mobile phones about then, nor any public phones for a few miles in either direction. We were parked slightly off the road in the gateway of a field with a track away to our left which disappeared away over the brow of a hill. The rain was easing, but the noise of the thunder seemed to be getting closer. I looked out to our right and pondered the gateway and track on the opposite side and was about to remark on the deeply rutted nature of the track, considering the rain we had just experienced was the first for a couple of weeks. Merv looked out of the left hand window.

'Fuck me. Quick. Move the fucking van!'

Glyn waved his arms about and replied,

'If I could keep this poxy thing going more than about three miles at a time I would, believe me.'

Merv pointed at the four Centurion tanks which were lined up in close order one behind the other. Each with its commander looking down imperiously at the stricken van and it's crumpled occupants. Merv whispered,

'Do you think they'd give us a push if we ask them nicely?'

A rather suave young officer in his camouflage gear asked us in his public school accent if he could be of any assistance as he was 'rather eager to cross the road and achieve our objective you fellows.' A few orders were shouted in a language I certainly didn't understand and a handful of similarly clad soldiers appeared and unceremoniously pushed our van out of the way. We made our humble apologies and they jumped back into their tin cans and sped away with a fairly unpleasant smell of exhaust fumes in their wake.

Of course, we were no closer to home and still with a van that was past its sell by date. Deciding we were not likely to get any further help from our nation's finest we resorted to pushing and bumping again. Another hour or so and we were limping back into town, looking forward to a hot bath, a change of clothes and something to eat. Merv and I were dropped off close to our homes, while the twins took the van back to their father's garage to park it up. Handy for the mechanics to try to bring it back to life on the Monday morning they thought.

Martin had had other ideas, as usual. Passing the garage in his car he spotted the van and turned onto the forecourt.

'You're back then?'

God he was sharp.

'Where are the other two? Only Phil and Nick thought you were due back by mid morning so you would be OK for a gig tonight in Warminster.'

Aaargh!

Martin came round to my place about half past four to tell me to get ready for six o'clock. We unloaded the gear from the van and with the help of a couple of his mates, who had sensible family cars rather than frog eyed Sprites or scooters, we got to the social club in Warminster to play for two and three quarter hours for about fifteen quid to an audience of not more than forty - and not one of whom was less than fifty. Cheers Martin. Rounded off the holiday nicely.

7. The Carnival is Over!

The week following our return from holiday was quite eventful. On Monday lunchtime Martin picked himself up off the floor of the garage workshop after he'd been told what it was going to cost to repair the van. Evidently, if we had pushed it the sixty odd miles home we would have been okay, but continuing to drive it when the warning signs that all was not well were quite clearly there for us to see, well… Martin took the only course of action open to him. He told them to scrap the heap of junk and asked what they wanted for the Ford J2 van that was parked up in the lot behind the garage where our old van was usually to be found. It was blue and it was slightly bigger than our old van, and it didn't have the remains of any light fittings on the roof. It did have a roof rack though. That was its drawback really, it looked more like a camper van than a bandwagon. Still, beggars can't be choosers and the price was right. Bloody cheap in other words. So a deal was struck.

In late August '65 Martin had got us a prime booking for Melksham's Carnival Dance at the Assembly Hall. Another support band and a headline act were to appear too but he didn't have all the details as yet. We were chuffed. We were still suffering in comparison to The Argonauts with the general public. We felt this would help us to persuade a few people we could actually play now.

We had had no change of personnel to date and our set had expanded from Chuck and Bo to include a load of numbers by The Kinks, The Yardbirds, The Animals and even The Pretty Things. We waited for news of who we would be playing with that Saturday night.

Eventually, the Carnival Committee signed Twinkle. That's right, the one hit wonder 'Terry'. It had been a hit at the back end of '64 reaching No4. She was not the 'hot' artist we had hoped for. Her backing group were called 'Boz and the Boz People'. Highly imaginative.

The appointed Saturday arrived and we got in early to set up the kit. The second support band, 'The Wanted', just back from a tour of Scandinavia, pitched up about six o'clock. They were a bit cocky and we didn't take much notice of them, we were watching the doorway awaiting the arrival of Twinkle and her entourage. The dressing room arrangements were fairly sparse in the Assembly Hall and Phil in particular was anxious to find out where she was going to be disrobing.

Time was getting on and the Carnival Committee were getting twitchy. Oh for a mobile phone in those days! Eventually someone managed to get hold of the London agent that had dealt with the booking. Twinkle was going to be a no show, she was double booked evidently - or at least that's what they told the Committee member who phoned up. But don't panic, Boz and the Boz People were on their way together with a replacement girl singer.

Naturally we were due on first. We changed into our gear and took to the stage. The curtain drew back and we were exposed to a hall three quarters full of people. 'Hi Heel Sneakers' 'Walking the Dog' 'Bring It On Home To Me', plus a selection of old Chuck and Bo and we were away. A good reception too, very pleasing.

As we got about two thirds of the way through our set two females entered the hall. One was blonde and maybe late twenties and the other had dark hair and looked about eighteen. Phil fell off the stage.

Okay I made that bit up. He didn't fall off the stage - just as well as it was a fair drop. The Carnival Committee were quickly in attendance and the girls were ushered to the side of the stage and then through to the dressing room at the side. There was no sign of Boz or any of his People.

The curtains closed after our last number. The Carnival Queen was now in the building and all sorts of worthies were falling over themselves trying to organise whatever was due next on the itinerary. 'The Wanted' should have been organising their gear ready to go on next but they were conspicuous by their absence. We moved our stuff back and to the side as best we could and wandered off to the dressing room.

The older blonde was deep in conversation with the lead guitarist of 'The Wanted' and it clearly wasn't going well. The Committee chairman came over to us and announced that Boz and the Boz People were no longer coming.

'So what's happening?' asked Martin, who had appeared from the front of the hall after taking the plaudits for masterminding the birth of a potential supergroup.

Negotiations with 'The Wanted' had reached an impasse. The blonde came over to Martin and asked where our manager was.

'That's me, darling.'

She was as hard as nails and probably hadn't been anyone's darling for some while. She was not a woman to mess with. She had asked 'The Wanted' for their play list to see if it was possible to find enough songs for her artist to appear. There had been enough songs, but the band wanted fifty notes to back her and she was not about to part with that much of her night's money to give to some jumped up band who had to go to Scandinavia to get someone to listen to them. So we looked at one another and had visions of us and 'The Wanted' having to slog away filling in the time from now until the end of the evening.

Martin said, 'They'll do it for ten quid.' (meaning us, with no prior negotiation). 'How many numbers does she need? Anyway who is she? Have we heard of her?'

The blonde A&R lady replied,

'Her name is Elkie Brooks and she's from Liverpool. She's our most recent signing and her first record came out last Friday. Let's see your play list and if we can find six or seven songs that she knows we might be able to do something to save this from being a shambles.'

Elkie then appeared from the dressing room and she was young alright. Her hair was cut in a Mod style and she was wearing a mauve jacket and mini skirt with matching shoes. Her legs (which all of us were looking at, not just Phil) seemed to go on for ever with the short skirt, and were contained in white tights. The material looked quite thick, certainly not silk or nylon. What it felt like I couldn't say, I didn't get lucky and nor did anyone else with her mother hen in attendance. She looked stunning.

Phil and Merv in particular joined in the conversation over the scribbled play list. We'd had to find a piece of paper and write down as many as we could remember, as we had never needed a play list before. Slowly but surely we heard the blonde and Elkie ticking off one number after another. They came to a halt at six.

There were a few difficult moments. They asked Martin if they could give us the 'spots' for a couple of other tunes so we could quickly run through them and add them to the list. Martin was stumped.

'Spots? What are they when they're at home?' The blonde realised she was fighting a losing battle.

'Can you read music?' she asked in the general direction of the five of us who were the subject of the discussions. Merv and I nodded, we both had studied piano (he was miles better than me) but the others didn't have a clue.

'Look' said Martin, 'we can do those six numbers. They know those well enough. If they go on with something they've never played before, they'll cock it up and your singer will look just as much of a prat as they will when it goes wrong. Best to stick to what we know.'

I told you Martin was a smooth operator, the blonde was like putty in his hands. Either that or she just wanted to get the six songs out of the way and piss off back to London before her fledgling artiste's career crashed and burned in this godforsaken part of the country. Whichever it was the songs were put into a running order.

'The Wanted' had gone on stage after a short delay and launched into their one hour set. We carried on the debate about what songs Elkie would sing right at the back of the stage behind the curtains. They were every bit as ordinary as I had expected them to be. The band that is, not the curtains, if you were wondering, they were orange. The curtains that is, not the band. Hope that clears that up.

The Carnival Committee were ecstatic. Everyone in the hall knew Twinkle wasn't coming. They knew there was going to be a girl singer top of the bill but what they didn't know was that we were going to be backing her.

After 'The Wanted' finished there was another short break while the Carnival Queen did something regal, probably presented a cheque to some organisation or other that was benefiting from cash raised during the oh so boring activities the Carnival Week inflicted on the local inhabitants.

Then the Committee Chairman pulled a fast one. So he didn't tarnish his reputation with the good townsfolk he told Martin to get us on stage to do a couple of warm up numbers and then give Miss Brooks the big build up. Oh and just announce the fact that the top name isn't here, nor her backing group, and that our little five-some, barely out of nappies in the music business, would be doing the honours. Thanks a bunch!

Back go the curtains again and we're into The Stones and The Kinks, to get the crowd into a state of euphoria. Muggins is the singer, therefore the poor sod left to make the announcements. I could feel the colour draining from my face, that clammy feeling on the palms of my hands as I clung onto the mike stand for dear life. My tongue stuck to the roof of my mouth. Nothing new there then, that was normal for virtually every performance in the first year or so. I made the announcement and there were groans of disappointment.

Were they because Twinkle's fan base was far wider than we had imagined and her legions of followers were all in the hall that night? Had someone heard a sneak preview of Elkie Brooks' first single and voted it a resounding 'MISS' on the Melksham Juke Box Jury? Much more likely dear readers, the groans were aimed in our direction. The first half the evening had probably been a fluke. Surely, they thought, they'll never be able to sustain it long enough to support this youngster, whoever she is.

I was unaccustomed to introducing top line acts, Elkie was my first. I usually got by with 'We'd like to do a number now...' followed by the artiste and the title, it served me well for over a decade. On this occasion the words came out pretty much in the right order and as I shouted

'Ladies and Gentleman, Miss Elkie Brooks!'

She burst through the curtains at the back of the stage and grabbed the mike from me and the lads struck up the first chords of her chosen opening number, 'Hi Heel

Sneakers' followed by 'Walking The Dog' and 'Bring It On Home To Me'. Strangely familiar isn't it? Well you have to remember she arrived half an hour into our first set, so she didn't know!

When the play list was being drawn up I foresaw a bit of a problem, but the blonde was too intimidating for me to mention that we had already played those songs, in that order. Actually, writing this now, it just shows what good judges of a running order we were if a future superstar and her A&R person came up with the same one.

How were those first three songs received? Remember what she looked like? Every one of the three hundred odd blokes in the hall was convinced she was singing exclusively for him. The single ones, plus a few that had left their wives in the bar for a few minutes, were crowded down at the front of the stage. As each song finished there was lots of cheering and warm applause all around the building, even the wives who had returned to claim their husbands agreed she was brilliant. She could sell a number, even an old standard like 'Walking the Dog' seemed as fresh as a daisy.

It's a bugger when you get old, your memory goes you know. Now 'Don't Let Me Be Misunderstood' was never next, but it was in there somewhere, possibly number five. We may have played 'It's All Over Now' and hang about, did she do something from Chuck or Bo? It could have been 'Around And Around' or 'You Can't Judge a Book'. Whatever it was they lapped it up. I even provided back up vocals on a couple of numbers without Elkie giving me the evil eye, nor Mother Hen, who was standing at the side of the stage with Martin. He was in his element. We were making him look good, working cheap for our home town and coming to the rescue when the evening was descending into chaos. We were ticking all the boxes.

Elkie finished her final song and the crowd yelled for an encore. Fat chance! We only had the six that she knew. She left the stage with her adoring audience of young lads, and a couple of old pervs at the front, making lewd noises in the time honoured tradition. We ploughed on for another half hour with the rest of our selection of rhythm and blues, until it was time to close the evening's entertainment. "Thank you and goodnight". Curtain down.

The Carnival Committee Chairman rushed onto the stage and grabbed the mike from me. Conspicuous by his absence when he thought things might go tits up, he reappeared when he realised disaster had been averted, and the sweet smell of success was drifting across the footlights from the hall where plenty of people were still mingling.

He thanked Elkie Brooks, 'The Wanted' and us for our efforts and brought the Carnival Queen back up on stage to wave to her subjects. Then, shock horror, he turned to Merv and whispered,

'The National Anthem'.

Merv looked at him.

'Nobody said anything about this pal.'

'Surely you know it,' squeaked the Chairman and, turning to the audience, he said,

'Ladies and Gentleman. The Queen'.

Merv was a little rusty on that one. It obviously didn't come up at Mrs Smith's in Grades One to Eight. I didn't do it when I was round her place either. 'Minuet in G' possibly, several arpeggios, a rap across the knuckles with a wooden ruler if your hand positions were incorrect, but 'God Save The Queen'? Rarely, if at all.

Bless him. Our Merv turned up trumps. A little falteringly to start with but in a key that was manageable for most of the crowd. Men stood to attention with straight backs. It wouldn't happen today, but most of the older ones had been in uniform either in the war or in National Service. The women in their best frocks, handbags on their arms as they were getting ready to make their way home had also been waylaid for these last rites. The young ones took their hands out of their pockets and cupped their ciggies in their hands to try to make out they weren't smoking and disrespecting Her Majesty.

Merv got through it. Big sigh of relief. Another box ticked for Martin. The crowd could go home.

The extra money changed hands. 'The Wanted' weren't, and trudged off home to Bristol. Elkie and her minder were spirited away by the Committee before Phil could get a word in, or anything else for that matter. They got into a large estate car and headed back to London. We had to get the kit down and out fairly sharpish as John the caretaker wanted to be in his bed. No time to wallow in the moment of how we had saved the day.

Of course, Elkie Brooks was destined for bigger things. But it would be a long time coming. She had a hard road to travel yet. Our paths were to cross again in April '71 at the Granary Club in Bristol, but that story is for another day children. Time for bed.

8. The Times They Are A- Changing

I always dreaded having any publicity photographs done. Not because of how we looked, although we were never a boy band it has to be said. But every time we did shell out a few quid for some photos someone left the band within a few weeks and generally we changed our name and switched our style of music. Perhaps if we had stuck to one style and just grafted on a new musician each time someone left we would have been better off. Who knows?

In truth, we had had some black and white pictures done in the youth club very early doors and they were no problem. The five of us stayed together with little or no friction for the first eighteen months or so with no musical differences or fallings out over women. Perhaps Martin kept the lid on it by getting us plenty of local gigs and it was still more a bit of a laugh than a serious attempt to make the big time. You can't take yourselves too seriously if you're playing gigs every other week in your own town, your friends won't let you get away with it, nor will the non believers. One glitch in your performance, a broken string, a dodgy amplifier, uncontrollable feedback, you name it, we had it and they won't let you forget it.

We had some colour shots done outside our new practice venue, a sports pavilion a couple of miles outside town in a less built up area as we'd become too noisy for the locals near the youth club. In fact, as we developed over the years, we got the elbow from here too. The smattering of bungalows around the sports field when we arrived had grown into a small village by the end of the Sixties and this was lived in by people who were not partial to Led Zeppelin, Rory Gallagher and The Groundhogs. C'est la vie!

No sooner had Martin started to hawk these colour pictures around some newer venues a bit further afield than two things happened. Gerry suddenly got the urge to turn us into a Donovan tribute band and Alan Price left The Animals. How the fuck are those two things related I hear you ask. Let me enlighten you.

Gerry had got us into The Kinks big time which was no problem really, because I found singing their songs a doddle. We had done all the early hit singles plus the B sides. 'It's Too Late' was the first song we ever recorded, in a flat somewhere in Bristol, on a Thursday evening. Why forty years later do I remember it was a Thursday? Heaven only knows but I would put every penny I have on that being right. Martin must have set it up, I think he was there when we did it, but I can't remember what happened to the tracks. I never heard them after that night, whatever they were, but 'It's Too Late' was definitely one of them. It sounded OK at the time too.

I digress (more often now than back then!) When Donovan recorded 'Catch the Wind' it passed me by, a total non event as far as I was concerned. I was listening to Howlin' Wolf and John Lee Hooker. Gerry was adamant we should add this song to our playlist. He was singing it, so fair enough, in it went and sometime later we added "With God on our Side' by Manfred Mann. Then one night we played at the Sergeants' Mess at Lyneham RAF base. We had been persuaded by Martin to play 'Help' by The Beatles and Merv took the lead vocal. The overall opinion of the assembled crowd was that it was fucking pants and I had to agree. Something had to give.

And so it came to pass brethren that the twins Malcolm and Glyn, and Merv and I travelled to Trowbridge one Friday night in the early summer of 1965. It was always best not to travel to Trowbridge with too small a party, it was a rough place then and it's no better now.

We took Phil along too and for once he stayed with us and didn't wander off prospecting. We'd read in the New Musical Express that Alan Price had left The Animals in May 'to pursue other musical interests', so it was out of curiosity as much as anything else that we went to one of the Alan Price Set's first gigs in the Town Hall. What we heard that night changed our lives, well, changed it for the next three years or so at least. Dramatic stuff isn't it?

When the curtains went back, there he was with his Hammond organ and Leslie speakers. Not that we were all that genned up on what it was that was making that awesome sound, we found that out later for ourselves. What struck us was the absence of any lead or rhythm guitarists, just a bass and a drummer and three cool looking dudes, on the far side of the stage from the lad himself, holding trumpet, tenor and baritone sax respectively. 'It's Getting Mighty Crowded', 'Ain't That Peculiar', 'Loving You is Sweeter than Ever' all come back to me as fresh as the day I heard them. 'Midnight Hour' too and Nina Simone's 'I Put a Spell On You' were belted out with the bass and drums as tight as any unit you ever heard, allowing Alan full rein to mesmerise the audience with his keyboard skills while the brass section filled in with rasping riffs that have hardly been bettered since.

We were dumbstruck. Chuck and Bo were history. All the British bands we had covered in the past eighteen months were passé. No way was I going to go back to Donovan, The Beatles and Manfred Mann protest songs.

That Friday was the night we first met Ian too. He was an itinerant roadie, a Londoner, in his late twenty's or early thirty's and not much over five foot. The next time we saw him he was with Georgie Fame and The Blue Flames at Ross on Wye. That's another story, so read on if you want to know what happened. Seeing him go about his work decided us there and then not to piss about with Martin or Glyn doing the driving, while we all then lugged the gear in and set it up once we had arrived at the venue. We were going to search for a roadie of our own. The small matter of payment was never discussed.

Alan Price had probably belted out three or four songs before he had a minor glitch with his organ or amp. It sounded fine to us but he was clearly not happy. He leaned back in the final stages of a number and bellowed "IAN" off mike and at the top of his voice. Ian scampered on stage with odd bits of kit in his hand and rectified the problem, temporarily at least. This rigmarole was repeated about ten minutes later, but fortunately for Ian this time he found the permanent fix and all was then sweetness and light in the Price household.

Merv had already decided his little electric organ wasn't going to enable us to replicate the sweet soul music we had witnessed. He also wanted a roadie to summon on stage by calling "IAN" at the top of his voice even if that wasn't his name. Malcolm also realised just how far behind he was in the drumming stakes that night. The bloke was superb. It was the economy of effort that was impressive. We knew loads of drummers who bashed the living daylights out of their drum kits, but this guy was rock steady and still filled in the gaps with twiddly bits (sorry, I was never a drummer) but his hands were hardly moving, not waving frenetically in the air like Animal in The Muppets. That Friday was probably when Malcolm started to think football might become more important in his life than being in the group. I started to think we needed another set of photos done.

Needless to say Phil had spotted an attractive young lady on the far side of the hall and went to investigate. Glyn was as keen as I'd ever seen him on the subject of music, he agreed we should 'do this kind of stuff, it's good'.

Miserable bastards that we were, we then set about planning how to break it to Gerry that, as Alan Price had jettisoned the lead/rhythm guitar format, he was surplus to requirements. For my own part I suddenly realised that what I had been singing so far in my career was bland and unfulfilling. All in all a good night.

By the time our next rehearsal night came around it had been agreed who was going to have a quiet word with Gerry. Typical blokes, we bottled it and nobody spoke to him apart from the odd grunt now and then through the first hour or so. He worked it out for himself.

'You fuckers don't want me in the group anymore do you?' he shouted eventually.

Glyn was there for the first time in ages, just spectating and probably wondering if there was going to be a punch up or whether a touch of the verbals would get the job done.

'It's not that Gerry,' said Glyn.

Fuck me I thought don't blow it mate.

'It's just that the lads want to play a different type of music and they don't need a guitarist for it. It's nothing personal. It's just one of those things,' he continued.

Amazingly, the petrol-head got it in one! He almost got Gerry believing we were gutted he had to leave and that was why we were all so reticent about telling him. That night when Gerry left we knew that in the cold light of day he would realise we had stiffed him, but we drove back into town more concerned about how we were going to do the gigs Martin had committed us to over the coming weeks and who we could get in to play in that brass section.

I put my key in the front door and as I trudged up the wooden hill to my bed the only thing I could think of was what the fuck was Martin going to do with those bloody photos.

9. Sweet Soul Music

Martin worked at a local engineering factory as I said earlier and his knack of finding transport, equipment, gigs, guitarists, photographers was phenomenal. Blow me down if he didn't come up with a bloke who had just got himself a tenor sax. That was Nick and he was the right age, wanted to play and was available. Result.

Well we had to meet him first and give him a try out. He came out to our practice hall and listened to Merv and Phil going through a couple of likely numbers. 'Midnight Hour' by Wilson Pickett, of course, which group didn't do that one, with or without a sax in their line up and 'Mr Pitiful' and 'My Girl' by Otis Redding.

Nick was a bit like Malcolm really, not a natural musician. I remember he struggled to get a consistent sound out of the reed he had been given when he bought his saxophone. It must have been an inferior brand and it had split. We weren't the best people to ask about buying kit accessories mind, Phil and Gerry always got cheap strings and Malcolm the ropiest drumsticks and snare drum skins. False economy, but money was short.

Once we'd got Nick sorted and tidied up our spare strings etcetera, to give the impression we were more or less a professional outfit, the real work started in earnest. Martin had managed to shuffle a few of our bookings, changing dates here and there, probably losing some for ever, but hey we were going through a major refit. We did do some gigs as a four piece. Martock in Somerset was one I remember. Merv filled in on organ as best he could on a load of numbers, clearly those numbers where Gerry's guitar had been crucial had to be abandoned but we somehow managed to get through an hour and three quarters with Nick appearing on stage for ten minutes in the second half to struggle through the songs we had learned. Merv had suggested we add 'Green Onions' by Booker T and the MGs and Nick found the right key eventually and filled in with some supporting notes. He was far from having enough confidence to launch into a solo in those early days.

The main thing was that he fitted in. His attitude was spot on, he was keen to learn and it was just as well. By now we were well into summer and I remember we went out to the practice hall virtually every day for a week. We may have taken a few days holiday, because I remember being there mornings about half ten to learn new songs! We used to take a record player along, with singles and albums provided by yours truly (I seemed to be the only one buying records). So we listened to Don Covay, Junior Walker, The Marvelettes, The Four Tops as well as Sam and Dave, The Temptations and of course Otis Redding and Wilson Pickett.

Over those few days where we had the 'crash course' on how to learn a new playlist, we also received visits from youngsters Merv was at school with and who had been in the school brass band with him. They were ex cornet and trombone players mostly and they could produce a note on a trumpet (borrowed from a bloke Martin knew who was in the Navy) but once again they lacked any real talent. Nor did they have that other ingredient you need if you're going to be in a band - desperation to make the big time. If you have that then nothing ever gets in your way as you strive to make it to the top of the tree.

Over the next couple of weeks we gigged in local venues, adding more numbers featuring Nick and reducing the number of 'fillers' from the old line-up. Then one night Martin said we should change the name of the band to something which reflected the type of music we were doing now. He thought if we kept the old name, people would expect us to carry on playing the Chuck and Bo songs plus The Stones and the rest of the more edgy English bands.

He had a point. We wanted a clean break, so Nick suggested 'Heart 'N Soul', which considering he was a new boy was pretty good for his first attempt. So good in fact that there was no further discussion.

Early that autumn, a Tuesday evening saw us with our new van, kit loaded on board, driving out to the practice hall. There was still work to be done on the new repertoire and more songs to learn. Martin had some news for us too. He was still prepared to be our manager if we wanted him, but he felt we had pretty well exhausted the local scene. We'd played virtually all the venues that wanted us. Most of them wanted us back but we didn't always want to go back mind, He had been in touch with an agency in Bristol to see if they would give us bookings further afield. They were ready to hear us play and if we were okay then they wanted to be our sole agent. That meant Martin's grafting in the local scene would be knocked on the head. It was time to take the plunge.

In a way it came at about the right time. We had become stale in the old line up if we were honest. The spark we got from the move to soul rather than rhythm and blues with a 'poppy' slant from the British bands charting through '63 to '65, meant we were up for a move to pastures new. Of course, if we'd known those pastures were in bloody Wales, and we'd spend the next couple of years going over the Severn Bridge nearly every weekend, we may have been less keen.

We did a couple of local gigs on the Friday and Saturday nights without incident. The J2 was just the job and Phil and Martin had fixed a bench seat into the back from a write off they had raided at a nearby scrap yard so we had a comfortable seat for four of us, plus driver, passenger and one perched on the engine cover in the front. The height of luxury. Saturday was Samuel Salter's Social Club in Trowbridge for the umpteenth time. Nick and Phil had brought along a lad called Dave who was home on leave from the Navy. He was a year older than me and had joined at fifteen and now he was on the aircraft carrier Ark Royal and had just finished a tour of the Far East.

Dave was a character and had loads of stories about his shore leave in Hong Kong. He had spent a lot of his spare time on board ship learning to play the drums and he played for the ship's orchestra. On this last trip they had even backed Sammy Davis Junior. Malcolm was a little nervous as he set up his kit that evening. I think he thought that Nick and Phil were trying to work him out of the band. Dave asked if he could have a go and Malc handed over his sticks a little reticently. Every drummer has his own quirky way of setting up his kit, at least the ones we used over the years certainly did. Dave tried a few rolls around the snare, up onto the two small tom toms mounted on the bass drum, then over to the floor tom tom. He stopped three or four times to make little adjustments and experimented to see if he was comfortable.

'Right. That should do it. I've no idea how you manage to play if you set them up like they were in the beginning!'

Then he launched into a five or six minute drum solo, pretty impressive stuff too, including one piece that showed his sense of humour as he rattled away on the snare drum as if he was in a pipe and drum band, bringing his sticks up under his nose in perfect alignment.

Malcolm was deflated.

'You might as well keep my sticks.' he said with a smile that belied his inner anxieties. Dave was happy with his work and had no wish to prolong Malc's agony.

'No thanks buddy. Come and sit here and see if they're set up better for you too. If not we'll tweak them again until we find the best set up.'

Malcolm sat down and tentatively tried to perform multiple rolls with the new set up and after a few false starts he had to agree it was a lot easier. "No bugger ever showed me how to set the kit up before."

Dave asked him where he kept his spare sticks. Malcolm didn't always have any and if one had broken we would have been stuffed unless we were playing with another band and could borrow one. When he retrieved some from the wooden crates Phil had constructed to carry the drum kit in back in the early days, Dave fixed them in place, ready to hand on the bass drum and suggested Malc never turned up without at least three sets of sticks.

'If one shatters because you've had it a while, and they get weakened by too many rim shots on the snare drum, or it just flies out of your hand on a warm night when your hands are all sweaty, then two seconds later you can be back on the beat and the audience won't notice a thing.'

'Cheers Dave. None of these would have thought of that,' said Malc, nodding in our direction as we sat watching the master class unfold. No sticks were broken that night but Malc was ready if they had.

As we were driving back from Trowbridge after the gig Nick asked if it would be alright if Dave came out to practice on Tuesday evening. Nobody had any objection. He was good company. I can't remember who it was who said it as we went our different ways when we were dropped off in town, but someone remarked that it was Dave's trumpet that had been borrowed for the trials we had had earlier in the year when Nick joined us. All those school friends of Merv's had used it before we rejected them one by one. It was probably Martin who went round to Dave's auntie's and asked to borrow it as Dave was obviously away in the Far East at that time. He was adopted and lived with two aunts as far as we knew. I never really knew his family circumstances, but maybe his early childhood was the catalyst for him joining up as young as he did.

Whatever his background he was there on Tuesday evening with his trumpet. He and Malc set the drum kit up in double quick time so we were ready to go at least ten minutes earlier than usual. Merv and Nick went over the tunes we had rehearsed the most and sorted out what notes Dave should be playing. He had bought the trumpet in London when he was home on leave a couple of years before. He had played the cornet at fifteen in the Navy and stuck with that for a couple of years before he took a fancy to the drums. His lip was a bit off to start with and he produced a few bum notes but, as the evening wore on, he got it together and it certainly added to the brass sound we were trying to achieve. Merv was keen to move on to something new to add to our play list, so it was agreed Nick and Dave would work alone on any nights we had off, getting him up to speed so he could get on stage with us as soon as possible. We were on our way to being a six piece!

The following night it was off to Stonehouse to try out for the Bristol agent that Martin had been in touch with. We were all working of course, Dave wasn't coming with us but we all piled into the van and eventually found the place with about twenty minutes to spare before we were due on stage. Not a good start!

When we got the kit out of the van and lugged it in through the back door of the hall we were virtually straight onto the stage, which helped. But with two other sets of kit already on there, we were hard pressed to find space to get our little bits and pieces in.

Martin had wandered off to let the management know we had arrived, find out the playing times and so on. He came back and said,

'You're on for about forty minutes. The other bands are 'Emile Ford & The Checkmates' and 'Sounds Incorporated'.'

Fuck me I thought. Two fairly big names. We've got to support them? The other lads had a few nerves too and we were a bit worried about the agent into the bargain. If we were only on for one set of forty minutes, what if the agent turned up late? He might miss us altogether. I was more concerned that we would be crap tonight with the two bands due on after us. Highly polished professionals to a man. Hell's teeth! Where can we get a bloody pint or two? No chance, we're on straight away.

We started with 'Down in the Valley' by Otis Redding, then '634-5789' by Wilson Pickett. 'Hold On I'm Coming', 'Mr Pitiful', 'Midnight Hour' and anything that showcased our Mervyn on keyboards and Nick's wailing tenor sax. Malc and Phil held it together and the audience reaction was more enthusiastic than the youth clubs and social clubs we generally played at. These kids knew the music we were playing and they liked it. Consequently we enjoyed playing to them. It showed on our faces as we finished off our set and everyone headed to the side of the stage to see Martin

He was alone. No sign of the agent.

'Mind you,' said Martin, 'I've only ever talked to him on the phone. I don't know what he looks like. He could be here for all I know.'

Somewhat dejected we trudged off to the pub down the road and had a few swift ones. We were partly drowning our sorrows, imagining the worst, that the agent had been a 'no show', and partly congratulating ourselves on the quality of our set. We wanted to get back to the hall though to see Emile Ford. We knew they had had hits a few years before, but you don't always get the full impression of what a band is about until you've seen them live. There was a crowd of kids at the front of the stage bopping along to the sound. Emile had them in the palm of his hand. Big bloke.

We watched him work his magic and then the stage was re-jigged again to allow 'Sounds Incorporated' room to get their large line up into position. The crowd were a little less enthusiastic it has to be said, when they took to the stage. A lot of instrumental numbers, as was their speciality, with organ and brass doing their thing, without ever sounding anything like the stuff we were doing. Perhaps without the big personality that Emile had, they were past their sell by date, and the kids couldn't find any character to identify with or anyone to focus on, if you get my drift. Even so the musicians among us stood and admired the way they did what they did. It was a throwback to '60 through to '62. This was '65 and the times they were a'changing. I wish I'd written a song about that come to think about it.

The night was coming to an end. People were leaving the hall and bands were mingling on the stage, breaking down gear and readying it for the various vans in the car park. Conversations between the two professional outfits were fairly amicable, they had probably crossed paths before around the country over the years. We had a chat here and there with members of each band although we were a little unsure who was from which band.

Martin came up to the side of the stage with a tall, stockily built chap, probably in his late thirty's, who was growing through his hair. He was a big unit and I would never have said he was balding to his face. He introduced himself as Howard, the agent and despite our earlier concerns he had been around all evening. He wanted to listen to us without us knowing he was in the building. He was convinced we could do business. He was part of a big Bristol agency that handled a load of bands and could give us access to venues all over the West Country and South Wales. We were all for it and so when we shook his hand and he promised to be in touch with some dates for our diary we had a spring in our step as we loaded the van and climbed aboard for the journey home.

Martin was a little quiet on the way back. Obviously the reality of his no longer running around with us week in week out was becoming all too concrete. He drove us back in silence as we chatted animatedly about the endless possibilities of life on the road to fame and fortune that stretched before us. As I always used to say to the lads in the band, when a setback occurred or a change was forced upon us by circumstances, 'life is just a bowl of poisoned cherries.'

10. Dance To The Music

It's strange how things turn out. In those very early days when The Argonauts were in their pomp, and ruled the roost as far as all the bands in the area were concerned, we were in awe of their lead guitarist Dave. He had been playing for a long while, even though he was a little bit younger than me. His dad Les was a pianist, pub trained rather than classically, if you like. He vamped with the left hand and sorted out the tune with the right. Very effective he was too. A lot of pubs and clubs had an upright piano in the bar, not always in tune mind, but it didn't seem to matter after you'd had a few beers. Les would be persuaded to knock out a song or two and sometimes people would sing along, other times they'd just carry on drinking and talking. He was about six foot three and well built so very rarely did anyone ask if he'd move on to another pub. Dave would tag along with his older brother John and eventually Dave, having taught himself to play the guitar, sat in with his Dad and they played to anyone prepared to listen.

Dave's talent for the guitar was soon spotted and 'The Footbeats' were born. Rock 'n Roll mostly and from there it was a short hop and a skip to Jason and The Argonauts. As a unit they were the best around, so it was no great shock when they turned professional and disappeared to Germany and the clubs and US airbases where other British groups had learned their craft on the way to fame and fortune.

After about eighteen months though, the hopes and dreams had turned to frustration and disappointment. Not an unfamiliar story of course. Dave had grown tired of the long hours playing to empty venues, the travelling around the country with tedious hours spent with little or no cash, setting fire to your farts to pass the time. He was a quiet homeboy at heart who had a gift for making his Fender guitar sound like magic.

So after their latest stint in Germany, they came home and Dave decided enough was enough. He started work back at the engineering factory, where he had been apprenticed several years before. You can probably tell where this is going can't you readers? He'd been home a few weeks when he bumped into Martin and Nick at work and caught up on the latest gossip. He knew we were without a guitarist and that Nick was playing sax. Martin told him about the Bristol agency and how the local gigs were being ticked off our itinerary and how he had taken a back seat as far as Heart 'N Soul were concerned.

We had played on several occasions at The Mendip in Atworth. It was a social club in another small factory just outside town. We had a longstanding date in our diary to play there on a Saturday perhaps three or four weeks after the audition in Stonehouse. Nobody told Malc or me but we turned up and started unloading the gear when Dave appeared with Nick and Phil and if it was okay with the rest of the band Dave wanted to sit in and play with us tonight. Merv was keen, and so was I, as we were well aware how good he was. We didn't know if he knew all the numbers we were doing at that time, so we had a quick run through our playlist and he knew over half already. It was just a case of sorting out which key we did them in and who was handling any solos on the way through. Dave filled in bits and pieces in several others and sat out any that were totally foreign to him.

The two and a half hours we had to play seemed to whiz by and the audience were happy enough. The Argonauts had played there fairly often and Dave was well liked and more popular than we were. Afterwards Nick asked Dave if he had enjoyed himself. He said "Yeah, brilliant. I like the stuff you're doing now. It's cool. It's up to you guys, I don't want to put anyone's nose out of joint. If you're not happy say so, but when are you playing again? I'd like to come along if you want me to." Daft question.

We had a practice session set for the Monday or Tuesday evening and it was agreed Dave would pick things up from there. Merv rang Howard and told him we were now playing as a seven piece. More and more gigs were being rung through to Merv in his office. He was working at a local solicitor's. Mr Taylor, the choirmaster worked there too. Small world isn't it?

The next few months were our introduction to the wonderful country that is Wales. My great grandfather was Welsh so I have my own reasons for not castigating them too much, but when you're travelling weekend after weekend in a foreign country you meet some lovely people and some absolute wankers.

Howard sent us to Tenby and Haverfordwest for instance, and as we engaged the locals in conversation (mostly male sadly) we were informed, quite abruptly, that as far as they were concerned Wales didn't start until you were on the road out of Cardiff. Places like Cardiff, Newport, Monmouth and so on weren't proper Welsh places see, they were English towns or cities that just happened geographically to be on the wrong side of the Severn Bridge.

Thank God the bridge had opened by the time we were gigging regularly in Wales, the long trek round would have put paid to those weekends away. What am I saying! Who were those bastards that robbed me of Saturday and Sunday, watching footy, or going to the pictures with a girlfriend for a fumble in the back seats or going for a pint on Sunday lunchtime. Sunday? The bloody Welsh didn't even open on Sundays in the mid '60s. Fucking road builders, why waste time on the M4 when the A4 and A38 could have had a few potholes filled in!

We had already had one change of name after Gerry left. The next one was a little while coming as, with the switch in the style of music we were playing, 'Heart 'n Soul' was appropriate enough. We had added Nick and the two Daves and lost Glyn as a driver without too many glitches. Howard was initially pretty happy with the name and certainly with the beefing up of our line-up. The more of us there were, the more he could justify charging and therefore the more he earned in commission.

The next member to jump ship was Malcolm and, to be fair, it didn't come as a big surprise. His football skills were much in demand and, after trying to do both during the 65/66 season, he decided he couldn't spare the time for the band if he wanted to play for the Town at the level they had reached in the various regional Leagues. Away games were in Devon or Cornwall some weekends so the time came for a parting of the ways. We knew another band in town that was hardly getting a gig anywhere to shout about and their drummer Pete was the obvious candidate. He was on our doorstep, with no commitments and he finished work at half four every weekday. Whether he could drum or not was incidental. Pete was the guy for us!

Malc wanted to be able to start pre-season training and all the bollocks these footballers need to do for ninety minutes of graft every weekend. So, not long after the World Cup Final in that glorious summer of '66, we got Pete to come along to a practice night. Malc was happy to take him through the numbers we were doing and once he had almost turned Malc's kit back to front, as he insisted on having his high-hat on his right rather than on the left like any normal right handed drummer, he was fitting in really quickly. After a few sessions over a three week period we were back on the road with a new drummer.

One thing Pete brought to the band was his madcap sense of humour. He was a cross between Freddie Starr and Norman Wisdom and he kept us in fits of laughter many a time on a long journey, or in an interval at a gig in some dodgy pub in the Welsh hills.

One night he nearly stopped the lads on stage playing altogether with just one line delivered with his deadpan expression. We were in Chard and there was a large crowd in the town hall that night, not because we were there, but because the half time entertainment was a stripper. She arrived in our dressing room behind the stage with her husband/manager/minder about ten minutes before we were due on for our first set. She was pushing forty with a big fur coat. She looked the part alright and he was a bit of a slimy git and started telling us what we had to do for him. As usual, Howard hadn't mentioned anything about backing a stripper.

Merv, Phil and Pete were delegated to provide her music. She wanted as few of the band on stage as possible. Merv and Phil were consigned to the far edges and Pete sat at the back. After all, most of what she intended to do would be facing the audience! We carried on with our own set as soon as the details had been thrashed out and after an hour of sweet soul music, the curtains closed to a smattering of applause. We made our way to the bar to get a drink and the stripper with her husband, in 'minder' mode went the other way. She was carrying what looked like a large gin and tonic and as she teetered by on her high heels I detected a slight wobble that suggested it wasn't the first of the night.

Our little trio returned to the stage and got ready. We went to the dressing room, but were refused entry as the town hall management was in attendance. Miss Whiplash or whatever she called herself was getting her slap on and anything else she needed to prepare for her act. Her hubby appeared and warned us off, standing in the wings as she wanted a clear run for the dressing room door after she had got her kit off. Yeah , yeah , yeah no problem.

The crowd were getting restless. We looked out front and they were ten deep at the front of the stage, all with a beer in one hand and a fag in the other. Safest thing probably, didn't want to have a spare hand at a time like that did they? We were in Chard, for heaven's sake. They were sons of the soil, mostly and short on conversation, shouting "C'mon darlin' get your tits out!!" and she was still in the dressing room!

The town hall bloke got up and did the honours and introduced her, whatever her stage name was, and with a roll of drums, our intrepid trio launched into 'Night Train!' All aboard! Twelve bar blues and Merv was away on his Hammond organ, giving it plenty. The lady artiste appeared at the side of the stage, still in her fur coat, the locals bayed for flesh and she began her act.

I won't bore you with the details. They're all much of a muchness aren't they? Long black gloves; check. Black stockings; check. Tiger-skin bra; check. Twirl the tassels; check. Pick up stocking from floor without falling off high heels. Rain check.

Slight pause while she takes a second run at that one. Got it! Check. Rub yourself up and down with stocking, turn to face Pete and bend over to look at audience through the legs. Check. A bit of prancing about on the acres of stage between Merv and Phil and then do a double take at the side of the stage where the discarded members (steady on) of the band are all stood watching.

Only the G-string left now. Make the crowd wait, remove it while facing the back of the stage, then a quick pivot on one heel and tadaa!!!

Her husband struggled with the curtain and although it had worked like a dream when we started our act, at the end of our first set and when our trio had struck up, it now refused to move, except oh so very slowly. She turned back towards Pete, not wanting to give the lads in the front row a close up of her bits any longer than was absolutely necessary. Merv and Phil were looking across the stage at each other trying to agree when the Night Train should pull into the station. Pete was about four feet from the naked stripper and looked across to the side of the stage and without a hint of a smile said,

'I ain't going to tell my Mum about this.'

The curtain had finally reached the centre. Her hubby shouted at her to get off. She gathered up her odd bits of discarded clothing and scuttled off towards the dressing room, running the gauntlet of the rest of us and the town hall chap who was trying to pacify her husband, and get us to move away, but couldn't resist a quick peek as she brushed past him and slammed the dressing room door behind her. Merv and Phil were laughing like drains. We were now free to join them on stage. The town hall bloke tried to fix the curtains while chatting to us and convincing himself everything had worked out alright really.

The stripper, now fully clothed, and her husband emerged from the dressing room, gave us a filthy look and left the hall at a rate of knots, never to be seen again. We all went back on stage for our second set and at the end of another fun packed evening we drove back home and dropped Pete off at his mothers' house. Cruel? Not particularly, he did still live there.

11. Oh Happy Day.

It was winter 1966. We had driven up to Cirencester in the van, with Phil travelling in his frog-eyed Sprite with Nick. Usual reasons, the van was cramped and cold, plus the sports car pulled the birds.

We arrived at the venue, the Town Hall from memory, set up our kit and found the nearest pub. I had my usual, a swift four pints of whatever bitter was on offer to lubricate my throat and loosen my inhibitions. As was often the case, we returned to the scene of the gig and found a handful of people scattered around the outside walls of the room. We began our first set and gradually a procession of teenage boys and girls trickled through the doors and things started to look up. We were going down pretty well with our soul selection, Wilson Pickett, Sam and Dave, Otis Redding and the rest.

In those days we were a six piece, with a crappy Hohner organ, drums, bass and lead/rhythm guitar, a tenor sax and yours truly on vocals. We finished our last number for the first half. Somebody pulled the stage curtains across and put an LP on to cover for the lack of a DJ. We hung around for a while chatting, deciding whether to go back to the first pub or try somewhere different. From the front of the stage appeared three girls, probably about seventeen but who cared in those days. I'd spotted them dancing around their handbags for most of the set but hadn't paid any real attention to them.

They introduced themselves and seemed particularly interested in getting up close and personal with the organist, the drummer and me. I wasn't complaining, in fact I wasn't saying much of anything. My tongue was stuck to the roof of my mouth and I was probably dribbling. She was a knockout. About five foot two with long black hair and dark brown eyes, which although a non swimmer, I could have plunged right into there and then. She was talking to me and I was the only person on the stage, it was magic. I thought I'd died and gone to heaven, or at least I fantasised about the 'plunging' part but not into her eyes. But wait. What's that noise? It's her mate leaving the stage at a rate of knots in floods of tears, Merv having told her to 'fuck off' as she was hanging onto his arm for grim death and he was feeling all righteous about his precious Rosemary, who was many miles away at University in Nottingham.

The third girl followed her mate, while the girl with me was looking after them with a puzzled expression on her face.

'Oh dear,' she said, 'she'll be a pain tonight now.'

'Why's that?' I enquired, a little concerned that my chances of a quick dip might be fading fast.

'She always has the organist.' said my new friend without a blink of those outrageously long lashes.

Lights went on in my head as I did the maths. It wasn't my voice, nor my boyish charm and good looks, not even my personality. Not even that in my stage trousers I contrived to appear to be hung like a horse, ye old rolled up sock trick. Nope. I was the singer. Ergo, I was it.

The decision was made. We went to the first pub again, Merv (alone), Nick, Phil and Dave (alone but not by choice). Pete was reunited with the caring mate and Little Miss Misery who tagged along in a sulk. I floated along behind with the first prize and a big grin on my face. We had a couple of bevvies and returned to the hall, which by now was heaving, well alright, it was fuller than when we left it. I extracted my tongue from the throat of my companion and we took to the stage for the second half. The hour we had to play seemed to drag, as the prospect of what would follow kept dancing in front of my eyes. Literally, since they moved from the side of the stage into the centre, for a better view of my trousers and Pete on the drums.

Little Miss Misery got picked up by a local lad, who perhaps 'got lucky' every now and then when a group turned up without the required keyboard player. A couple of slow ballads and a rousing finish saw our visit to Cirencester enter the last lap. The curtains closed yet again and the kit was hastily taken down and put into the van. Phil disappeared with Nick in the Sprite and the rest of the lads had to hang fire while Pete and I found a quiet spot to say our goodbyes. Not to each other, of course, but to our two young ladies.

The reality and the fantasy have blurred over the years. She was beautiful, that was undeniable, I offered up a prayer of thanks to the Big Man for not making me a keyboard player and went for it. You have no idea how urgent it is for those sat in the van waiting, to get home. On another night, in different circumstances, they would be quite happy chilling out in a transport café until the sun came up, but not when you've pulled and they haven't! A couple of bases were reached successfully but any thoughts of 'plunging' were not on the agenda sadly. The usual promises about getting together again next time we played there were made but we never did. They never turn up the next time anyway. A thousand gigs experience proved that over umpteen years. So back to the van it was, envy all over the faces of those inside as I climbed in the back. Home James.

12.You can keep your 'Welcome in the hillside'

What memories of Wales can I dredge up that might interest you? One of the longer weekends I can remember was in April 1967 and we had played in England on the Friday evening, where it was is beyond me, but it was a late one. By the time I rolled in it was about four in the morning. On the Saturday afternoon, just after lunch we set off towards Cardigan. We arrived in Cardiff at about five o'clock and stopped at a garage to fill up with petrol. We had met a fair bit of traffic on the motorway and the A48 the other side of the bridge, so we'd had a fairly frustrating journey so far and there were plenty more miles to travel until we got to our gig.

The guy on the pumps was in his fifties at a guess and was keen to chat. He pointed a greasy finger at the side window to get us to open up, so he could stick his head in and get at the guys sat in the back as well as the lucky ones in the front.

'What about Jarret then?' he asked in his obviously local accent.

We didn't have a clue what he was on about. He wouldn't let it lie though, he had clocked us as English as soon as we had pulled up at the pumps I reckon.

'What about Jarret then? He showed you English boys isn't it?'

The word English was rather cruelly emphasised I thought, considering we were travelling many a mile to entertain some of his fellow countrymen and women. As we didn't have a fucking clue what he was on about, he grew more agitated and a few unpleasantries were exchanged with those inside the van, mostly those in the back. They were keen to get moving so they could get to the gig and extricate themselves from the confines of the seating arrangements we had cobbled together in the back of the van. The seats were comfortable in our previous existence but with the two Daves having joined things were getting decidedly cosy.

While these unpleasantries were flying back and forth I was the mug sat by the open window in the front. The petrol attendant was carrying on about someone, or something called Jarret, sticking his finger in my chest and leaving a dirty mark on my brand new Ben Sherman. He had a habit of spitting when he was angry which I noticed more than once. I'd had enough so I wound up the window and the final two or three gobs landed on the outside of the glass rather than on yours truly.

That made him even more upset as he clearly thought we were pissing off without paying. He started banging on the outside of the van, shaking his fist and generally making himself look like a prick. This brought some younger bloke in a tie out of the office to see what was going on. He came round to the driver's side and asked what the trouble was. Malc was driving that stretch of the trip and he just offered the bloke some money to pay for the petrol and said it was a problem with the language. We didn't speak Welsh so we couldn't understand what the bloke was on about. The office chappie looked at him a little confused at this but took the money and returned with the change.

'Cheers mate.' said Malcolm and made to drive off.

'What about that Keith Jarret then, nineteen points in his first international!' called out the younger bloke as we pulled away. Fuck me, they were all at it.

We had to stop in Swansea to take a piss, get some fags and a paper to check the footy results. Bloody banner headlines in the Sheep Shagger's Gazette 'England Routed by Schoolboy', rugby - who knew, who cared? We must have stood out like spare pricks at a wedding as being English, because we couldn't even get back to the van from the place we had stopped for a break without some lads on their way out to the pub or local hop calling out,

'What about Jarret then?' from the other side of the road.

We managed to drive the rest of the way without being spotted and arrived at the venue in Cardigan. There was no escape. Now we were really in Wales, into it deep. We were up to our necks in it. The entire Welsh rugby union fan club was in Cardigan that night and every single one of them just had to come up and say something, either while we were setting up, during our first set, in the break, ad infinitum.

The only bright spot on the horizon was a tall well built girl with long dark hair. She was wearing a dark red polo neck sweater and a camel coloured trouser suit. She didn't appear to be with anyone except a couple of female mates, so I chanced my arm and brushed through the Welsh fifteen to track her down to the bar. I was in luck, she had seen our second set all the way through and she was impressed. So, as there were plenty of hands spare to break down the kit on the stage, I took the opportunity, as Phil had done on many occasions, to give the young lady a tour around the inside of our van.

Now as the kit was on the stage there wasn't much to see, so I sat her down on the back seat and went in for a snog. No early problems except for the sweater which appeared to end about eighteen inches below the belt which was keeping her trousers up. Her tongue was all over the place and things were starting to hot up. She quickly assessed a forlorn struggle to remove anything worthwhile in the time available before the lads arrived to load up the gear and switched her attention to my zipper. Game on! Considering the fact that she was a big girl, and the cramped situation the back seat afforded, she was remarkably dextrous, (good with her fingers, in case you were wondering) I was counting backwards from one hundred (impressive eh?) in anticipation of what was to follow, when there was heated activity on the outside of the van, which tended to distract me. I had reached about seventy three when the whole evening went pear shaped.

A female voice yelled

'Mwfanwy,' accompanied by a banging on the side of the van, 'Gareth's here!'

I was half in and half out of my nicks at this juncture and I couldn't have given a flying fuck, quite frankly whether Keith bloody Jarret himself was there, or Max Boyce, with a male voice choir into the bargain. The word 'Gareth' seemed to have an instant cooling effect and her hand, her tongue and everything else that was in contact with my body was swiftly removed. She was away out of the van like a greyhound out of the traps.

Curses, foiled again!

The lads were wheeling amps and speakers down the ramp at the side of the building and so I was not alone long enough for Gareth to know for certain which of us had been playing around with his girl friend. We had the kit in the van in no time flat and were all ready to make our way on to the next gig in Tredegar on Sunday.

'How much was it we were getting tonight?' Phil asked. Not enough I thought but didn't articulate it as I could sense a little tension.

Merv said, 'Bollocks. I thought you were sorting that Ted when you disappeared'

I denied all knowledge of any financial dealings. Anything that may have happened in the past twenty minutes or so, or that might have if bloody Gareth hadn't arrived was freely given as far as I was concerned.

As we made our way gingerly up the ramp back into the building to search out the manager, I caught sight of my female companion, now on the arm of a man mountain. Fair play, she didn't drop me in it. Just as well, he would have killed me! She obviously did let on we were the band that had played there tonight, and that we were English, because Gareth informed us that he and his mates had just got back from the Arms Park after seeing the match.

'What about that Jarret, then boys?' Limited conversationalists, the Welsh, don't you think?

We managed to pick up the cash and get away unscathed. Phil had a brainwave and asked the manager of the place whether there were any bed and breakfast places locally he could suggest we try, even at this late hour. Phil wasn't keen on trying to sleep in the van, considering how crowded it was on the trip down into Wales. The bloke gave us an address about three minutes drive away. He reckoned we would get in there no problem. We decided we could afford for three of us to get a proper bed for the night. The rest would stay with the van.

Right enough, the door to the terraced house was opened by a hard faced elderly Welsh dragon who took our cash up front and herded us into the single rooms on the first floor. It was cheap enough but as we were 'out of season' she wasn't doing breakfast. We had to be out by nine sharp. I don't think any of us slept much. It was a case of 'hot and cold running water in all beds', namely, bloody damp. The other four in the van were better off, at least they could cosy up against one another for warmth. Perhaps not, we were close, but not that close.

Anyway, we were all up and set to leave by nine when Phil drove the van round to pick us up. They had spent the night in another side street and hadn't fared much better. It was a cold night but at least they hadn't seen any sign of Gareth or his mates wandering the streets looking for trouble. They were tucked up in a warm bed and probably thought we were sensible enough to drive back to England. Howard had had other plans.

We found a café open in the first or second village we drove through and went in for a long overdue breakfast. There were a few locals in and they were able to take the piss out of us something rotten. Not knowing any Welsh meant we didn't get the specifics but it was obvious that we were the cause of their amusement. Seven Englishmen looking like they needed a good night's sleep, several needing a wash and shave, dressed in gear that marked us down as 'beatniks' or whatever passed for modern terminology in a place so far from civilisation it made our little market town look like the centre of everything that was 'cool' and 'happening'. Of course they were amused. I strained to listen to their conversation to see if I recognised an odd word or phrase. No sign of Jarret' or any reference to the 'rugby' as far as I could tell.

We devoured the fried breakfast, which was just what the doctor ordered, paid up and left so we could get out of deepest Wales and head for the delights of Tredegar. The journey this time was uneventful, although as we went east the weather took a turn for the worse. A bright, sunny start was replaced by grey, overcast skies and drizzle. When we stopped after about sixty miles to stretch our legs it was cold and the dampness seemed to just hang in the air. The rain wasn't actually falling, or so it appeared, it was just there in front of you. It was a brief stop, for a pee and to pick up a paper, I won't bore you with the headlines on the back page. When we finally arrived in Tredegar, the weather had improved slightly, but the town was so depressing it dragged you down into its miserable self such that even if the sun had been panning down it would probably have appeared dark and oppressive everywhere you looked.

Perhaps all mining towns were like that, I don't know, this was the first one I'd ever visited in daylight - if you could call it daylight. I checked my watch a couple of times and sure enough it was mid afternoon. There were virtually no cars or people on the streets, the buildings were blackened by time and industry and any shops that hadn't closed down were shut anyway as it was Sunday. So why were we here then we wondered?

A short drive around the empty main streets brought us to an imposing Victorian building which had a large board on the front with gold lettering, faded and peeling it goes without saying, which informed us that this was the Tredegar Miners' Institute, or some such title.

'That's the place' said Merv. 'That's the name on the contract Howard sent me I'm positive.'

Inwardly, we were all hoping he was mistaken, but there seemed to be an inevitability to it. It was Howard's little joke, I think, a long tiring weekend with a decent enough gig to start with, something not too dusty on Saturday evening, then a shit hole to finish up in on Sunday night.

As we were following Phil's old principle of arriving early in order to set up our kit, have a practice and then troll off to get a bite to eat and a few bevvies, we looked around in vain to find a caretaker or someone in a position of authority to let us in. Fat chance. They were probably sleeping off their Sunday lunch after Chapel. So we parked up and wandered the streets, and then the side roads, searching for a café that was open for business. Zilch. It was back to the van, dry the damp drizzle from our faces and clothes and sit rereading the papers for a couple of hours before there was any sign of life.

Around six o'clock we ventured out and about again and found a café open that served a reasonable pasty and chips, with bread and butter on a side plate no less, haute cuisine for us weary travellers. We got back to the hall in time to see that the doors were open and a steady stream of middle aged and elderly people was filing in. Great! We found the head man on the Committee who told us where to bring in our kit and what the running order was for the evening. We unloaded the van, got set up and had a quick sound check, then we headed for the bar. Yes, hallelujah, even on a Sunday night in Wales they had a bar!

We got served and then headed off to what passed for a dressing room to have a chinwag about the running order. We were on first for forty five minutes, followed by the bingo, then the comedian and then we went back on again for another forty five minute set. All over by half past ten, kit in the van by eleven, home by one o'clock. Job's a good 'un! Sunday nights eh? This line up was more like a cabaret, with bingo to replace the novelty act. A quick dash to the bar for a refill and we were up on stage ready to go.

The hall was laid out with tables and chairs in long straight lines and, fair play, virtually every table was occupied. There was a smattering of the younger girls of Tredegar but for the most part it was 'grab a granny night'. Never mind, we could still enjoy the evening. We ripped into our opening numbers with great gusto and the response was immediate. The head man from the Committee was up to the side of the stage, showing a remarkable turn of speed, to ask us to turn it down a bit.

'C'mon lads, they can't hear themselves talking over your lot now, can they?' he said.

Ah, it wasn't a cabaret then, more a recital, background music to the drinking, smoking and nattering. We carried on with our volume much reduced and got through the set without any more interruptions.

As we finished the Committee man came on stage with a small folding table and chair and asked for a mike to be left on so he could use it for the bingo. Once he was set up he returned with his bag of balls and a tray and he was off and running.

We went to the bar for a beer and found we were virtually on our own, except for a handful of lads and lasses who considered playing bingo beneath them. The rest of the audience were apparently glued to their chairs surrounded by a smoke haze, spellbound, as Dai or whatever his name was, called out the numbers. We decided the excitement was too much and trailed back to our dressing room to have a rest. Merv wanted to see the comedian anyway who was changing into his stage gear in the cramped space put aside for the artistes. He was in his forties I would guess and was quite a cheerful soul, which was not what we expected. Rumour had it that real funny men were always long faced miserable bastards unless they had a mike in their hand and an audience. He introduced himself and we were splitting our sides with laughter right away. I always did that every time I saw Tommy Cooper, I don't know about you, but as soon as he appeared on stage, even before he spoke I was helpless. This bloke though was a different kettle of fish.

'Hello lads,' he said, 'what are the crowd like then, okay? My name's Wit Munday by the way.'

After that, we had to watch his act, to see if it could be as bad as his choice of stage name. We needn't have worried, he was pretty awful. All his jokes were as old as the hills although the delivery in his Welsh accent made a few of them seem funnier than they really were. He

99

tested the water with a couple of pale blue ones and changed tack once he caught sight of the Committee man making his way to the stage, leaving his wife at their table. She looked decidedly sniffy. Obviously Sunday night was not a good night for a risqué joke in Tredegar. So poor old Wit Munday ploughed on, digging himself deeper into a hole from which there was only one escape. He wanted to finish with a song and get off. We were at the bar again, getting a beer to take on stage for our last set so we were in no position to help him out so he sang unaccompanied, except for the catcalls and whistles from around the room. He legged it to the dressing room.

'Tough crowd tonight boys,' he said as we returned to get our bits and pieces and get back on stage.

'They were okay with us in the first half.' replied Merv.

Wit Munday folded his suit and put it in the holdall with the rest of his kit.

'You won't be offended if I don't stay to see the rest of the show will you boys? Goodnight,' he said and disappeared into the night without a backward glance.

We trooped back on stage, checked our volume was at the required level and launched into our final set. Blow me if Dai Laffing wasn't on his way forward again! Now what?

'OK lads you can turn it up a bit now, we'll push a few of the tables back and we can have a bit of a dance see?'

We did see. Things were taking a turn for the better. His missus was on her feet and, having knocked back several brandy and babychams, was giving a fair impression of a gogo dancer on speed. The place was suddenly jumping. Even the young ones tore themselves away from the bar and joined in with the throng at the front of the stage. Of course, we thought it was a shame we had to stop after forty five minutes when we had suddenly cracked it, but every time we announced,

'And this is our last one for tonight folks.' they kept cheering and shouting for more so we kept going until eleven o'clock or just after. Then it was, 'thank you and goodnight.' Quick, get the kit down, get paid and get out of here.

At least they had stopped calling for more but that head Committee man wouldn't let us get away with it that easily. He leapt up onto the stage and grabbed my mike and asked for a 'big hand for the band'. Once they'd got that out of the way they toddled off home and we were left to get on with packing up. The head man's good lady was giving Malc the glad eye. He was scared shitless and she was on the way to being legless, all in all not a promising combination. Her husband was either used to her trying her luck with young men or oblivious to the fact because he had imbibed to the same extent and was past caring. It did occur to me, sat on the edge of this little scenario, that it seemed strange she was the one who got all prissy when Wit tried a couple of dirty jokes and yet after a few more drinks she seemed intent on doing the wild thing with our drummer.

The Committee man came up with the cash at last, after lots of stories about groups and 'turns' they'd had in the Club over the years. Malc disappeared for as long as possible with as much of our kit as he could manage - she wouldn't give in easily though this one. Hubby suddenly dropped a Performing Rights form on Merv that we had to fill in, itemising the songs and composers we had featured during our act. Load of old bollocks. We only filled perhaps a dozen in over a decade and nearly every one we did was fiction, so how the original artists or composers were supposed to get their true benefits, God only knows. We never met a band who admitted doing them properly.

Merv had to find a table to write on and borrowed the Committee man's pen. He suggested we move back into

101

the dressing room and Malc made for the door, but she was too quick. We decided to drop him in it and shuffled in behind Merv and closed the door, leaving Malc ashen faced on the side of the stage with his escape route cut off by a woman intent on mischief. Filling in the form took a while. Longer than usual as Merv had a lot of help from Phil, myself and Nick. He was quite taken aback as we normally took very little interest in things like that.

When the form was completed to the Committee man's and our satisfaction, it was time to leave. A final sweep around the dressing room and stage for any missing bits and bobs, then into the van ready to leave. Where was Malcolm? He appeared from a kitchen area behind the bar and legged it out of the hall and into the front seat.

'Let's go! You bastards. Thanks a bunch for leaving me with her.'

'Was it like waving a sausage in the Albert Hall?' Dave asked

Malc said she had grabbed hold of him and virtually frog marched him to the furthest part of the place away from her husband, stuck her tongue down his throat and started to massage his balls.

'I don't like women,' he had told her, 'I prefer blokes.'

This attempt to escape her clutches had been in vain however as he continued, "She grabbed my hand and shoved it up her skirt and told me not to worry. I'd soon change sides once I'd had a real woman. She was a nympho! What were you lot fucking doing for so long anyway?"

As it happened he had been able to keep her at bay for long enough to enable us to get out of the place, so he did what every News of the World reporter did, when sex was offered to him on a plate on a story, he made his excuses and left. We pissed ourselves laughing at his predicament and headed out of Tredegar and onto the road back to the Severn Bridge. Naturally our plans to be home relatively early were shot to bits now so we got over to the English side and dropped into the Services. Seven lots of eggs, bacon, sausage and beans were eaten on a table surrounded by hairy arsed truckers doing the same thing. We were regulars so the staff knew where we were headed, what we were likely to order and how little money we had left at the end of the weekend to pay for it with. We nearly always had to dip into the gig cash to get us home fed and watered, plus some petrol on the last leg.

Tired and weary, we dragged ourselves out of the Motorway service station and back into the van and an hour later I was walking up the pathway to my front door. About a quarter to four on Monday morning and I was home, having left at about half four on Friday afternoon. I padded quietly up the stairs.

'Goodnight son,' said my mother. I dropped off to sleep wondering if she was a light sleeper or whether she never really settled until she heard my key in the door. Three hours later I was woken by the alarm and work beckoned. Ho hum.

Just one weekend in Wales, one of dozens over the years but that one stuck in my mind a little more than most.

13. Please Mr Postman

Returning to the subject of Young Farmers and their ilk, we played a lot in Devizes in the early days. Fair play to them, they had a lot of venues, and events were being put on elsewhere too, all the time. We did a gig at the Town Hall with The Avon Cities Jazz Band for the Young Conservatives one Friday night and that was the night we were spotted by the Devizes branch of the Young Farmers. Pretty much the same crowd really as it turned out. They asked us to play at Pewsey one Saturday night and we arrived, set up and played our stuff. It was during the early Heart 'N Soul days before the two Daves had joined up, so there were just the five of us. During one of the instrumentals, probably 'Green Onions' I jumped down off the stage and started dancing with a real cracker of a girl who I recognised from one of the offices at the Avon where I tried to hold down a day job. She was unphased by this strange bloke splitting her away from her girlfriends and after the dance finished and I had to get back for the next song, she seemed genuinely sad to see me go.

Hope sprang eternal. After we had finished playing I returned to where she was and asked her name. It was all going swimmingly, when two or three lads arrived from the bar, where they had been drinking quietly, rather than get involved with all this dancing malarkey. Probably talking about a young heifer they had their eye on or some such.

'Hello' says this lad as he put a protective arm around Jude, as she had turned out to be. 'Were you any good? Sorry we weren't listening.'

I wanted to punch his lights out, but the way Jude reacted to his arm around her waist told me all I needed to know. I was history! As I tried to think of a way to back off gracefully, she came to my rescue.

'They were brilliant, Martin. And in case you were wondering, we work together, okay?'

Suitably put in his place, he introduced himself as Martin Butler and while we were doing the rounds I found he had two other brothers there too. All from a big farming family around Devizes. The other lads had joined in the crowd of us in the middle of the dance floor, partly to see if I needed any help, partly to avoid carrying the kit out to the van for as long as possible. Mostly it was Merv and the twins who aspired to belong to the county set and mixing with the Young Whatevers was just the ticket. We chatted for twenty minutes or so until the caretaker got twitchy and wanted the place cleared so he could get home to bed. Martin and his brother Pete were keen to carry on the conversation and we agreed to meet up in The Bear in Devizes, one evening in the following week.

As you will have read in other stories, there were a few sports cars about among the band members and our close friends, so we piled into the cars and shot up to Devizes on the Wednesday night. A couple of beers in The Bear and Martin and I seemed to be on friendly terms. He was difficult to read though as he had a strange sense of humour and he didn't give a lot away about himself. There were several other non family members in as well as our crowd and at the end of the evening Pete Butler suggested we take the cars for a spin. Not every one was up for it and only a handful of cars remained.

'Where do you want to go?' asked Chris our roadie who had his best mate Ralph with him as usual.

'Oh just up to London, have a spin round Leicester Square and come back.' says Pete.

'You are joking!' said Chris.

He wasn't. Off they went, leaving The Bear at half past ten (closing time then mind). There was no motorway until Maidenhead in those days so it was A4 all the way to the 'new road'. They were still up there in about an hour and twenty minutes. Stopped for a coffee in a late night place in town, cruised around the half empty streets, then bombed back down the deserted roads, taking about the same time to come home and Chris and Ralph were in bed by a quarter to two. That was the first trip with that crowd and the start of a long hot summer. Any nights we weren't practicing or playing we were driving out and about mixing with the sons of the soil.

Because they were a social bunch it was only a matter of time before they pitched up at one of our gigs. They drove to Ross on Wye for one of the Saturday nights when we appeared on our own. Another lengthy round trip, with a few beers on board. I tell you we were fucking lucky the thousands of miles we travelled without a serious mishap. So were they. While we were in Ross that night Martin asked if he could sit in on drums while we were tuning up and doing our sound check. It was okay by us, we thought it would be a giggle. He picked up the sticks and after a few false starts he was into the first song like a good 'un.

'You've done this before' said Phil, never slow off the mark.

'I'm very rusty. It's the first time I've picked up a drumstick since I finished playing.'

Wait for it! You want to know who he played for don't you? Well, he wouldn't tell us that night. He waited until a weekend or so later, when he had picked me up and taken me to his parents' house after we'd had a beer in The Bear at lunchtime. A couple of the other lads were in the car behind us. We pulled onto the drive and went in. His parents were still out to lunch somewhere and Martin disappeared to his room and returned with a couple of records by Dave Dee, Dozy, Beaky, Mick and Titch.

'You don't like that crap do you?' I asked him.

'That was who I played for,' he said, 'when they were Dave Dee and The Bostons. We came back from Germany about fifteen months ago and I quit because I was tired of the merry-go-round and I couldn't see us making it. They send me a copy of each new single when it comes out just to show me I was wrong.'

Whoops! Again I wanted to find a way to get out gracefully, but instead I ploughed on.

'Which were you then?'

Martin explained that as Dave Dee and The Bostons, it was true, they had done the rounds for several years with a good deal of success, but nothing chartwise. The record company had come up with a wizard wheeze. Why not re-brand them with a catchy name. What are your nicknames? I was 'Tinny' from Martin so the original idea was Dozy, Beaky, Tinny and Titch. I was planning to tell them I was jacking it in so I didn't pay a lot of attention to it anyway, but we had a roadie called Mick who had been with the band for a while and when I handed in my notice, they asked me if I could give him a couple of lessons, just to see if he might make it. He was passable and rather than try to get someone else they didn't know from Adam in, Mick got the gig. The rest, as they say, is history.

Was he bitter? I told you he had a strange sense of humour and I didn't quite know how to take him sometimes. Perhaps he was, and that was how he coped with it. Black humour usually masks a troubled soul doesn't it? We stayed mates for some time longer than the rest of the band were involved with the 'sons of the soil'. None of us ever fell out, it was just the gigs were more and more frequent, distances longer and getting up for work in the morning was hard enough, without an extra trip to London thrown in midweek -just for a coffee. As the hits for DDBM&T continued I wondered how he would stay sane as each single and album dropped through the letter box. When their time passed and only compilations and Butlins and Pontins remained, perhaps he was able to go to work on the family farm with a happy heart. Whether Jude was with him I never knew. Didn't see either of them again.

14. Seven Drunken Nights

Another holiday on the south coast where most of the band went away together was in August 1967. Earlier in the year, as we were now mostly playing well away from home, we took the opportunity, when it came up, of accepting a sort of 'residency' in two venues in town. This gave us one Wednesday each month in each, so we were seen by any locals who bothered to turn up every fortnight. This was popular with all three parts of the equation, as we enjoyed a gig in town, the places were usually packed and the people who ran the gigs had no complaints either.

We had met Chris and Ralph at one of the venues, the local Conservative Club. Chris was in charge of the records and Ralph was his sidekick, I think they probably had no great pretensions on the DJ-ing front, but it was as good a way as any to get off with a few birds. 'Any requests, just come up and see me' seemed to work for the most part. Crowded dance floor, music pumping out and several ladies getting up close and personal to shout their record of choice in your ear was far too easy for them it appeared, when I saw them at work on the first gig we did there. We chatted to them in the break for a few minutes, then again at the end, and it was evident that they enjoyed our style of music. The soul sound was well represented in the stack of records that Chris had at his disposal, even if he had to keep the latest chart stuff handy as well. 'Although I don't much like some of it, you've got to give the kids what they want', was his philosophy.

After the second or third month we were seeing more of them socially into the bargain and Chris suggested we needed a regular couple of roadies to get us to and from our gigs, leaving us to concentrate on our playing, while they humped the kit in and out of the venues.

As you probably remember Glyn had drifted off to do his rally driving and have a life, which meant the driving was shared between the two or three of us who had a licence, and could get insurance, while we all mucked in with getting the kit in and out of the van and setting it up or breaking it down. The offer from Chris and Ralph was too good to turn down, especially as they didn't want paying! They reasoned that if they wanted to see us anywhere other than the Cons Club, they would have to pay to get in, this way they could get into some clubs and college gigs they wouldn't normally have access to. Plus the talent on offer would be better as well. While we were playing, they could make it clear they were with the band and use that to attract the women. Cheeky bastards! Phil probably wondered if his 'gigs to birds' pull ratio was in any danger of slipping and weighed it against not having to work all day, then drive to some far off town to play a gig, struggle up a couple of flights of stairs with Merv's Hammond organ….. and fairly quickly said "OK you're on. When do you want to start."

As the year dragged on the idea of a week off gigging became irresistible. Howard was piling on the pressure with more and more distances to travel, using the argument that we had outstayed our welcome at some of the local venues, and anyway we needed to expand our exposure if we wanted to build up a big enough fan base to turn professional. I wasn't convinced. We were covering a wide selection of American and British soul songs and as the Sixties wore on there were changes on the horizon, We were unlikely to break through as we were, unless we wrote our own material and developed our style into something more original. None of that meant we were any less popular in our own small way and the gigs were coming thick and fast, so we didn't have the time to do the soul searching that we clearly needed to.

The idea of a week in Bournemouth was mooted and there were as many as ten takers from the band and our entourage. Chris and Ralph were up for it and, as Malc was going, even Glyn came back into the fold for the occasion. Rich, another lad who we had all known for yonks on and off, was in our crowd socially that summer and he was keen too. The plan was to find a camp site on the edge of the New Forest, in the Christchurch area and drive into town for our entertainment. As on the previous holiday I told you about earlier, a couple of lads were unable to get time off or were otherwise engaged, but Merv wanted to get down at the weekend if at all possible. It was the end of the month so the Monday was the Bank Holiday and he was going to drive down and seek us out.

Transport was not a problem this time as we didn't need the van for any mid week gigs. We kept the diary free totally, so we could just hang out with each other and any crumpet that crossed our paths. I wasn't convinced of the pulling power of our previous old van with the sign on top, but Chris and the other lads upped the ante this time. Chris drove a brand new MGB GT and Rich had a MG Midget, Phil had his old frog-eyed Sprite and Glyn used his rally car to tow his parents' caravanette. This was pretty naff when it was set up, but it didn't detract from the overall effect when it was collapsed and stowed away in towing mode on the drive down and back. I went in the car with the twins and, as Glyn had removed the rear seats to install his rallying 'bucket' seats and roll bar etcetera, I was on my own on the hard floor in the back. I was prepared to put up with the discomfort on the trip down as I wanted to sleep in the caravanette - I was never keen on the camping lark at the best of times. The twins and I, together with Merv, had been to Weymouth camping in 1963 or 1964 and with pouring rain, gale force winds and insects crawling inside every nook and cranny it put me off the outdoor life for good.

We arrived on the Friday evening at the campsite our research had designated as the centre of operations and I leapt out of the back of the car to start organising my bed for the night. Easier said than done. Although Malc and Glyn had slept in the van on holiday with Mum and Dad on several occasions, they hadn't a bloody clue how it transformed from the flat pack on wheels into a gypsy caravan. Typical! We were still at the early planning stages when the others arrived on site and Nick was the practical one on hand with advice, Twenty minutes later we were up and running. Nick was installed as bunk number four.

We were surrounded by the various tents that the rest of the group had managed to beg steal or borrow and a camp fire was lit. Out came the ubiquitous camping gaz stove and the sausages. Several burnt offerings and some inedible charred ones followed, then we were off in convoy to the nearest boozer on the main road into Bournemouth. It was a big country pub with a sizeable car park and a fair selection of ales, plus a decent juke box livening up the evening. We decided its proximity to the site meant that this was now our 'local' for the week and settled in for a session. As it was now fairly late on the Friday night we just pootled into the outskirts of Bournemouth to find a chippy open so that we could feel as if we had actually had some food inside us after our pathetic efforts earlier. Then it was back to camp and our first night's sleep.

Four adult males in a caravanette in the middle of August was on a par with the Black Hole of Calcutta. Tight for space, smelly and baking hot. We survived, but it was a struggle. Nick decided to go back under canvas for the rest of the week. It helped, but then Rich caught a cold and asked to move inside with us. Terrific! That was a recipe for disaster. The hot sweaty conditions might have helped his chesty cold, plus something you will read about in a minute or two, but the rest of us took a cold home at the end of the week.

The weather was set fair on the Saturday morning and all weekend we drove into and around Bournemouth, on a quest for decent boozers, women, entertainment, women, something to eat and of course, women. The sports cars helped, particularly late at night after the pubs and clubs chucked out. We would be cruising the streets with the tops down looking for girls needing a lift home. There was no shortage of takers and we were ferrying the better looking ones to the Chines or out towards Southbourne and so on. In exchange for saving them the cost of a taxi we received various gratuities in return. Usually not much more than a snog though if we were all being honest. Rich was not having a lot of luck on that front, whether it was his cold in 'da doze' or something I couldn't say, but it was getting him down.

After the hectic weekend we were all up and about reasonably early and got ourselves along to our local. After a cold beer the world seemed a better place, certainly after another sweaty night trapped in the caravanette with Rich and his snuffles, even more so when you added in the fairly basic washing and toilet facilities in the concrete block about fifty yards from where our tents and vehicles were situated. And multiplied ten fold when, as a consequence of the primitive cooking in house plus numerous takeaways, that block seemed even further away when you were taken short. But hey, that's the magic of camping in England isn't it? I'm buggered if I see the fascination.

Bank Holiday Monday in late August has always been popular. Probably because it's the last long weekend before Christmas and people feel the need to drive miles to sit in the car trying to find a parking space, then search the beach for enough room to lay out a towel, just to catch those last rays of summer sun. Even in 1967, when there were no where near as many cars on the road as today, I'm here to tell you it was heaving. Cars were bombing down the road to and from Bournemouth and Christchurch, looking for that pot of gold. We sat in the cool of the pub with a cold beer, listened to the juke box and watched the world go by.

'I wonder if they've got any arrows?' asked Ralph.

'What would they have a dartboard for if they didn't want us to play?' said Nick.

I looked at the crowd of locals and fellow holidaymakers at the bar and thought that perhaps us taking up a fair percentage of the available floor space to throw a few darts might be stretching the landlords' hospitality a bit far, but Ralph ploughed ahead anyway. Two well used old sets of darts, with fat bodies and sparse feathering left on the shafts were produced and we were on the oche before you could say. 'Let's play darts!'

Teams were selected and the games began. It has to be said neither of us were very good, I couldn't remember the last time I had played. Nevertheless with the beers coming at regular intervals, the darts improved and the atmosphere among our audience was encouraging. Chris and Ralph were winding people up as they were clearly the better players and there was more laughing and piss taking than actual darts for some of the time. I found myself at the board chalking the scores most of the time as my number skills from my days in banking, and the accounts department, where I was presently employed came into their own.

It was half past one and gone when the door flew open and there silhouetted in the doorway was a large young man in a smart jacket, open necked shirt and cravat, the dark glasses completing the rather noble look. It was Merv. As he looked at the assembled gathering watching us at the dartboard, he assumed his upper class telephone voice and asked,

'Hello, you fellows, what are you doing mixing with the hoi polloi and playing pub games to boot?!'

Because I didn't want to be chucked out in the next thirty seconds I thought rapidly and moved forwards bowing and said, "Welcome your Highness." The other lads caught on and followed suit and someone made their way to the bar to order him a drink. There was hardly a seat in the place but by gentle persuasion we encouraged a few couples to 'budge up' and Merv found himself perched in a window seat with a lager and lime, with his newly found acolytes hanging on his every word. It worked a treat. When I went off to the bog a few minutes later I was intercepted by one of the bar staff who said the landlord wanted to know who he was!

'He's a Middle Eastern prince. His family are in oil and he's here at college in Bath.' I said. 'But don't make a fuss. He's trying to have as normal a stay in England as he can as part of his education.'

Satisfied for the time being she scuttled away to tell the boss and I carried on to drain a drop off. When I got back, the darts marathon seemed to be forgotten, so I made my way back through the crowded bar to listen to Merv finishing his story of how he managed to track us down.

'It was frightfully busy on the road, but as I came along the main drag I spotted the motors in the car park. All lined up side by side it was an absolute doddle!'

Since opening hours were less liberated than they are today, we were fast approaching closing time and several of us realised we couldn't keep this pretence up a lot longer, so we surprised the landlord by going before he called time and, more importantly, before we screwed up!.

We spent the rest of the Bank Holiday in Bournemouth where Merv could relax at last along with the rest of us and after a very pleasant day and part of the evening he drove back home, leaving us to enjoy the rest of our holiday.

The next visit to the local was interesting of course, it was virtually empty on the Tuesday lunchtime and the landlord was keen to ask about our visitor from the previous day. We were prepared for him though as we had decided at breakfast (burnt sausage, crispy bacon and indescribable eggs in case you wondered) that we wouldn't come clean. We opted for the tap on the nose and 'no comment' approach and suggest he would drop us like a hot brick if any publicity about his stay in this country entered the public domain. He bought it.

We made the most of Tuesday as it was forecast to be the best day of the week weatherwise. Rich was still in the throes of his cold, more on his chest than ever, so a visit to the chemist was called for, so that the rest of us could get some sleep in that bloody caravanette. We hit the beach and then got a meal and had a few beers early in the evening, planning to drive back to the camp site to wash and change ready for a late trip to town to see what developed. We were in a park I think, with perhaps an open air bar, or a café or whatever and Rich was chatting up a young waitress and looked like getting somewhere for a change. She finished at nine and had a mate there too who was not bad either. Nick made his move and before we knew it they were sorted for picking them up in Rich's car after work and going for a drive.

Whether it was Rich who was in a rush to get the action started as soon as possible, or whether they had struck lucky with a couple of real goers, I'm not sure, but the rest of us were hardly back at the camp site and into our shit, shave and shampoo routine before the lads turned up with the girls. Rich warned us all off of returning to the caravanette for a while and disappeared inside. Nick was in Rich's car, discreetly parked under the trees almost, but not quite, out of sight of prying eyes with his young lady. We left them to it and as most of us were pretty near ready to hit the town we wanted to get moving, of course, so we were very childish and tried to stop Rich's fun before it got too hot and heavy. If we weren't getting any why should he?

As quietly as about half a dozen blokes could creep up to a parked vehicle, having had three or four beers, we gathered at the end of the caravanette where there was a small square window. If we stood on tiptoe to look inside the van we could make out two shapes on one of the bunks. Through the said square window children, we could see the young lady fully clothed (curses, foiled again!) and Richard naked to the waist. The trip to the chemist had supplied him with a jar of Vick. Rather than popping to the shops for some Angel Delight or something similar for him to apply to her upper body, he was using our sleeping quarters, not to get his end away, but to get this girl to apply Vick to his rather hairy chest! Who said romance was dead?

Perhaps the girl was anxious that this unexpected foreplay was a precursor to something kinkier to follow, or maybe us pissing ourselves outside the van had something to do with it, but things went downhill from there. Nick was the one most miffed as he was well away

119

with his bird when her mate burst from the caravanette wiping her hands on a tissue and it was pandemonium. We were accused of being perverts. They were convinced they had been conned into coming here for a gang bang. Nick was still hoping something could be salvaged and calmed his bird down enough to stop them calling the law and they settled for a taxi back to town, which Nick and Rich stumped up for. Nick was spitting feathers. We finished getting ready but Nick and Rich were not in any mood to enjoy a night out, so we only dropped into our local for a couple and had an early night.

The mood was still a bit dark and heavy in the morning, but at least we had had a better night's sleep. The Vick had helped Rich, although the extra whiff on the inside of the caravanette, mixed with all the others, made an interesting if unattractive combination.

Our mood matched the weather because Wednesday was muggy and thunder didn't seem far away. As bridges needed mending we didn't do too much that morning except chill out at the site, a bit of tidying up and move a couple of our tents to better locations. As the week went on we found people moving off home so there was more room and we thought we might as well use it.

In addition to all the camper vans and tents, there were quite a few static caravans. One really old one, that looked as if a good gust of wind would finish it off, was about ten yards away from our circle of tents and vehicles. The only person we saw during those first few days was an old chap, probably pushing eighty, shabbily dressed and looking generally unloved. He hadn't complained about the comings and goings at all hours, nor the noise that half a dozen or so young lads are inclined to make just by being awake. As a result we never had occasion to talk to him. That morning he shuffled over and started to chat to us.

'It's good to see you lads on holiday enjoying yourselves,' he said. 'I heard the commotion last night and ...'

We all began to apologise for waking him up but he waved his hand dismissively. "None of that matters boys. Just don't let it fester. Get it out in the open and sort it. Life's too short to let an argument spoil your holiday."

We all felt suitably told off and the mood lifted almost immediately. He said his name was Bert and he had lived there with his wife ever since he had retired from his business up in the East End of London. Wife? What wife? After the introductions had been made we were starting to wonder how long it would be before we could get rid of Bert and drive down to our local to start the day off right - now we were all talking to one another again, Bert latched on to Rich. Whether he knew somehow that Rich had been the catalyst for the row the previous night, or maybe he had been looking out of his caravan window all the time, I don't know but Rich and Bert were in deep conversation just a few yards away from where the rest of us were clustered around what was left of our campfire.

'Won't be a minute lads.' said Rich and disappeared into Bert's old van.

About ten minutes later he reappeared. He didn't say a lot at first and, as the rest of us were eager to get up and running for the day, we didn't get the full story until we were sat in the pub with our first pint of the day.

'What did he want then Rich?' I asked.

'He wanted to shift a couple of sticks of furniture around to make it easier for him to get around in there to care for his wife Doris.'

So there was a wife then.

'I was a bit scared at first,' Rich continued, 'it's as dark as night inside there. Everything smells musty and when we had moved the stuff around she called out and asked

121

who was there. Bert took me along to the bedroom and there she was, sat in bed naked to the waist. She's over eighty with hardly any hair and it turns out she's blind and bedridden. Bert is the only person she will let anywhere near her to care for her. She wanted me to sit on the bed and hold her hand because it isn't very often they have company these days. We talked for a few minutes about my family and where we lived, stuff like that. She said she and Bert had been there twenty years and they had had a pretty full social life when they had first moved down from London. The last few years had been a struggle and Bert hadn't had the chance to go out on the town for a long time. I jokingly said he could come out with us one night, but could she trust him not to run off with some dolly bird. She told Bert she would be alright on her own for a couple of hours if he really did want to go out and ... um, well, sorry fellas but if he's serious, then we might be lumbered tomorrow night for a while. He'll probably be home by nine anyway so it shouldn't cramp our style too much.'

Terrific! We wondered if Rich was joking, then whether he was getting his own back for last night, and in the end we reckoned Bert would pull out with some excuse or other and we'd be off the hook. The rest of the day was spent dodging heavy showers, although the thunder never materialised and the temperature stayed high, it was one of those days when you couldn't get comfortable. The heavy atmosphere was one thing on our mind, but the spectre of Bert in his glad rags shuffling about with us in Bournemouth on the Thursday night was uppermost for the majority of us I reckon.

We returned to the campsite, where Doris and Bert were shut up tight in their van, but Doris was giving him an ear bashing about something or other. We assumed it was to do with us taking him out and were even more convinced we would be spared what we anticipated would be an embarrassing evening. We got washed and changed ready to go out.

'Where shall we go then fellas?' asked Rich.

Anywhere with music was the general consensus, so we set off to Bournemouth in convoy, had a swift pint in a pub near the pier then asked the young lad serving the beers if there were any live bands on somewhere handy. He pointed up the hill and said,

'"I think they've got something on up there tonight. Not sure who though.'

Where he was pointing was a club on top of the cliff, where the International Centre was built many years later. That night it was 'The Peddlers', a three piece band who had limited chart success but received loads of critical acclaim. We didn't really know what to expect. Although I had read a review in the NME of a gig they did in London, as I say, their singles output wasn't picked up on by the radio stations until later in the Sixties.

We were knocked sideways it has to be said. With Roy Phillips on Hammond organ and just bass and drums they produced an awesome sound. Did I say 'just bass and drums'? The drummer did a solo for six or seven minutes that served to confirm to Malcolm that he had made the right decision in retiring to play football. Boy this guy was a natural. The bass and drums unit was as safe as houses which left Roy to improvise to his heart's content. Great sound from the organ, distinctive voice, all in all we were convinced they were the next big thing. Of course, there was a jazz influence to some of the stuff they played and Merv was back on that old bandwagon again, wanting us to include some jazz in our set. I suggested we were unlikely to have the musicianship to emulate this lot and while Malc and Glyn agreed, Merv was a tad miffed. Later on when we got home we did dip into some early Georgie Fame tracks which I had bought and included some in our set

123

for several months but we never pursued that line in any great detail. Most of the places we went on to play in over the next couple of years thought it was a pretentious load of crap anyway.

So, thoroughly chastened, with The Peddlers sound ringing in our ears, we made our way back to the campsite eager to pass on the inside knowledge, when we got home to the rest of the band who hadn't holidayed with us, that we had glimpsed the future. Sadly for The Peddlers that 'next big thing' tag we labelled them with proved to be wide of the mark. Why are fame and fortune so fickle? Three brilliant musicians crafting tunes to a standard that fellow band members can admire, but only dream of matching, never make it to the top, while some absolute no talent wankers have half a dozen number one hits. Please note the next band mentioned is purely coincidental.

Thursday morning dawned and there was no sign that Bert's contretemps with Doris had left him grounded. He was up and about in plenty of time to catch us before we crept off to the pub and called out to his new friend, Rich,

'What time tonight then Ada?'

Excuse me? Where did that come from? Rich said it depended what he was planning to do. If he was up for it we could go out about nine and go clubbing. He was more keen on an earlier start, say half past seven, and going for a meal in a restaurant in town. He said,

'It'll be my treat Ada, don't worry about a thing.'

He seemed so adamant, we were fairly confident it would cost us a few quid each, plus another quid or so to get him pissed up. Then we would have to get him safely back into his caravan to his missus. Well, Ada would have to obviously, as they had become such good friends.

'Stands to reason,' I said.

It was another iffy day so we took a drive around the New Forest, found a pub for lunch and a beer, then cruised around the streets of Bournemouth and Boscombe before going back to the site to wash and dress up for our night out. By the end of the day the weather was improving and by early evening the sun had broken through the low cloud and it was warm in the pleasant sunshine. We all decided to go for the best trousers we had with us, a clean shirt and tie, with a leather or denim jacket to top it off. We looked the dog's bollocks. Rich went over to Bert's van, still half expecting him to be a no-show, and knocked on the door.

'Come on in Ada,' cried out Bert, 'Doris wants to say hello.'

He disappeared inside and came back with Bert in tow. He may have had a wash and shave, but his clothes were still pretty shabby. An old pair of beige trousers, which hadn't seen an iron on them in a decade, complete with stains from who knew what. A faded orange shirt over which he wore lighter beige top zipped up on the last six inches or so. This too had seen better days and was all stretched and baggy, particularly the pockets, where he kept all sorts of things, keys, fags, tins of this and that from the camp shop, bottles of milk. They all got stuffed into this top's two pockets willy nilly. Naturally it was finished off with grey socks worn through on the heel and a pair of ancient yachting shoes. Proper man about town he looked. Who's going to let us in looking like that I thought.

We were all going to pile into the cars and squeeze Bert in with Ada (sorry Rich) in his MG Midget. In the days before drink and drive limits it was so, so different. No seat belts either. Bloody hell we took some risks and we never gave it a second thought. Anyway, Bert bless him suddenly looks up and says,

'Why don't we all get in my motor, we could probably all fit in?'

What motor? We had never seen him drive since we were there. He took Rich over to the other side of his old van and there, under the trees, was an ancient Armstrong Siddeley. It turned over first time on the crank, yeah it was that old, and purred into life. Chris walked round to the front of the car and looked at the windscreen to see if there was a tax disc. It ran out at the end of the month. Phew!

'In you get Ada, you can drive.' said Bert. 'Come on lads don't stand on ceremony. You five in the back and we'll fit three on the bench seat in the front.'

Two minutes later we were off up the road towards Bournemouth. The ride was smooth and, although the seats had seen some wear and tear, the old car attracted quite a few admiring looks as we cruised into town.

'What do you think of it Ada?' asked Bert.

'It's brilliant.' he replied. 'The band could do with something like this to arrive at gigs in.'"

We all laughed as we remembered the hours spent crammed into the old van, rattling about all over the West Country and South Wales.

'One of my boys is bringing me a newer car down from town tomorrow, give me twenty five quid and it's yours!' said Bert.

The lights changed to red just in front of us, Rich braked hard. It was very quiet in the car. Was he kidding? What would a classic car like this go for, a couple of hundred? What did he mean, 'one of my boys'? A son perhaps. Or had we underestimated him when he said he had retired down here from the 'family firm' in the East End of London. The lights changed and we pulled away.

The matter was left there, hanging, as we arrived at the town centre and looked for Bert's restaurant of

126

choice. I can't recall the name now but it was a big hotel and we parked in front. We piled out and walked up the flight of steps to be greeted by a uniformed commissionaire, complete with top hat who Bert acknowledged as if he was an old friend. We got through the revolving doors and were ushered into an ante room off the main foyer and reception area by a middle aged bloke who may have been the manager. I hung back from the main group, huddled in earnest conversation around the hotel chap and Bert, to admire the furnishings of where we hoped to have our meal this evening. It was a bit up market from our usual transport cafe and I seriously doubted we could afford to bail Bert out when it became clear his ambition to pay for everything exceeded the contents of his pockets.

I needn't have worried. The conversation was at an end. The manager had politely declined our presence on the grounds that a couple of us were not wearing ties. But we were on holiday. It was only Rich and Malcolm that had brought a couple of ties each, and we had borrowed them to get most of us sorted. So Bert was okay to pass muster and not us?

'Fuck 'em,' said Nick, 'if our money isn't good enough we'll go somewhere else.'

Brave words mate. I wouldn't bet on it not turning out to be our money either I thought as we traipsed back through the revolving doors and down the steps to the car.

'Where to now then Bert?' asked Rich.

Bert was full of apologies for us not being allowed in and vowed never to go back to the hotel, but he was a bit reticent about suggesting any alternative. As we drove away and up the hill we saw a place called The Barrister's Brief on the left hand side of the road and a couple of parking spaces somewhere handy.

'Let's try here,' said Malc, 'I'm getting hungry and I don't want to drive around Bournemouth all night looking for somewhere.' We agreed.

We parked the old car and wandered into the restaurant more in hope than expectation. The head waiter was at our side in a flash. Here we go I thought, ever the optimist.

'Good evening, gentlemen. Have you reserved a table?'

We don't normally have to matey, not in the sort of establishment we usually eat. We normally move the plates, cutlery and other rubbish off the table and sweep the fag ash off the melamine with a sleeve. Perhaps the other place had phoned ahead, but this chap had a new wheeze for getting shot of us, since his buddy had already used the 'no ties' angle. Bert took charge as if he'd been doing it for more years than we'd been alive. He fished a fiver out of his trouser pocket and slipped it into the breast pocket of the head waiter's crisp white shirt.

'We didn't have time I'm afraid. I'm sure you can find us a suitable sized room for the rest of the evening.'

A fiver to me was half a week's wages back then and it must have been fairly significant to the head waiter as with a click of his fingers a couple of young lads appeared, similarly well dressed, and we were whisked away to a room at the back complete with a small bar and a table that seated twelve. We were in!

'Will this suffice sir?' asked Bert's new friend. Bert was certain it would and we were not about to disagree with him. We all sat down and two young waitresses filed in with the menus and wine list. The young lads took drinks orders and disappeared to the bar to fill them then, after a short time while we got our first drinks of the evening down, the orders were taken for our meals. The wine waiter was summoned by Bert and three bottles of red and three of white of Bert's choice were ferried out to our table. Well it was a start at least.

The remainder of the evening was spent eating and drinking in a convivial atmosphere, where Bert held court telling us about his early life in London before the war. His family were in the fish business plus a little import and export on the side. During the war he had been stationed nearby and although he wasn't prepared to go into too much detail, in case the statute of limitations hadn't run out, he told us he'd stayed on into 1946 after he'd been demobbed, as the campsite where we had been staying had been a wartime airstrip and planes of a 'non military nature if you get my drift' he told us, landed there at night with cargoes from overseas to be transferred to London for sale on the black market. He reckoned he and the people he'd been involved with had made a pretty penny and naturally, when he had retired, this had been his first choice when looking for a place to retire to.

We had finished off the six bottles that had arrived with our starters. The main courses were long gone. We'd nearly all opted for steak and chips, so don't get your hopes up for a description of something of a cordon bleu nature, it would have been wasted on our palates. Bert had the Dover Sole, you can take the man out of the fish business and you can work the rest out for yourselves. As we wondered whether we could manage a pudding, (there I go again showing our lack of class) Bert was ordering more wine. Okay, we all thought, we might as well order something to help soak up all this alcohol so off we went into another course, then cheese and biscuits, cigars for those that felt the need and brandies or Irish coffees. Oh my gawd we were going to pay for this in the morning! What if we had to pay for this TONIGHT! That was a sobering thought as Bert ordered a bottle of Scotch to take home. The time had also come for the bill to be brought to the table.

The head waiter put in an appearance, fussing around the staff as they cleared away the final debris from our table. We were all well pissed and Bert was almost asleep. The bill remained on the table, just to his left, in between him and Rich, who had been told where to sit as soon as we had found our way to the table oh so long ago. "What's the damage Rich" someone asked.

'You don't want to know.' said Rich out of the side of his mouth in an attempt to keep Bert from sussing we were concerned.

Bert seemed in no rush to leave and was polishing off the dregs of a large brandy in a brief moment of lucidity, before telling us yet another story from his time in the RAF during the war. We heard how he met Doris. We heard all sorts but we didn't hear the rustle of folding stuff and a kerching as it was stashed away in the till of The Barrister's Brief. Midnight was fast approaching and we were almost reaching the point at which the head waiter would have telephoned the local constabulary when Bert unzipped his old top, reached into the breast pocket of his faded orange shirt and produced a wedge of notes of several denominations thicker than any I have seen before or since. How much was there I don't know, We didn't count it.

'Pay the man Ada. Give him a few more on top for the girls and boys. They earned it.'

Rich gathered up a few notes and compared what he had in his hand to the bill in front of him, took one more and gave it to the head waiter, who I swear to God bowed and thanked us all profusely for honouring them with our presence. We got to our feet a little unsteadily and made our way out into the warm night air and over to the Armstrong Siddeley. Bert was lagging behind with his bottle of Scotch and had to be helped into the front seat and pushed along to the middle so Chris could get in on the passenger side. Rich was to drive. He had a sneaking feeling Bert wouldn't have wanted anyone else to drive the old bus so he had perhaps had about one or two glasses of wine less than the rest of us and only one brandy but he was still only barely able to cope.

We got back to the campsite in one piece, thank goodness. The only problem was the Scotch. Bert had decided he didn't want to wait to get it home before he opened it. He must have had a swig or three in the restaurant or in the gents, because Chris and Rich suddenly realised when we turned sharp left and then right into the camp site the front seat was wet. "Bloody hell Bert have you pissed yourself?" asked Rich. Bert was snoring and dead to the world. Chris found the bottle on his side of Bert with the screw top off and the remainder of the contents leaking out at a fair rate of knots. What a waste of good whisky!

Rich parked the car, after a fashion, and we manhandled Bert out and carried him to his caravan. Doris was awake and started shouting at him.

'What time do you call this? I suppose you've had too much to drink? What will happen to me in the morning, did you think of that while you were out having a good time, eh?'

Rich was delegated to go and quieten her down and he promised to get up and see to her in the morning if Bert was not up to doing it. She was a bit tearful then and apologised to him for being the way she was, she didn't want to be a burden and so on. She wished she was still up and about and had been able to go with us and Rich had to tell her where we had been and what we had to eat and how much we had enjoyed Bert's company.

'Well dear,' she said, 'I hope it didn't cost you too much to look after the old bugger. Thank you for taking him out.'

Time for bed I think. Don't worry Bert, we won't tell her if you don't.

There were a lot of sore heads in the morning. We went without breakfast and our usual trip to the local. It was a warm sunny morning and we sat under the trees by our tents and drank strong black coffees and felt sorry for ourselves. About eleven thirty we saw the new car arrive. It made us sit up and take notice, that's for sure. The driver had pulled up by the reception lodge and was talking to the guy on duty, who was pointing over towards us and Bert's old van. He was about thirty years old, maybe six foot tall, with short blond hair. He was wearing a dark blue Italian suit, sunglasses and looked a bit like Steve McQueen from a distance. He also looked as if he could handle himself, if you know what I mean. Just the way he walked and his posture, it was dead cool. Did I tell you what he was driving? It was a pale blue Chevrolet with chrome all over the place, recently registered and just his sort of car, Steve McQueen that is, but Bert! Why on earth did an eighty year old bloke want a car like that?

Mr Cool drove over to the caravan and without a look in our direction, as we stood or sat there open mouthed, got out and walked to the door, knocked, then waited for the invitation to "Come on in, John!" Oh, so Bert was still in the land of the living then, good. John went in and we saw or heard nothing for ten minutes or so, then John came out to the boot of the Chevvy and picked up a cloth wrapped package from inside. "Fuck me is it a sawn off?" whispered Nick. We had to agree it was about the right length and again, without a sideways glance John was back inside the van. As we debated what it might have been, the caravan door swung open and John was back out in the open air. He walked towards us with the same package across his arms, but now it had been opened.

'The Guv'nor wanted you to know if you wanted this,' he said, 'I brought a couple down but he won't be able to eat them on his own.'

He lowered his arms and displayed a beautiful sea bass on a tray of crushed ice.

'It came ashore this morning lads. Hope you like it.'

All thoughts of sawn offs were dismissed and the twins set to trying to rescue what passed for our camp fire. A lot of opinions were offered as how best to cook it. None of us had a clue really, so John put in his five-penny-worth and we just did basically what he told us. As I say he looked like a bloke who was used to getting things done. As he stood smiling at our culinary efforts, Rich asked him whether he was driving the Armstrong Siddeley back to town. John shook his head.

'The Guv'nor said he offered it to you. If you don't want it I'll take it to the nearest scrap yard and go back up on the train.'

We had the same conversation as last night, but although it was a snip at twenty five quid it was a lot more than we had between us, taking into account what we needed for the rest of our holiday. We told John it was a no go and he shrugged and went back to the van to say his goodbyes to Bert and Doris. Then he was off in the car, leaving the brand new Chevvy alongside the van under the trees. I thought the birds in the trees now had the best thing to shit on in the south of England. I wonder if they knew?

We only had one day left of our holiday. We spent a couple of hours playing crazy golf in the afternoon, did a little shopping for pressies to take home to family and friends (honest we did really!), then at night it was back to the local where they had been missing us, then on to the club on the cliff top so we could watch Amen Corner (the next band to appear after The Peddler's remember?).

In those days they were only just nibbling away on the edges of the charts. I think they were promoting their first single that night 'Gin House' and although we knew they were from Cardiff, we hadn't heard them. We were keen to compare our sound against their line up which included Andy Fairweather Low on vocals (quite a high voice girls if you recall), Blue Weaver on keyboards, two drummers and assorted guitars and brass. Whether there were seven or eight of them in this embryonic stage I don't know. We watched and listened to their set but we didn't come away with as favourable an impression as we had the earlier night. If anything we thought if we beefed up our brass section and tightened up our rhythm section we could match anything they were likely to come up with.

When the night was over we left the club and assumed we would probably never see Amen Corner, or any of the band members again. We didn't think they had that certain something to make them a household name. Our success rate at picking winners was pretty piss poor and our paths did cross on three more occasions over the next few years. So we were wrong on both counts.

We had another late night ferrying young birds out to the outskirts of Bournemouth and, as we knew we were off home in the morning, we were reticent to go back to camp, so we kept cruising around the town centre in the vain hope that there were some late night revellers still to emerge from some nightclub or other who were gagging for it. Fat chance. But we enjoyed the drive around with the top down, the fresh air sobered us up if nothing else. Reluctantly we drove back and slept as well as we could, knowing that a cracking week's holiday was at an end.

Tents were taken down, the caravanette was collapsed and tidied away under the tarpaulin cover. Cars were topped up with petrol where necessary and we said our

134

goodbyes to Bert. Only Ada was allowed in to say cheerio to Doris. Then we set off in convoy out of the campsite, turned for Christchurch, heading up and away from the New Forest and back to the sunny climes of West Wiltshire.

15. Wheels

I've told you about our problems with transport. Vans that broke down after struggling with far more weight than they were ever designed to carry. We took large amounts of gear, and several people, over crazy distances and expected second hand vehicles to go like the clappers. Well, one day in maybe 1967, when weekends were mostly spent in Wales, Phil and Merv had a brainwave. Not a good sign. They saw a two tonne Bedford St John's ambulance parked in a lay-by on the road out of town, with a 'For Sale' notice on the windscreen.

'That's what we need,' shouted Merv as we drove by in our clapped out J2 on the way to Street to visit a music shop to buy guitar strings and drum sticks. There was probably a new organ there too that Merv had his eye on. Phil chimed in with his five pennyworth.

'Yeah, that would solve all our problems. Let's see how much they want for it.'

All the way down to Street and back they discussed how to convert it into the epitome of a band wagon. It was still there in the lay-by unfortunately when we drove past on the way back home. A quick shit, shave and a shampoo and we were off to Trowbridge in the evening for a gig in Gloucester Road. Everyone else had to be dragged into the discussion, not in the audience mind, just the rest of the band. Fed up with the J2 letting us down, and various turkeys we had borrowed while it was off the road, there were no dissenting voices. A deal was

137

struck in the week and for twelve pounds it was ours. No tax or insurance. Virtually out of petrol. Terrific.

We transferred it to the yard where we had negotiated a lock up for the J2. The twins' family garage had an open air compound where we had parked for free for a while, but their dad wasn't so keen on the 'free' bit and we were concerned about the 'open air' and the lack of any real security. Knowing the J2 was OK for the time being to get us where we needed to go, we spent a couple of weekend mornings working on the Bedford.

Phil calculated the space required at the rear of the ambulance to stack the kit and a wooden partition was put in place. Then we had a slight problem. The double doors at the rear gave access to the kit, but there was only a sliding window between the front seats and the business end of the ambulance.

The bulkhead between the front and rear compartment was difficult to cut through to say the least, all five of us took it in turns with a hacksaw and eventually carved a large enough oblong hole for Merv to get through with little difficulty. This meant it would be a breeze for the rest of us. Phil then discovered quite by chance that, on measuring the available floor space, it was almost a perfect fit for a king size mattress. We didn't have one at that particular moment but one materialised very quickly.

We had an interior light, of course, which we got to work again and we were ready to try her out - in more ways than one. Again there was a slight drawback. This model of Bedford ambulance had a window on either side. Indeed they were quite large windows. Whether the St John's Ambulance people used this as a demonstration model, so that passers by could see the unfortunates on the stretcher stations inside (which we had removed by the way) as they were being patched up or covered up, depending on the state they were in, I could never work out, but privacy was at a premium.

We were playing in Corn Street in Bristol on the Saturday night when we had completed the extreme makeover on the van, so we filled her up, transferred the kit over, piled on board and set off. The old van showed an impressive turn of speed once you got that two tonnes travelling. We rolled into Bath with Phil driving and Nick riding shotgun beside him up front. The rest of us, plus a couple of girlfriends, were in the back with the light on and as we approached Cleveland Bridge traffic lights we saw what we would have to contend with. Anyone on the pavement was turning their heads, doing a double take, then staring into the goldfish bowl. If they were old they just stared. The younger ones fell into two camps. They either realised we were a group and wondered if we were famous and ran alongside the van, waving and shouting at us, asking where we were playing and so on, or they realised we were a group and took the piss something chronic, with all the related hand signals you can imagine. Our girls asked if we could turn the interior light off. Twelve quid? A bleedin' bargain I reckon! Game on!

For about three months this was our intended 'passion wagon'. On the face of it we had all the ingredients, the only way in or out was through a relatively small hole, that was blocked off by whoever was sitting in the front passenger seat. We had a comfortable mattress to rest on during our journeys, to sleep on overnight at those far flung outposts of Welsh Wales that we found ourselves in and with any luck we could entertain some female companions into the bargain.

Where did it all go wrong I hear you ask? Insurance was costly. It did fifteen to the gallon on a long run, half that if you were flooring it on the motorway. It used oil in tanker loads. We picked up two Welsh birds at a bus stop in the middle of nowhere and ran them into the next town and that was it. Oh and there were always fumes in the boudoir that were so strong you were frightened to go to sleep in case you never woke up. It had to go.

So after half a dozen assorted vans either borrowed, hired or owned at great cost to ourselves, we eventually saw sense and bought a Ford Transit. The Transit was the ubiquitous bandwagon of the era. If I had a fiver for every Transit Chris flashed our lights at on roads and motorways all across the country I could guarantee Champion's League football at my beloved St Andrew's. Well, maybe not that many but one helluva lot.

Short or long wheelbase, with large wing mirrors or without, rusted out or in pristine condition, they slogged up and down the length and breadth of Britain for year after year.

Chris drove a brand new MGB GT as I mentioned before, so he was used to the flashing of lights to acknowledge a fellow MGB owner. We started doing it to Transits, regardless of whether they had company names on the side or 'J.Smith & Sons Painters & Decorators'. A lot of van drivers obliged, but several looked at you as if you were bonkers.

When we first took possession, we had to get a comfortable seat to fix in the back, so it was back to the scrap yard to find a suitable item and put it in securely. We had loads of space in the back for our kit when we were still the Copperpot Band. Even more once we were down to just the four of us with Elijah & The Goat.

Chris had a few concerns about safety and later on he welded a grill to the back door windows and attached a steel bar that went right across the back doors. This deterred the 'chancers' who knew the secret of 'popping' a Transit door off in no time flat to remove your kit while you were parked up overnight. The steel bar came in

140

handy too, more than once. We had a problem with a promoter at one venue who was trying to short change us on our money for the night. It was a no contract job and we had been told it was thirty quid, he swore blind it was only twenty. Chris went out with some kit, put it in the van, then returned with the bar and asked the bloke if he was absolutely certain. We got the thirty quid.

Although the van was 'roomy' compared to some of the crap vehicles we had had to put up with, there were some weekend trips when there were six or seven of us, and nearly if not all were going to have to sleep in the van. Chris and Ralph would finish work early, get a lift from Chris' brother-in-law or another mate and go to Bristol to hire a long wheelbase Transit. What a palaver that was! If you told insurance companies you were using a van as a band vehicle, you could either forget it or pay through the nose, even for third party, fire and theft. They would have had no chance if they told the garage they wanted a van for the weekend, to get a group up to the Midlands and back, with seven passengers and a ton of equipment. So they were picking up vegetables, cabbages usually and transporting them locally from growers to suppliers. Low mileage and hardly any weight to speak of. That worked most of the time, although we had to switch garages at least once, when they got suspicious of the frequency that a couple of long haired youngsters popped in on a Friday afternoon. How many bloody cabbages were there in Wiltshire anyway? So it was 'moving a few sticks of furniture into my new flat from my parents' house, mate', for some weekends.

Chris got some wing mirrors from a lorry that had found its way into the scrap yard. They were nigh on two foot long and when they were fixed into place Chris had no problem seeing what was behind him, except for that night in Chard when Pete had a full frontal from the stripper. To get to the stage door we had to reverse the

Transit through an archway. It was a tight fit. Ralph was at the back directing Chris and all went well until the front end of the van needed to get through. There was a scraping sound, followed by a bending of angle iron, then the tinkle of broken glass. Chris used a few expletives and then with commendable strength, bent the still intact left hand mirror flat against the van. The Transit cleared the gap with inches to spare.

When we got the van back home, it cost us a few quid in repairs, but it was a small price to pay for the coolest mirrors on any Ford Transit we met on our thousands of miles of motoring. On those middle of the night times when we passed a bandwagon on a country road and stopped for a chat, it was nearly always. "Where did you get your mirrors? How much were they? Oh we gotta get some like that!"

16. Someone chanted evening

Trips into Wales weren't always weekend long slogs mind you. One venue we played early on in our time with Howard's agency was the Top Spot in Ross on Wye. The owner was an entrepreneur named Harvey Fear. There were gigs there on Friday and Saturday nights from what I can remember. Fridays were for top line bands and a supporting group. Saturdays were generally just for one band carrying the thing on its own, playing for say two and a half hours. When you were supporting on Friday you might get two   spots either side of a name from the charts.

The first time we went there was on a Saturday. I think Dave, the trumpeter, was back on board ship, so we were one short but we were feeling fairly confident when we eventually found our way to the venue. That trip was an awkward one, a couple of ways to get to it, but no matter which you tried it always took longer than planned.

We pulled up alongside the doors at the side of the hall and prepared to unload the kit. A guy turned up in a Roller and sauntered over to us. I took an educated guess and asked,

'Mr Fear?'

He looked at us with a smile on his lips, which didn't quite extend to his eyes.

'You took your time. I don't like my bands to be late. I was just going to call your agent and tell him you were a no show. Still, as you are here now you may as well play tonight.'

Bloody hell! We were no longer confident. We were nervous. We didn't want to upset Howard so early in our association by getting a reputation for being unreliable. He disappeared via the main entrance and reappeared two minutes later when he threw open the double doors with a flourish. We had that kit out of the van, onto the stage and set up in record time. Sound checks were rattled through and we awaited our playing times from Mr Fear, before we allowed ourselves the luxury of a little wander up the main street of the town.

Once he had strolled down and given us our start time for the first set, which was one and a quarter hours long, we walked off into town. We found a pub and settled in for a couple of beers and a chat. The venue itself was impressive. A good sized elevated stage, a large dance floor and at the end, stairs led up to a mezzanine where a long bar stretched virtually the whole width of the building. That was always a problem if you played a venue laid out like that. Architects, you listening? Never design a place with the bar directly opposite the stage. The bar staff can't hear a fucking thing when people order their drinks. It slows up your chances of getting a drink so it can't be good, okay? Less drinks sold equals less profit. Bad news.

We trotted back down the steep hill to the club in plenty of time for our scheduled kick off, because we didn't want to upset Harvey any more than we had already. We changed into our stage gear two at a time in the tiny dressing room at the side of the stage. It was maybe eight feet long, but although it was four feet wide by the entrance door it was about two foot six at the other end. Weird. Possibly the smallest we came across in all the venues we played.

At the appointed time a spotlight on the stage flashed on and off, so we knew Harvey was upstairs somewhere indicating we should get our arses in gear and start playing. We got on stage and ripped into our first song. The lighting was of a higher class than we were used to, pure white spots and coloured options too. He made us look good. When Merv started the introduction to the song, he was picked out unerringly with the spot and I felt the heat from the lights when I started to sing the opening words. Impressive. As we got through that first number I noticed a box at the front of the stage, pretty much in the middle, with a green strip shining back at me from the bottom. As I wondered why this eerie unflattering light was illuminating my shoes considering how the rest of the stage equipment was so hi-tech, the centre strip, an amber light came on. Green? Amber? What on earth is coming next I wondered.

What a prankster he was that Mr Fear, and no mistake. About halfway through the second song and the amber strip went out. The larger red strip came on and before you could say 'what the fuck's going on' our drummer was left playing the drums on his own. Nick had a brief muted toot on his saxophone, but we had to admit, we were stuffed. The audience were obviously in on the joke, because although they jeered and wolf whistled for a few seconds, they took it pretty well. Clearly they didn't think this interruption was permanent. Harvey Fear strolled towards the stage at his usual pace and beckoned Phil towards him. Phil then relayed the message to the rest of us as Harvey strolled back to wherever his control box was. "We're too loud" said Phil, "He can cut the power to the stage whenever he chooses. If we want to carry on, we need to turn it down."

We turned the volume down on the amps, power was restored. We finished the first set and the good children of Ross and surrounding areas gave us a pretty good round of applause it has to be said. We headed for the pub. There were some unhappy campers among us. What right did this bloke have to treat us like kids, with his traffic lights system. We'd never come across anything like it before. We weren't that loud anyway. After a couple of beers it didn't seem to amount to much so we went back to the club and passed the rest of the time waiting to go back on for our second stint of one and a quarter hours, checking out the talent. Fruitless exercise that night.

The Top Spot was always a 'cheque to the agent' gig, so we were a little apprehensive what Howard might say about what had gone on with Harvey that first time we played there. We resisted the temptation to whack the volume up in the second half and tell him to stuff it when the red light came on again. The second half went without incident in fact and all in all we felt we had gone down okay. As long as he didn't get all pissy with us when we were getting the kit down and away, we'd be alright. He never spoke to us even. He was busy up on the mezzanine with his bar staff and bouncers, getting a few stragglers away from the bar and the dregs of their glasses. We just got on with clearing away, loaded up the van and chatted to a few of the crowd who came up to pass comment, find out if we were coming back, where we were tomorrow, next week etcetera. The usual stuff. Merv just popped his head back inside the loading doors and called out,

'Good night. We're off now then.'

Harvey Fear just raised an arm and gave a lazy wave. Was that good? Or was it bad?

Would you believe it? It was good. Howard rang Merv first thing Monday (in other words almost lunchtime) to say Mr Fear was very impressed and wanted us back on a Friday night as soon as possible as support band to a top name. Bring it on!

We did a few Saturday evenings as well, on our own again, in between the brushes with the big time Charlies. Because of the type of music we played, American soul that is, we attracted a more 'Moddy' audience, not just in Ross on Wye, but in general. Naturally, even in the dustbowl of culture that was Melksham circa the mid Sixties, there were Mods. They came to all our local gigs and a few of them were mates. When we were playing one of our regular non-agency gigs in town (don't tell Howard I like my kneecaps!) we must have been asked where we were playing that following Saturday.

'Ross on Wye,' said Merv, who seemed to have an affinity with the Mods, not that he could carry off the clothes, not with his physique, but there you go.

'Where the fuck's Ross on What?' said one of the half dozen or so lads who had gathered around Merv's keyboard.

'Wye' said Merv.

'Because we want to know where it is, so we can come and watch you again, you're alright.'

Bloody hell. Praise indeed from anyone from our own neck of the woods.

Suffice to say we travelled to Ross one Saturday evening, set up and had a quick run through. We were on time and we had the volume under control. Dave was back home on leave so we were up to seven. We were cooking with gas. Harvey Fear was in a good mood - the traffic lights appeared to be switched off. We had noticed this on Fridays too, the chart bands never got any warnings as to the level of their volume nor were they cut off in their prime. Funny that. We popped up the road to our usual boozer and had a couple of bevvies. I don't think I had any more than usual, nor anything exotic in the way of shorts. I certainly wasn't on any

147

illegal substances. But when we got back to the hall the posse from our hometown had just arrived, with reinforcements. There were a few more bodies climbing out of the Minis, all neatly dressed, and all obviously under the influence of uppers or downers, or possibly both. Although I wasn't indulging somehow the mood caught me and, when I walked onto the stage to pick up my microphone, something alien took over and my mind went on a trip into the unknown.

We rattled through the first couple of numbers without a break. Normally, I just mumbled something along the lines of 'We'd like to do a number now...' so the audience wouldn't have missed much. After the final chords of the second song had died away I began to sing the introduction to the next song "The Letter Song" by Joe Tex. When I say sing, it was more of a chant. If you are a rock cake you know what I mean, or even if you have ever heard the old joke about the pilgrims in Rome listening to the Pope wittering on in the distance and one turning to the other and asking what his Holiness is saying. 'Blowed if I know, let's get closer to find out' says his mate. When they make their way through the masses they get close to the Pope and can hear him as he walks among his flock, making the sign of the cross and chanting in Latin. 'What did he say?' asked the first pilgrim. 'I don't know what he meant by it' said his mate, 'but it sounded like – 'I can beat you at dominoes'.

If you know what that sounds like, when it's sung, then that was how this sounded. "Good evening. We'd like to do a number now, by Mr Joe Tex. This one is called 'The Letter Song', with the last words in each sentence switching from a monotone to a rise and fall in pitch. Mr Taylor would have been able to describe it better, but hopefully, you get the idea. Instead of thinking I'd lost the plot, which the boys in the band did, the audience lapped it up. They had seen us before, but

148

suddenly we were the dog's bollocks. The Melksham lads were well impressed. Mind you, given the glazed expressions on their faces as they danced together at the side of the stage, they would have been anyway. The rest of the night was a blast. Every song we did was greeted with applause and when we took our half time break we had to do an encore before they would let us off stage.

Chuffed to bits, we had a couple of beers in the hall. Phil reasoned if we couldn't pull tonight, we never would. Plus, we had the home boys to talk to as well. They were making the most of their association with us and had a few young ladies in tow. There were still a few to go round so we needn't have worried.

Most Saturdays saw around four hundred in the crowd. That night there were perhaps a few less, but even so a fair proportion greeted us as we got back on stage for the second half. No, they didn't cheer wildly, they intoned in the prescribed manner "Welcome back." We couldn't go wrong that night.

Where the inspiration came from to make that introduction that way, who knows. Totally off the cuff, but it was a winner. We used it in other venues and it went okay, we never overdid it and gradually it ran its course and I went back to the same old platitudes. The next time we were at Ross on Wye on a Friday evening the chart band we supported asked us what it was all about, because they were watching as we went on and even before I had got to the microphone the crowd were chanting "Good evening". The bass player asked us after our set,

'Is one of your blokes a vicar or something?'

'Defrocked, since you ask.' replied Dave the trumpeter.

So who were these bands we supported on Friday nights I hear you ask. The best known was Georgie Fame and the Blue Flames. Do you remember me telling you about Ian, the roadie for the Alan Price Set? Well, this was when we met him again. It was a spring evening in '68 when we arrived. Ian was already there with his long wheelbase Ford Transit. He was off loading amplifiers and speakers and called out a hello as he trotted inside the hall, with what seemed like a quantity of kit that three of us might share between us. When he reappeared he saw us starting to unload Merv's organ, which we always placed at the back of the van, last in first off, as it weighed a ton.

'Leave it lads, if I was you. This stage isn't big enough for both of you. Your bloke might as well use Georgie's.'

He was stood by the open doors of his van and was getting himself into a harness arrangement that looked complicated, but was designed to allow him to carry Georgie Fames' Hammond organ on his own!

He moved the organ into position at the back of the van, back towards him, hooked himself on and took the full weight on his chest. He then turned slowly and waddled into the hall, where we followed in awe. He rejected all offers of help from the seven of us, saying he had it covered.

'I've got a system,' he said, 'thank God this gig doesn't have stairs. They can be a bastard.'

Now when I tell you Ian was about five foot three, certainly no taller, it was impressive. When we carried Merv's Hammond into a venue, on nearly every occasion it was one body on each corner! We tried to emulate Ian and double up on carrying bits of kit in from our own van, but I did myself a mischief very early on and retired to the pub up the road. Partly to heal my wounds and partly to get a drink to ease my thirst from the drive up to Ross.

We had been later than we had intended so were tight for time. When I was joined by Phil and Nick they were a bit concerned.

Phil said, 'We're not sure Merv should play Georgie's organ. What if it's set up differently and he can't get his pedals or stops sorted out. It could be a disaster. Anyway, what's Georgie going to say when he gets here? He may not be keen to share his instrument with a relative amateur like Merv.'

The rest of the band joined us and we had a couple of quick beers and faced the prospect of going on in about ten minutes without having had a sound check. Merv was a bit later joining us and he too was a bit tentative about his prospects, as Ian was still trying to get all his kit on stage and working. Merv had last seen him muttering, with wires and leads everywhere. He thought it best to leave him to get on with it, without him asking if he could have a little tinkle, as it were.

So back we trotted, changed into any stage gear we weren't already wearing and got up onto the stage. The place was heaving because of the main attraction that night, and there were possibly a load of newcomers too, because there was no discernible 'Good evening' from the depths of the hall.

Merv sat on the stool in front of Georgie's Hammond organ and Ian twiddled a few knobs and assured him everything was OK. You know what number we were starting with, all together now, 'I Can't Turn You Loose' by Otis Redding. Well that opening riff is pretty memorable at the best of times, but when Merv ripped into it with the loud pedal down as far as he usually did with our equipment, he nearly took the back wall of the hall out. Loud? Fuck me, it was brilliant, a totally different sound from his own Hammond. I turned round to look at Merv and he had a grin on his face that was as wide as the Severn estuary.

'Sorry lads.' he shouted, but the rest of them were concentrating on their own instruments and joined in and away we went.

151

Merv eased back on the volume a tad, but the impact of that first song on the audience meant the night was going to be a breeze. Merv even suggested we put back in one of our older numbers, Alan Price's 'I Put A Spell On You' which he sang, because his vocal range was higher and it seemed to fit better with him playing the organ bits as well. That went down a bomb too.

It was the traditional format. We played two sets either side of the top band who did anything between forty five minutes and an hour. We came off stage and tried to get into the dressing room. It was cramped at the best of times, but with three brass players and a drummer and guitarists from the Blue Flames either in there, or stood just outside, it was decidedly cramped. They chatted away to us as we threaded our way in or out. The brass players gravitated towards one another and guitarists compared instruments, all pretty amicable stuff. Then Speedy Acquaye, the conga player, appeared from the bar with a drink and his smile lit the place up and talked to everyone of us as if we were old friends and equals.

Georgie was either still in a limo on his way to the gig, or in hiding in Harvey's office. Ian was busying himself on stage repositioning their kit and moving leads and wires about again. As the Blue Flames mounted the stage there was a movement on the far side of the hall from the dressing room and some security guys appeared with Georgie Fame in their midst. He climbed on stage, sat at his organ and began to count the tempo of their first number. No false start because his volume had been tampered with, no adjusting stops to combat Merv's time on his beloved keyboard. Just sweet soul music. Magical minutes spent watching a master at work. The crowd were gathered at the front of the stage and as the Blue Flames showed us what a tight, professional outfit should be like, they paid homage to the craftsman on the

Hammond organ. The only chart songs they did were 'Get Away' and 'The Ballad of Bonnie and Clyde' but it was enough. That fifty minutes was gone in a flash. They departed to wild applause and we got ourselves ready to take their place to round off the evening.

Speedy was still smiling. Georgie had disappeared as swiftly as he had arrived, without a backward glance. We played the majority of our second set with assorted Blue Flames personnel at the side of the stage. Trips to the bar and time spent chatting to some adoring females wrenched them away for a few minutes at a time, but it was because we tried hard to hold our own, in the face of such talented musicians, that persuaded them to give credit where it was due and not merely adjourn to the bar.

We finished the set and climbed down from the stage where Ian and a couple of the brass section were standing. While they were chatting to Merv about his keyboard skills and complementing Dave on his guitar work, I changed shirts in the dressing room and looked to find a spot to cool down. Speedy was deep in conversation with Nick and Dave the trumpeter, so I looked for Pete to see if he wanted to push through the crowds to get to the bar for a well earned beer. He was dismantling his kit in anticipation of us packing it into the van and heading off home. So I decided to do the journey alone.

When I was upstairs on the mezzanine I saw Georgie similarly making his way slowly to the bar. I spoke. Nothing controversial, just how much I'd enjoyed his set and cheers for letting us use his organ. He blanked me. He didn't see our sets, so he didn't know me from Adam, so maybe it was understandable. He was homing in on the bar and seemed a little distant, euphemistically speaking that is. He had that all too familiar look these days. Shot to bits, spaced out, wired, whatever it was he was not with us anymore. A bit miffed, thinking what an arrogant sod he was, I veered to the right and made for the opposite end of the bar to him. I was accosted by a drunken lad in his mid twenties maybe, who wanted to talk to me. He grabbed my arm, told me how much he enjoyed us, not just tonight but the other times he had seen us and asked me if I was going to watch the National tomorrow.

He said he was a stable lad. Not so stable at this time of night obviously, but he still had his hand attached to my sleeve and I wasn't going anywhere. If I wanted to make some money he told me to back a horse called Red Alligator. Naturally I had never heard of it, I was never really interested in racing. Most sports passed us by when we were driving up, down and across the country, it was difficult to become an expert on any of them. I thanked him profusely for the inside information, hoping he would let go and I could get to the bar. He needed a refill so we both decided to go our separate ways at about the same time. I got a beer and wandered back to the stage. Never saw Georgie again. By this time the kit was nearly all down and away, I'd practically forgotten the name of the horse and it was time to bid farewell to Ian and the Blue Flames.

All the way back in the van I tried to remember the horse's name.

Forget it,' said Nick who did back a couple of gee gees in his time, now and then, 'it's a lottery, the National and the Derby. Most regular punters give it a miss. It's the only time in the year the housewives put a few bob on and the odds are all over the place.'

Suitably chastened I gave up trying to think of the name and fell asleep. When I woke up we were outside my front gate. I put my key in the lock, turned it and went in.

'Goodnight son.' said Mother.

As I settled down in my bed it came to me 'Red Alligator'. I put my bedside light back on and wrote the name on an envelope from the tax man. The rest, as they say, is history. I gathered up my loose change and a couple of notes, withdrew a fiver from the bank in the morning and I had eight quid. When the bookies were open I placed it all on Red Alligator. There was no flicker from the face of the middle aged woman behind the screen to give me a clue as to whether I was a mug punter or an astute backer of a good thing. When I looked at my betting slip, my heart sank. Twenty five to one! Bloody hell. Some tipster that piss artist was. Inside information my arse.

'He'll walk up, you mark my words.'

Yeah right. I wandered into the George for a beer, barely having enough for my pint of Watney's Starlight with a dash. Regulars, Barry and Len (of whom you will read more later) were there as usual, papers open at the racing pages, studying the form. I kept my mouth shut but listened in vain for a mention of Red Alligator as the object of their shrewdly placed bet. Someone else joined us and he mentioned thinking of doing Red Alligator each way, along with a couple more just to give him something to follow as the race unfolded.

'Keep your money in your pocket.' said Len.

It was getting worse. I was financially embarrassed into the bargain and rather than accepting a beer from them when I couldn't return the favour, I drank up and trudged home. Was I going to watch the National on the telly, asked my old man, who had just got out of bed after a night shift.

'Not got time Dad. We're off to Hereford tonight and they're picking me up about three o'clock'

Dad said to have a safe trip and not do anything he wouldn't do.

Mother put fish and chips on the table, standard fare for Saturday lunchtime, bought from the shop either by me or my younger brother Bob. There was all the usual build up on the black and white, eighteen inch Bush (now there's a prospect) telly before the big race. With about a week's wages on a long shot I was more interested in getting the grub down my neck, having a quick wash and brush up, getting changed and standing outside our front gate on the pavement praying that the van was already on the way.

Of course, as I was outside by about twenty to two I would have had a long wait. I wandered up to Phil's place and waited for the van with him. He didn't ask why. He was biting his nails and trying to work out how late we could leave it before starting the trip to Hereford, so he could know the result of the National before he left. I pointedly asked him why, since he normally took no interest in horse racing, or any sport much except for rugby. Evidently, he had five bob each way on one of the joint favourites, the last of the big spenders.. The van turned up bang on time, we piled into the back and were on the road about forty minutes before the race started. Red Alligator strolled into the winner's enclosure around about the time we were moaning about having to contribute towards the toll on the Severn Bridge.

We found out about my good fortune when we arrived at the venue. The caretaker knew the names of the first three home and I was chuffed to nuts. Phil was not so fortunate, his modest flutter had failed to register on the bloke's memory banks, but he was almost positive it hadn't made it all the way round. The evening passed pretty much problem free, I don't remember a lot about the gig itself, just a few moans from the lads about my winnings still being in the bookie's and, as I was so strapped for cash after scraping together all my loose change to get my stake money together, I was in no position to buy my own beers.

The moral of the story is I suppose that if you get an inside tip from someone associated with a stable like that you should always act on it, you may regret it if you don't. But you should only bet what you can afford to lose. I was very lucky that day and on cool reflection I realised it. In the last forty years I have hardly put a bet on since.

The Krowats. Left to right: Phil Wheeler; Ted Tayler; Gerry Cooper; Malcolm Phillips; Mervyn Osman. (From a practice session at the old Canberra Youth Club, Melksham.)

Heart 'N Soul. Left to right: Nick Fido; Phil Wheeler; Dave Shott; Dave Lane; Ted Tayler; Malcolm Phillips; Mervyn Osman. (After a wet afternoon on the Downs in Bristol.)

Copperpot Band. Left to right, above: Ted Tayler; Dave Shott; Dave Lane; Pete Ayliffe; Nick Fido; Phil Wheeler. Below: Another action shot to complete the line-up! Mervyn Osman on the extreme right (plus his Hammond organ!) Both pictures from a live performance again at the Canberra Club.

Elijah and the Goat. Left to right: Dave Shott; Pete Ayliffe; Ted Tayler; Phil Wheeler. (A practice session at Melksham House.)

Bucephalus. Left to right: Dave Shott; Phil Wheeler; Paul Seemayer; Ted Tayler.

Bucephalus. Left to right: Phil Wheeler; Dave Shott; Paul Seemayer; Ted Tayler. (Both pictures from a wet afternoon in Cumberland Basin in Bristol.)

17. Winter wonderland

We're still in Ross on Wye for the next leg of our trip down memory lane. The trip back from the Georgie Fame gig was uneventful, but it wasn't always like that. As I said, there were a couple of ways we could go. We were up there one Friday backing The Herd, who were just breaking into the Top 10 with 'I Don't Want Our Lovin' To Die'. Phil drove the van with Pete and me via Cirencester and Gloucester. This was '68 again but the weather was decidedly dodgy.

The other four lads were coming by car and although Merv agreed to drive, he wasn't happy. It had snowed on the Wednesday night when we were at a gig in Melksham. No problems there, on our doorstep. It had snowed on and off on Thursday, then frozen overnight. By the time we left late Friday afternoon it was a challenging drive for those buggers on the Monte Carlo Rally, let alone your average driver. Merv took the car on the motorway route, arguing the roads would be more likely to be clear at least until the Bridge. Then they could make their way up via Chepstow and Monmouth. Phil was a bit concerned that the van had been temperamental for a couple of weeks and didn't want to risk it on the motorway. Terrific.

As with most British weather, the snow had been patchy. As we headed towards Cirencester the gritters and snow ploughs had been out on the main roads at least and progress was steady if unspectacular. The further north we went however the deeper the ruts in the compacted snow became and by the time we reached Gloucester it was snowing again. With the street lights on and all the streets in front of us twinkling their welcome mat at us, Phil looked at his watch and said,

'Fuck! We're going to be late if we don't get a move on.'

Despite Pete and me suggesting we were happy to arrive in one piece and Harvey Fear have a pop at us again, rather than end up in the nearest A&E, Phil put his toe down. There was virtually no traffic anyway, and maybe the law were tucked up somewhere warm, but the old van responded magnificently. Of course, with a fifteen hundredweight van, fully laden with all our kit plus three adult male passengers, it was just as well we only needed to travel in straight lines and were not called upon to stop suddenly or make any swift sideways movements. Otherwise, we wouldn't have survived to tell the tale.

We rattled into Ross on Wye just about at the appointed hour. Merv had pulled in about twenty minutes earlier. Their journey had been pretty much as Merv had predicted, up to the bridge that is. The winding A466 to Monmouth had been a bastard, with black ice, snow drifts, bare stretches and lots of local traffic determined to slow them down. The town itself had only a light covering of snow and this was pretty much churned up by both the motorised and pedestrian traffic. We unloaded the van and set up on the stage, where we were joined after about ten minutes by a flustered roadie from The Herd who had suffered a fairly horrendous trip from London. Not delayed so much by the weather, as the east of the country had missed the worst of the snow, as by the traffic leaving town on Friday afternoon. The other band members were just behind him in a car, he said, so we awaited their arrival with interest. Not because we were fans, in fact we had barely heard of them before the record hit the charts, but we wanted to see what all the fuss was about regarding this Peter Frampton bloke. A 'pretty boy' who was the 'face of 1968' or some such. We knew when their car turned up, because that was when a load of teenage girls appeared out of nowhere to launch themselves at the car as soon as a door opened and someone had the temerity to step outside. The bouncers moved in pretty sharpish and four lads shot through the doorway.

Greetings were exchanged and the 'face' was full of himself as per reputation. Yeah okay, compared to the rest of us he was a good looking bastard, but didn't he fucking know it. We were the support band and we were put firmly in our place. Kit was ordered to be moved here or there according to the whim of the chosen one. We had seen it all before so we pissed off up the pub for a few bevvies before we were due on stage. It was snowing, not a lot to speak of but it was there all the same. When we sloshed our way back to the hall ready to do our thing it was a little thicker in the street lights but we weren't really paying it a lot of attention, we wanted to get up there and show them what we were made of, plus we were fairly confident the crowd would be with us, based on past visits.

Of course, we had reckoned without the 'Frampton factor'. The hall was heaving, as for Georgie Fame, but the average age had dropped five years and there were about twice as many women as there were blokes. Phil was positively drooling. So was   I and even Merv allowed himself a licking of the lips. Sadly, their hearts belonged to another. We played our set with loads of gusto, included a few new songs we had added since our last visit, but we were only the support band and the girls in front of the stage were saving their lungs, and who knows what else for The Herd. When we strolled off the stage to enthusiastic but sparse applause from the regular groups of lads who tried to battle their way towards us to congratulate and commiserate, we knew the night would belong to the chosen one and his buddies.

We didn't go back to the pub for a change. It was still snowing for one and we were hankering after a cast off from the throng of girls clustered around the stage. You never knew your luck. We got a beer and stood waiting for The Herd to strut their stuff. They took to the stage and it was bedlam. When Peter Frampton checked his mike with a 'testing, 1 2 1 2," a couple of girls fainted. Oh Pleeeease! Then they launched into their act. It was very professional but they struggled to hold it together because of the noise coming back at them from the audience and, as the set progressed, it became more and more ragged. They rescued it once they trotted out their chart buster and a grand finale where his nibs did some vocal pyrotechnics which sent the girls over the edge once more. But as chart bands went we had played with better. They departed the stage in a flurry of bouncers and admiring females and we made our way forward through the crowds to retake the stage for our second set. The Herd had been spirited away to the Top Spot's equivalent of the 'Green Room' and the girls were left with no-one to scream at.

We had more success in the second set getting through to the audience. The regulars had enough shoulder room now to get to the front and occupy their normal spaces. The numbers dwindled from the mezzanine and dance floor as per normal as our closing set continued and we finished off with a couple of up tempo numbers and said our farewells. The Herd's roadie joined us on stage and we mucked in clearing kit away and ferrying it outside to the vans.

The weather had closed in even more and Merv and his passengers got in his car and pushed off as soon as possible. They decided to go back the same way they had come, trusting to luck on the A466 still being 'passable with care' as Harvey Fear had indicated when he came down from his office to see us off the premises. Phil, Pete and I got into the van, started her up and pulled away slowly up the hill out of town. Phil was a little more circumspect on the way back than he had been on the way in. It was a close thing but we made it up the hill and out, following The Herd's roadie in his Transit, edging his way tentatively towards his idea of civilisation in London.

We watched as his tail lights disappeared from view and the snow continued to fall, that may have been the time when we decided to buy our own Transit. As we continued slipping and sliding our way to Gloucester and the dreaded Birdlip Hill, little did we know that Ross on Wye was now cut off from the rest of the world. We were the last two vehicles to get out for over forty eight hours. As it happened Birdlip was not nearly as bad as we feared. The patchy nature of the snow, and the fevered attempts in the past couple of days to keep this problematical bit of road open, had meant the accumulations of snow had been minimal. 'Passable with care', Harvey had said and passable it was. We trundled on towards Cirencester, looking for a garage, just in case one might still be stupid enough to be open. Phil was getting a little worried we might need the odd half gallon to be absolutely sure of getting all the way back home. Now he tells us!

One thing we discovered over the years was that if you were in a reasonably large town, with a manned police station that was open overnight, you could drop in, and as they had a handful of cars at their disposal, they also had jerry cans of petrol. Provided you were prepared to pay slightly over the odds you could buy sufficient to get you home. All part of the service Sir! When we got as far as Tetbury, where the snow was about nine inches deep and drifting in a bitingly cold wind Phil approached the roundabout that would take us to Malmesbury, then on to Chippenham and home to a warm bed. The large building on the corner was the police station. Slowing to take the turn Phil suddenly had a brainwave. "I wonder if we can get petrol here?" The van stalled as it waited for an answer.

Tetbury is a small town. Even in 1968 its police station probably closed at five o'clock on a Friday night. This was a bad move. The van refused to restart. We may or may not have been running on fumes for the last few miles. The van still played dead. Pete huddled into his big coat for a little warmth. It dawned on the three of us pretty quickly, that the old van, despite it playing up now and then, did have a heater which worked. It was now about half past one on Saturday morning. We had no heater. It was fucking cold.

We considered our options. We had gone out prepared for bad weather, so we had warm clothing, big coats, hats and wellies. Exactly, no bugger would stop if they saw us dressed like that. We looked like half The Dubliners on a UK tour.

'We ought to push the van off this roundabout and up the road a bit,' said Phil, 'we're blocking a main road. We might get a fine.'

'Bollocks,' said Pete, 'I ain't getting out of this warm van to push it a few yards up the road.'

It seemed a tad churlish to mention that the effects of the heater were dissipating fast. We were sat in an increasingly cold van, blocking the road. My feet were starting to feel strange. I should have been warm in all the layers of clothes I had put on. I had borrowed my Dad's boots and put three pairs of socks on for a start. My body and head were warm, but my feet were frozen.

We sat there chatting aimlessly about all sorts of crap to kill time. It was now about two o'clock.

Pete suggested we took a walk up into the town centre to see if there was anywhere warmer for us to shelter. We left the discomfort of the inside of the van and walked about two hundred yards into a bitingly cold wind. Shop windows were ablaze with fluorescent light, but they were about as much use as a chocolate teapot. There was a public phone box too, which Pete decided to see if the three of us in our big coats could squeeze into. Secretly I reckon he wanted us to huddle together for warmth and was too proud to ask outright. We pressed all the buttons to see if we could get any loose change, like you did in those days, and tapped out any old set of six numbers to see if you got a ringing tone. Very childish. At a few minutes after two in the morning the couple of hits we got weren't home or were asleep and not about to answer the phone, so that was another few minutes towards the morning and we were no nearer getting into our warm beds.

We got back to the van and, despite the cold, managed to drop off for a while. I woke up with a start and cramp in my big toe, which Phil and Pete thought most amusing. Huddled up as we were there wasn't a lot of room to get my foot out straight and I was going through some strange contortions trying to get myself back to normal. As the morning light fought its way through the still threatening snow clouds, we heard the sound of the first vehicle to appear in either direction for many an hour. It was a rather large articulated lorry and it was directly behind us. It couldn't get round the roundabout because we were stuck right in the throat of the exit road it wanted to take. The driver got down from his cab and strolled across.

'Can't you move this fucker? You're blocking the highway.'

The highway! Phil told him our tale of woe. He even suggested we let our handbrake off and he could push us up the road for a bit to let him through. The driver wasn't having any of that. The driver disappeared back to his cab. His engine was working, ergo, so was his heater, but he never invited us in for a warm. Even though we had told him we had been there five hours. Bastard! Let him wait.

As it got progressively lighter, you can guess who was next on the scene. The Old Bill? Actually no, it was a milkman. He was doing his round on foot for the most part. His float was down the road where the snow had mostly blown away. It had only drifted in pockets, just our luck to hit one of the worst. We chipped in a few coppers each for a pinta and, although it was cold and had to be shared three ways, it was manna from heaven. That was when the law arrived.

'You're obstructing the highway sir,' one of the patrolmen offered, 'you can't stay here you know.'

Pete replied, 'Unless we get some petrol and get this van started we'll be here 'til Spring.'

That did the trick. A tow rope appeared from the boot of the patrol car, which just squeezed past us on the other side of the road, then we were   dragged out of our resting place and about two hundred yards down the road to a garage. We panicked a bit as we scoured the forecourt for signs which might have indicated '24 Hours Service' but there weren't any. Phil was confident we could get home on a gallon. Having bought the pint of milk, we were struggling to find any more cash and I can't swear to it , but I'm sure I recall four pence in old money being handed over by one of the boys in blue to complete   the   transaction.   Aren't   our   policemen wonderful!

Once we were fuelled up, we had to bump start the van as she wouldn't play ball with the starter motor. It would have been a comical sight if anyone had been stupid enough to be about that early. Phil was at the wheel. Pete and I, in our big coats and wellies, were at the back pushing the van trying to get up a head of speed on a slippery slushy surface. As we were clearly fighting a losing battle, the two patrolmen and the milkman, who had reappeared with a freshly replenished crate, joined in. The van increased speed rapidly. Phil started her up first time and off we trundled towards home.

Mother was up and about by the time I walked in. She had been concerned, naturally, as she hadn't heard me come in. 'Coldest night since 1947, they said on the wireless.' 'Really Mum? I would never have guessed.'

18. Who let the dogs out?

Just one more Ross story left really. This didn't involve lousy weather, just a lack of petrol and a brush with the West Country county set. We were supporting the John Dummer Blues band that particular Friday night, with Dave Kelly on slide guitar. I thought they were pretty good, I was always into that bluesy sound and they were okay in my book. It was the sort of music I listened to at home, when I had got fed up with the sweet soul music that I had to hear over and over in order to get the lyrics down. The rest of the band thought they were a bit old hat and went up the road to the boozer. I watched a fair bit of their set, keeping my liquid intake up by popping up to the bar upstairs for reinforcements.

After we had played our second set, we had a chat with the other band while we took down our various bits of equipment and stowed it away in our respective vans. For a reason that escapes me now only a couple got into the van, while the other four of us decided to go back in somebody's car. Which of them drove up to Ross on this trip I can't remember, but we bombed off back towards home without a care in the world until, when we got to about a half a mile from Kemble airfield, the car slid gracefully to a halt, having run out of petrol. All sorts of recriminations followed. Why didn't you fill up before we left? There wasn't anywhere open! I thought we had enough to get us back home! There was a garage open when we arrived in Ross last night! That was nearly eight hours ago!

None of which altered the situation. Fortunately, this was the summer of 1968 and it was pleasantly warm, unlike the Tetbury incident. We decided we may as well get our heads down until sun up, see if someone drove past so we could hitch a lift into Kemble, then either buy a can of petrol, or phone our old roadie Glyn, to see if he would pop out with a gallon, The latter was a last resort as he hadn't been with us for ages, although we were fairly sure we hadn't pissed him off to the extent that he would leave us stranded.

Dawn broke on the countryside and a low mist crept under the hedgerows towards our car. The sun was weak at that unearthly hour but promised a fine, warm day ahead. After being cramped up in the back of the car for four hours and more, the three of us were all in need of a leak. The two in the front were making us wait as it was a two door and we weren't going anywhere until they let us out. When the need struck them too we were all out of that car in a flash and over the five barred gate and into the field. The high hedgerows shielded us from the road but there was no traffic at that hour anyway.

Suddenly, out of the mist, appeared several dogs accompanied by a group of middle aged ladies and one or possibly two blokes. What they thought of five blokes at various points along the hedge with their backs to them I have no idea, but nothing could have prepared us for what the lady at the front called out.

'Are you beagling?'

'Sorry,' said Nick in his best telephone voice 'what did you say?'

The cut crystal voice asked again, 'are you going beagling?'

Well, when you're knocking the drops off after the first overdue pee of the morning, the last thing you want to be doing is shaking with laughter. It's a man thing I guess, can't do two things at the same time. I for one, laughed like a drain, popped the honourable member back out of sight and got a wet leg, which made it difficult to move towards the gate with anything approaching a cool dignified manner.

As the advanced party passed by the hastily reassembled group of early morning hedgerow fanciers, the pack of beagles appeared from the next field. We were now nearly all back by the gate, trying to effect a quick exit, but the dogs wanted to play and also sniff along the stretch of hedge that we had frequented. How this influenced the rest of their morning's excitement we were not going to hang around to find out. Over the gate we climbed and the dogs split into two, some carried on along the road side of the field, stopping briefly here and there, some came to the gate and peered through the bars at the retreating town folk with strange attire.

We still had the fuel problem to sort out but at least we didn't have an audience for this item, once we got back to the mini. With the sun rising higher in the sky, there were suddenly cars on the road again, admittedly the first half dozen were going away from our required destination, but eventually a Land Rover type vehicle came along and the chap answered our frantic waving by slowing down and asking if he could help. Obviously a member of the farming community, his first thought was what we were doing out here in the Wild West at such an early hour. After his first question, which was why we were out of bed on a Saturday morning when he had heard all today's young people lazed around in their pit until lunchtime, he said,

'Ah. I suppose you've come out to watch the beagling have you?'

We had to admit we hadn't and that we would very much like to get into a bed at least until lunchtime to catch upon the sleep we had lost cramped up in the mini all night. He took one of the lads into the village and even dropped him back with the can of petrol, before leaving us with a cheery wave. Nice bloke.

19. London's Calling

Did I tell you about the time we worked for the Kray family?

Yeah right! Well I have bored loads of people to death with this one over the years. But it was true. Honest.

We had been slogging away up and down the West Country and South Wales for a couple of years when out of the blue Howard, our agent in Bristol, phoned through a booking in London. Saturday night in a nightclub called Sybilla's in 'Man in the Moon Passage', just off Regent Street.

The money was OK without being special, but we were chuffed to nuts. It was our first booking in London. I had read about the club in the NME or Melody Maker and when it was set up the money behind it came from George Harrison and William Piggott Brown, a well known amateur National Hunt jockey. There were others too I've no doubt, but those are the only names I remember.

In those early days the 'beautiful people' were much in attendance. A-list definitely. By the time we played there it may well have lost its cachet as the place to be and be seen at. Nevertheless we set off early in the van with all six of us crammed in with our kit. We parked in an NCP car park just off Leicester Square and headed for The Golden Egg. We knew how to live in those days!

Once we were replenished it was opening time at the pubs in the Square,. Just across the corner from the Blue Boar, which we had all heard of, was a place next to the

ABC cinema that looked like the back end of HMS Victory. Memory tells me it was called The Captain's Cabin or at least one of the bars was. There was probably a Crow's Nest upstairs too. We settled down for a lunchtime session.

On the pavements outside we watched the passing traffic, both motorised and human. Those who had been without for a while kept shouting, 'Look at that!' 'Bloody Norah' and it was obvious there was a quality gap between the crumpet on the streets of London and the meagre offerings in West Wiltshire or even Bath. The not so desperate ones were car watching and, as well as a black taxi every two or three cars, there were the obligatory Routemaster buses plus Rollers, Mercedes, E Type Jags, Jensen Interceptors and the odd Aston Martin thrown in for good measure. Time passed very easily.

'I could get used to this,' said Nick.

Two people stood out among those thronging the pavements. One was a twenty something singer with a few items strapped about his person. He was clearly a one man band and as the crowd thinned we got a better look at him as he had quite a few coins dropped into his tin can. How good he was we couldn't tell from our vantage point inside the pub but later that summer we saw him on 'Top Of The Pops'. It was Don Partridge, who had that Number One with 'Rosie'. He was good but it didn't stop the law from moving him on as soon as a crowd built up around him. Typical.

'Can't have people enjoying themselves Sir can we? More than my job's worth. Move along please!'

The other guy never made the big time as far as I know. He came trotting along the pavement pushing a small pram. He was in his sixties maybe, with a powdered wig. The shorter courtroom variety rather than the full jobby. He wore Regency clothes I guess you

174

would call them. Three quarter length frock coat, trousers to the knee, white stockings and black shoes with a buckle. In the pram he had a wind-up gramophone. When he was happy he was clear of the law for a spell he produced a record, wound up his gramophone and on he went with his act. He tap danced and minuetted across the pavement like a good 'un.

He had us out of our seats and onto the streets. We just had to watch him up close, he was magic. Not a word was spoken. Just a nod as people dropped their money into the bottom of the pram and then he was off, trotting away to his next pitch, keeping a little way away from the police as they ambled towards us.

All too soon it was closing time. We had a wander to Carnaby Street to buy some clothes and watched a few more street entertainers - but the less salubrious sort. Dodgy geezers flogging Swiss watches and French perfume, plus the usual 'Find the Lady' merchants. We avoided spending or losing any money as far as I recall. Then we made our way back to the NCP car park.

Phil was always the optimist. He had this idea on the way up that we would get there early and ask if it was alright for us to set up and have a practice for an hour or two. He reasoned that the place would be occupied by cleaning staff or whatever and we could finish about six o'clock then find somewhere to eat. We would be playing two one hour sets and as everywhere closed down before twelve on a Saturday night we would be on the road back to the sticks by half past midnight. Wrong!

We got the van out of the compound and drove the short distance to the venue. It was a nondescript building with no obvious signs that it was a nightclub of some distinction. As we pulled into one of the last parking spaces almost by the front door, a powder blue Jaguar zipped past us and pulled up by the kerb. "Prick" said our Mervyn.

Fortunately, the driver didn't hear him. He jumped out of the car and scurried towards us. He was in his late thirties possibly, tanned with thinning dark hair. His white shirt was open to the waist and had an enormous gold medallion hanging around his neck. I know it was big because, even though he was moving quickly, it didn't swing about, it just hung there motionless as if it was tied in place by his chest hair. That was impressive too.

'I couldn't be this lucky boys,' he said in his broad London accent. Not something we yokels heard too often except on the big screen or on the telly. 'You the band what's playing here tonight?'

Phil appeared from the back of the van and started asking if this bloke knew whether there was anyone we could ask about setting up for a practice.

'Shut up Phil,' said Nick, 'this bloke wants to know if we're playing here tonight.'

Again the bloke appeared not to hear him. He was in a rush to tell us why it was his lucky day bumping into us in mid afternoon, when we weren't contracted to arrive until nine pm. Sorry? He was the agent that had booked us through Howard and he was in the shit. Prince Rupert and his band were due to play in Farnborough that evening and he'd had a phone call telling him they were pulling out, as young Rupert was poorly.

Prince Rupert was a relative of Prince Buster as I remember. So it was an all West Indian Ska, Blue Beat and Soul ensemble. The agent said, "The bastard won't fucking work in London again. In fact if I get hold of him he won't sing again either. I'll chop his poxy balls off."

Moving on. He outlined his plan. If we did him a favour and drove to Farnborough in Hampshire, got there for seven pm., played for an hour and a quarter, top of the bill, with a support band and a DJ he would pay us forty quid plus the thirty we were due in Sybilla's. We

176

did the maths. More money than we had earned. Big problem, we didn't know how to get to Farnborough, how far it was or how good the support band would be. Could we find our way back here in the dark? Were we being stiffed? Was this bloke sending us off just to get shot of us so he could slip his own band in as a late replacement, effectively 'blackballing' us as far as the real agent, and even Howard, was concerned.

We nodded agreement to everything he said, despite our reservations and set off. The time passed quickly on the way south as all the doom and gloom merchants poured out all of the above 'what ifs'.

We arrived in Farnborough at about seven and reached the venue by half past. Thirty minutes late. Why is there no one about to ask directions when you need them. If I had a fiver for the number of times we asked an old bloke on the street where such and such hall, college or club was and they replied, "I don't live here, I'm only visiting my sister. I haven't been well..." (once they started on their fucking life story we closed the window and moved on), I would be writing this sat on a beach in the Bahamas.

Clearly our agent friend had contacted the venue. Once we pulled into one of the car parking spaces in front of the extension to the pub in the middle of Farnborough, half a dozen scooter boys gathered around our van and rather than filling us in, offered to help us carry our kit inside. A refreshing change from some places we had played. Chatting to the lads, they were all mad keen on the soul music we were playing at the time and said that the place would be heaving by the time we went on. The venue bussed in teenagers from local villages to keep the numbers up and this was the place to be on a Saturday night for miles around.

We were set up in next to no time and did a quick sound check. Then we went next door to have a few bevvies. It was pretty busy anyway with locals and they were a bit snooty as well. We thought how good looking we must have been as they couldn't take their eyes off us all the time we were in there. We downed the first pint and wandered off to find a quiet boozer. Once inside, and with full glasses, we chatted about how our day was going so far and how a few of the doubters had been put in their place.

When we were ten minutes or so away from going on stage we made our way back and had to push our way through hordes of parka clad youths and rather tasty females to reach the main door. The lads earlier were spot on. It was packed, with the ones outside still trying to get in.

The support band was just closing its set. We were impressed. They had a different line up from us. Lead, rhythm, bass and a drummer, all singing in close harmony - so close they were almost touching. We hated that sound, but they were good at what they did. Being a mod band, they were a bit like the English Birds if you ever saw them, not the American Byrds. They were something else.

We were just the six on stage that weekend. Merv on his Hammond organ (with Leslie speaker), Phil on bass, Dave on lead, Pete on drums. Nick was on tenor sax and I was on vocals as usual. We got the big build up from the DJ and ripped into "I Can't Turn You Loose" by Otis Redding. Followed up with 'The Letter Song' by Joe Tex and 'You Don't Know Like I Know' by Sam and Dave. We were off and running.

The hour and a quarter sped by and, as we were unaccustomed to headlining, we were able to leave out any 'iffy' numbers that we had done to death or only just learnt. All in all we felt we had done OK. The reaction was fine from the crowd. The floor was a seething mass of humanity dancing away, all the usual suspects. The cooler Mod lads in a corner dancing on their own, too hip to pick up a bird and dance with her. The single girls dancing around their handbags in twos and threes, while those couples that were there were clung onto one another for grim death on the crowded floor. A few songs from the DJ and adverts for next week, then it was 'everybody out. The coaches are here!' The law were in attendance by now too, making sure everybody was up and away before any trouble broke out. They were too knackered to start anyways.

Ten minutes later we were packing our gear away. Into the van and after an appreciative chat with the lads in charge of the gig plus their thanks for us filling in at the last minute, we were away back to the Big Smoke. Naturally, we had to scramble around in our pockets for some petrol money to get us back. I seemed to contribute most of it, same old story.

The trip back was more eventful than on the way down. Every forecourt had cars and scooters on it, with kids spilling out 'chilling' or arguing and we picked the quietest one to fill up. When we were about twenty miles away from Farnborough we saw a car on its roof just past the forecourt of a garage. There were lots of lights, cars, scooters and police.

'Move along please sir', one traffic cop said to Phil, 'nothing to see. Two dead. Typical Saturday night on this road. Too many young kids driving too fast, usually on pills. This one was speeding by and saw some mates, turned onto the forecourt, nearly ran a few kids down, narrowly avoided creaming the pumps and flipped over as he tried to get back on the road without hitting a lorry that was driving by. Take care now.'

We pulled away to the sound of the ambulance siren coming up behind us and, suitably chastened, we headed back to London's night life. For us 'hicks from the sticks' it was a riot of sounds and colours and people enjoying

179

life well after everything had shut down tight in our local towns and city. Man in the Moon Passage was still there. It hadn't disappeared like some figment of our imagination. We parked in a space reserved by a couple of judiciously placed traffic cones, courtesy of our agent we found out later, then went into Sybilla's for the very first time.

We had seen nothing like it. The club was small and dark. Some walls were mirrored, to give the illusion of space and the lighting was muted. A DJ sat by his twin decks in the right hand corner and the mellow sounds of Curtis Mayfield (while still with The Impressions) wafted across the room. Amen to that. The dance floor was empty, not that many more than fifteen to twenty people could have got on there at the same time anyway. To the left of the dance floor was a mirrored partition which separated the dancers from the rest of the club. There was a tiny raised dais in front of this partition and we speculated how we would get a seven piece drum kit on it, let alone anything else.

As we walked on through to the rear of the club, we could see a few people sat eating a meal, still in semi-darkness. We noticed the area was sectioned off into several larger and smaller booths. We were looking for the bar and the bogs as the journey back to town had taken its toll, one way and another.

We were intercepted by a couple of waiters, who turned out to be Greek, who told us we were not permitted in the restaurant as we were not customers, merely the hired help. It wasn't said in so many words but we got the message. They pointed us towards the bogs and said we could put our stage kit in a storeroom which was in the far left hand corner of the club, close to the kitchens. The guitarists were setting up on the tiny stage and cursing frequently as there were wires everywhere and they kept bumping into one another.

One of them came over to where we were chatting to another, younger friendlier waiter and asked where they could get a drink.

'"Coca cola. Ten shillings please.' the young man said, with a straight face. How he kept it up I'll never know. Who said the Greeks never had a sense of humour?

Only he wasn't joking. They had no beer on the premises. Only wines and spirits plus the obligatory mixers. No alcopops in those days kids and in case you were wondering, ten shillings is 50p in new money. Today, coke at 50p wouldn't be sniffed at but I remember taking the wife out a few years after this and buying four pints of bitter, four port and lemons and some chips on the way home with only a pound in my pocket, and managing without having to ask her to put her hand in her purse either. So you can tell what we were up against.

As it was now around eleven fifteen we were stuffed. All the boozers were closed and it would be many years before any shops would be open past about six pm on a Saturday night and, if we could have found a garage open, it would have sold petrol and diesel and hardly anything else. They had us by the short and curlies. We had pretty much used up all our spare cash on the petrol we bought on the way back from Farnborough, so it was a handful of shrapnel our Greek friend got in exchange for a couple of warm cokes. I got first dibs as I had to attempt to sing for a couple of hours again having given my all in Hampshire.

As the first mouthful reached its resting place, my bladder reminded me where I needed to be before too long. The gents was back towards the exit and, having entered, I realised I was not alone. An elderly chap who had the appearance of a gentleman's gentleman ushered me to the urinal, rather like an usherette pointing you in the direction of a vacant seat in the cinema, but without the torch of course. In here it was lit up like a Christmas tree. It was compact and bijou in there with lots of tiles and mirrors, elegant fittings in front of where I stood for bloody ages wondering if I could trust the bloke behind me. Naturally I couldn't pee either, but eventually I managed a pathetic dribble and resisted the temptation to knock the drops off in case I upset my companion with a couple of stray splashes on his immaculate flooring.

Moving away from the urinal with as much composure as I could muster I found myself face to face with the old retainer, who was holding a towel in one outstretched hand and gesturing with the other to the sink with the gold taps. As I washed my hands I looked around to see if there was a 'Noel Redding was here' scratched onto the surface. Not bloody likely. Not while this chap was about that's for sure. Once I had dried my hands the towel was taken from me and discarded into a clothes basket. One per person? Their laundry bill must be more than I get a week I thought as I returned to the semi darkness of the club. My attendant said,

'Thank you, Sir. Good evening,' as I left and I panicked as I wondered whether a tip was in order. I sincerely hoped not as after chipping in for the coke I was skint.

I relayed my experiences to the rest of the lads and naturally they disappeared into the loo 'mob handed' to see how many towels they could use up. Typical.

When we gathered together again in the store area cum dressing room, we had a limited view of the restaurant and drinking area. One table of four provoked some whispered discussions. Phil said the two women looked like fashion models or debutantes, really classy birds. Their two male companions were an Indian guy in his late twenties and a taller, older bloke who had his back to us. Nick said he looked like that 'Lawrence of Arabia bloke, you know, what's his name - Peter

182

O'Toole?' I snorted. You must be joking. What would he be doing in here?

The young Greek waiter cleared their table, which included the essential ice bucket and empty bottles of champagne, and returned to the kitchen. After the head waiter had visited the table, and obviously received a generous tip, he was in a much better humour and even lowered himself to come over to us to show us the cheque for his four guests.

'Very nice man.' he said 'Always pays the bill, never his companions.'

The cheque was drawn on Coutt's Bank for a ton and signed Peter O'Toole.

'Told you,' said Nick to me, and to the head waiter, 'who was the other bloke?'

'I cannot reveal his name but he is the eldest son of a leading Indian family.'

We were keen to know what they ate and drank for the bill to be as high as it was. But the head waiter tapped his nose and walked away, but as he reached the doors to the kitchen he turned and said,

'The food and drink came to just under forty pounds. Mr O'Toole is always very generous.'

With the time approaching midnight we were summoned by the DJ and went through the format for the rest of the night. We were to play two forty five minute slots, with a fifteen minute break, during which he would play a few tracks. No problem. Apart from the cramped stage area that was. Ah well.

People were drifting through from the booths with their drinks and were joined by newcomers who had only just arrived, presumably from some other late night haunt, because chucking out time was long gone based on West Country time. We launched into the same set we had used down in Farnborough all those hours ago. We reduced our volume once we saw the reaction of the crowd and gradually persuaded a few couples to get onto the dance floor. What they made of us was difficult to read really. They were all over twenty five for sure, no youngsters, nor was there anyone over the age of say forty, possibly forty five.

That in itself was a big change for us, we were more used to youth clubs, colleges and working men's clubs. So I was on my best behaviour, not popping into the audience to pull a bird and dance with her during an instrumental, hoping to catch up with her later. There were two reasons for this, I didn't want to get filled in by an irate husband and I was knackered.

As the dance floor became more crowded, we were squeezed even further back onto the dais, but it did give us the chance to do some people watching. O'Toole was long gone but a few familiar faces sashayed past.

'I've seen her on the telly,' said Nick.

'And her,' said Dave the guitarist.

Merv was working his little fingers to the bone on his organ (Don't go there, his Hammond organ!) and gesturing with his head towards a gangly six footer who was boogying away like a good 'un. His face was his fortune as they say. Made for radio maybe but nevertheless it was Jeremy Lloyd, who later in the '60s appeared on 'Rowan and Martin's Laugh In' and is perhaps best known for co-writing 'Are You Being Served' and 'Allo Allo'.

Whether Joanna Lumley was with him then who knows, but it was clear the vast majority of our audience were 'luvvies' or in the entertainment business in some shape or form. This was their watering hole, where they did their winding down after a show until the early hours. Our two sets passed relatively quickly and the applause at the end was warm and pleasing. The DJ thanked everyone for coming and encouraged everyone to move quickly and quietly out of the club in order to avoid too many complaints from the neighbours.

Why did Joanna Lumley crop up? She was married briefly to Lloyd. Most blokes would reckon he was a lucky bastard for that reason alone. Lucky? He was invited to LA for some function or other to join up with Sharon Tate and her entourage. He overslept. They went back to her place and were wiped out by Charles Manson and his followers. Overslept! Now that's what I call fucking lucky.

Anyway back to Sybilla's. With the last of the stragglers making their way out onto the empty streets we took down our kit for the second time that night and wearily loaded it into the van. The effects of the eighteen hours we had just gone through were catching up on us and the thought of driving the many miles home to Melksham was too much for our drivers. We climbed into the van and slept as best we could until dawn broke and the city began to stir itself ready for a leisurely Sunday morning. We made our way home in a much more subdued manner than on the way up, that's for sure, but we were richer for the experience and couldn't wait for the chance to do it all over again. It made a refreshing change from bombing over the Severn Bridge every bloody weekend on Friday night and dragging our arses into work on Monday morning after visiting some of the God awful venues the Principality had to offer.

What the fuck has all this got to do with the Krays I can hear you say!

On Monday, I was back at work and Merv rang. He was the main contact for our Bristol agency at that time and Howard had rung him in a pretty good mood, for a change.

'Well done lads, for Saturday,' he said, 'you've done yourselves a good turn there and us too. The club liked you and want you back in the near future. The agency also said their boss was very impressed with how you helped him out, no questions asked. He'd tried a couple of London bands and they wanted more money so he's kicked them into touch. Not a bloke you want to get on the wrong side of, if you know what I mean. He's ringing me later in the week with a list of places we can book bands into, with you going in first as a reward for your efforts. The cheque's in the post for both gigs, we've agreed to split our commission fifty fifty on this one. You did us a favour, we'll do you one.'

This was not a common occurrence believe me. The money duly arrived and at the weekend some contracts turned up in the post. Merv brought them along to the gig on Saturday night, something he didn't usually bother to do. It was usually 'dates for our diary' as it were. The heading on the contracts told us all we needed to know. The main director was Ronnie and Reggie Kray's father Charles. We never enquired what the name of his gofer was. We liked our kneecaps just as they were thanks very much!

20. Little Drummer Boy

Pete had another of his madcap moments on Bonfire Night in Abergavenny. Maybe sixty-eight, can't be sure, but I know it was November 5th. We were on one of our weekend breaks in Wales and had been in Abergavenny since just after lunchtime. It may be okay on a summer's day, but that Saturday it was raining, the clouds as grey as the slates on the rooftops of the dark red brick buildings. It was as depressing a place as I had been to that autumn. We had plenty to choose from given that we were back and forwards over that bloody bridge nearly every weekend.

The Top Club was not the happening place it perhaps aspired to be, so we played our first set to a half empty dance floor. It is always difficult to raise your enthusiasm levels when it turns out like that and consequently our performance was below par. We went up the road to a pub for our interval in dribs and drabs so maybe four of us were halfway down our pints when Pete walked in. It was a real spit and sawdust bar with no trimmings and the clientele was sparse too, and a bit rough looking - not the sort of bar to walk into on your own. We were English, of course, they had spotted that fairly quickly, so rough they may have been, but thick they were not. It was wet and cold out so winter gear was de rigueur. We had our long coats, assorted hats and looked a motley crew I'm sure. For whatever reason, I had left my hat and coat in the dressing room of the Top Club and was only wearing a suede jacket, on top of my stage clothes.

The door swung open and in walked Pete. He was about five foot four at the best of times but he had put my coat and old Homburg on, topping off the ensemble with a three inch wide white plastic belt This normally held his hipster flares up, but it was now holding the coat together and, because of his size, when he turned to close the door carefully behind him he revealed a significant pleat down the back that made him look more like the Hunchback of Notre Dame than anything else. The coat trailed across the tiled floor as he made his way to the bar.

Before he could order, the door opened again and in came the other band members, dressed normally thank goodness. They had stood back to enable him to make a grand entrance, but now they were ready to get a beer in and join us. As they walked in some local scallywags decided to throw fire crackers into the doorway and run off up the hill. Highly amusing!

Nick kicked the only one to make it inside the bar back outside and closed the door. Pete was not to be messed with though and he swished his way back to the door and went outside. With the fire crackers jumping around his feet he shouted up the hill at the group of lads gathered at the top.

'Dobbut!' he cried, 'dobbut boyos. I know your mothers. I'm going to tell on you.'

Whether it was the thought that Pete actually did know their mums, or the sight of him that put the fear of God into them, I don't know, but they scarpered like the hounds of hell were after them. Pete came back in and went to the bar to order a pint, still talking as if he had a speech impediment. (not the done thing these days I know, but back then we still watched comedians on telly and laughed at jokes about the Irish and all shades of colour, so tough, it was the way we were brought up).

He got his pint and we sat around a couple of tables having a beer and laughing at Pete trying to sit on a bar stool without removing the coat. It lifted our spirits at least and when we got back to the Top Club we were in a far better frame of mind to do our second set. Just as well, the place was heaving.

No two sets could have been more different. The dance floor was packed and we were back on form. After the manager paid us our money, he was chatting away trying to find out when we could come back again. We asked why it was so quiet in the first half. "Oh, everyone was up the playing fields for the big bonfire, see?" Well we did see now, but it would have helped if he had told us earlier.

Pete had his serious side too, as I recall from a gig we did in King's Lynn or Wisbech one Sunday night. We had played our first set in a pub in the town centre and we were besieged by a couple of young groupies. As we had half an hour's break we were just going to the bar to get a drink and sit quietly and think about the meaning of life - and dread the four and a half hour trip home and having to get up for work in the morning.

However these two groupies had other plans for Pete and me which, in the past, I would have gone along with. Pete was going steady and wasn't keen on mucking it up with a one night stand, even if it was hardly shitting on his own doorstep. I had started seeing someone too but when Pete said to me at the bar that he was going to give this golden opportunity a miss, I thought 'what the heck, I'll go along with it for the time being'. Pete said his philosophy was 'True to one, Mister. True to one.' That philosophy cost a fair few opportunities over the following months, not all golden of course, there were several dogs too, but all in all it was for the best in the long run.

189

21. Reflections

A lot of the venues I'm writing about are long gone. Anyone who was in a group back in the Sixties will tell you the same. Groups were a fairly new addition to the entertainment scene. At least the three guitars and drummer format was new. Previously there had been skiffle and folk groups, small dance bands. In the fifties of course the big bands held sway, they played the large venues while pubs, clubs and village halls, works canteens and the like were inundated with all kinds of two to say five piece combos with little or no amplification.

With the electric guitar came the added volume from a sudden surge in the production of amplifiers. Not just the volume of units required to satisfy the number of groups that were springing up but the volume of noise that could be produced that a lot of smaller venues found impossible to cope with. I don't know how many groups were playing in the UK in '65 but when we signed up for the Vincent, Rudman & Amigo agency there were two hundred bands in the Bristol area alone.

When we visited Sybilla's in '67 we saw a DJ featuring for the first time as an integral part of the evening's entertainment. Mostly there would be two bands in the larger halls and just one in the smaller venues with a record player to fill in the gaps. Or they would just whack up the volume on the juke box if there was one.

We didn't really appreciate the threat that the DJ posed to live music as the Sixties rocked and rolled into the Seventies. The Musician's Union did and, bless them, they tried to stem the tide with 'Music should be played live' stickers for your car or van window. Too little too late.

Mind you the DJ had several benefits over the groups. He played a wide range of music, including the Top 20 and most groups followed a particular style which didn't suit all tastes. He didn't have as much kit to set up or need to make as much noise with it. If he was a resident in a particular venue and therefore probably local, he didn't have to travel far. Some bands were notorious for failing to turn up and, as we knew to our cost, they travelled anything up to 200 miles to reach a gig to find the clientele would have preferred Country and Western rather than Hard Rock.

Dance bands and the like could play 'Happy Birthday', 'The Anniversary Waltz' and 'God Save The Queen' at the drop of a hat. A DJ could very quickly add records like that to his collection. Ninety percent of the groups that sprang up in the Sixties were only set up to play what they wanted to play. Rhythm and Blues, Pop and all the perceived 'old hat' trimmings went by the wayside.

The clincher was that the DJ worked cheap, so one by one the smaller venues disappeared from the available places for bands to learn their trade. The disco took over and for a decade the music scene was crap until Punk turned everything on its head again and kids started to play live music again. Hallelujah!

22. Noel, Noel, Noel

One of the venues that has survived through to the present day is Salisbury City Hall. We played there four or five times in all. The most memorable was the first without any doubt as that was the night we first met Noel Redding.

We had arrived to support a group from Brighton, or somewhere down South anyway, called The Loving Kind. They were a three guitars and drums line-up and we were still traipsing around with our Vox AC30's, so Phil and Gerry were all agog when we saw the Fender amps on the stage. Rather like the ubiquitous Stratocaster, they just oozed class on the stage alongside our rather twee looking kit. Being a professional set up they had arrived ages before us and their sound checks were done and dusted so there was no sign of the group's personnel.

We got our kit set up and ready to go on first, then found our way to the dressing room in the dark recesses of the stage. Of course, being a 'proper' stage, for theatrical productions and the like, there were mirrors and lights aplenty.

We chilled out for a while. For whatever reason we had been tight for time that evening so we had no time to pop over the road to a boozer for a couple of beers. The manager stuck his head round the door and suggested we pull our finger out and get on stage. We did our forty five minutes to a sparse but enthusiastic crowd and when the curtains closed (very posh) we popped back to the dressing room to have a breather.

We planned to watch The Loving Kind do their headline spot, or at least as much as we could put up with. If we had time we'd have a couple of quick ones before we went on to wind up the night's entertainment.

As we walked in through the dressing room door, we came face to face with the other group. They had been in town for a 'beer up', were all set to go on, but one guy asked Merv,

'Where's the bog, mate?'

Merv started to tell him, it was out the door, down the back of the stage, half way up the side wall was a doorway through into the corridor and the bogs were on the left hand side.

'Fuck that.' said this bloke.

He turned away and walked to the hand basin under a mirror surrounded by dozens of light bulbs. He turned on the cold tap and proceeded to piss in the sink. We averted our gaze as clearly the four foot mirror gave an all too graphic view of his activities and we didn't want to upset his mates who were also likely to need the bog before they went on stage.

It may have been a common occurrence where this group came from, but it was the first time any of us young country boys had seen the like I can tell you. Of course, you learn from your elders and these guys were just a bit older than us. Every opportunity we got from that night onwards we took similar advantage of any sinks in our changing rooms.

As they were due on stage, there were only brief introductions and promises to watch our short set after they had played. Then they were off and running. Very professional. The guy who pissed in the sink turned out to be playing lead and singing back up vocals. We appreciated they were far more polished than we were. It was the late summer of '65 and we were just shy of two years experience. We had seen enough after about half a dozen numbers and slipped over the road to a nearby pub. The Loving Kind were playing to a crowded hall. The pub was pretty much empty. Ah well, that's show business!

We got back in time for their last three or four songs and then it was our turn again. True to their word they stood in the wings and watched us play our closing numbers. The crowded hall was thinning out and before the curtains had closed after our final number it was rather like the pub had been about an hour previous.

The Loving Kind got cracking on breaking down their kit and loading it in their van. Being pros, instead of a clapped out vehicle like ours, they had a Ford Transit, short wheelbase variety. Rather than push off back to the smoke or wherever they were headed, like most bands we supported, they hung around while we shoehorned our kit and ourselves into our old van, chilling out and chatting as if we'd known them all our lives. Eventually, we said our goodbyes and we both set off in opposite directions home.

We only got first names of course. Why bother, you were probably never going to see each other again. Phil had been working on that premise with the young ladies for a while, the rest of us were trying to keep up, but he was holding aces. I felt like I was dealt threes and fours all the time although the dealer favoured me a few times as you have read already.

Probably because of the 'sink' incident I remembered the name of the guitarist and that was Noel, and another guy was Pete but apologies to the rest of the group. As I say, we were probably never going to see each other again anyway.

Wrong! A couple of months later we were coming back along the A303 from somewhere the far side of Andover and out of the mist came a Ford Transit. We were almost past one another, having flashed our lights at the van and had them flash back in recognition of another band wagon on the road, when someone in the back yelled,

'They're pulling over. Stop. Let's wander back and see who it is. I'm sure we've seen that van before.'

Of course it was Noel, Pete and the others. So the next half hour was spent discussing where we had been in the last couple of months and what was it like tonight. They told us they had been at the Top Rank Ballroom in Cardiff and it had been pretty good. We recounted our experiences in Aldershot or wherever it had been. They sympathised as they had played there too, in the distant past. Once again it was a warm friendly conversation.

As the chilly early morning air took its toll we wished each other all the best and carried on our journeys. It was not long before Noel moved on to better things. He got a call from Chas Chandler to come for an audition.

Of course the story goes that he thought Chas Chandler wanted him to audition for The Animals.

'No way man', Chas said, "it's a new band with a fantastic young black guy on lead guitar. I want you to play bass.'

As '65 moved into '66 we continued to grow in experience and played further afield. But we tried to watch Top of the Pops on Thursday evenings if we possibly could. We saw the Jimi Hendrix Experience make their debut and on the Friday, as we all met up to spend a long weekend in Wales (again!), the main topic on the agenda was the bass player.

'Fuck me,' said Phil 'did you see Noel last night. He's made it. Lucky bastard.'

As the years passed, we kept track of people we had come across on the road who were obviously on the way up. Several were plucked from relative obscurity to join a headline band, as Noel did. Others whose careers we followed appear elsewhere in these stories.

Phil and I were the only survivors of the group that had appeared at Salisbury City Hall the next time ours and Noel's paths crossed. It was '70 or early '71 when we heard that Fat Mattress was appearing one Friday night at the Devizes Corn Exchange. This was the group Noel formed after his time with the Experience had come to an end. Pete was still there from memory with lots of different musicians and totally different music from his previous style. Not really my cup of tea, but Phil and I went along with the other two guys in the band to meet up with Noel again.

Mind you after the highs and lows (well documented) of working with Hendrix we didn't think he would have a clue who we were, maybe even what day it was if all the stories were true. We needn't have worried. After their set, and as the roadies were clearing the kit from the stage, I approached Noel and said,

'Hello Noel mate. Remember me?'

He took one tired look. How many hundreds of wannabees had bent his ear over the past five years? A female might have grabbed his attention as Noel's reputation with the ladies was almost as legendary as Phil's. Then realisation dawned.

'Alright mate, how the fucking hell are you Ted?'

Phil joined me and it was 1965 all over again. We chatted about the times we had met. Noel said there was at least one other night when we hadn't, they'd seen us on some dual carriageway and we had acknowledged them by flashing our head lights but they had sat in the next lay-by for half an hour waiting to no avail.

'Posh bastards now then,' they thought, 'too good to mix with the likes of us.'

He wanted to know whether we were still playing. We took him through our various changes and said one of the first things we had done once we could afford it was get ourselves a Ford Transit. It was outside the hall

197

complete with its huge wing mirrors. He was impressed and chuckled when he heard we had nearly lost them for good previously in Chard when Chris had reversed the van through the archway and the archway won.

Anyway, back to the Corn Exchange. Once Noel was up to date with our situation we asked about his time with Jimi Hendrix.

'What was it like playing those bloody great football stadiums in the States Noel?' I asked.

He grimaced. 'Left me with a bit of a problem mate, the doctors don't know if it will be temporary or permanent.'

We thought he was on about his hearing with the amount of kit they were using but we were mistaken.

Noel said, 'We used to get the crew to set up our Marshall amps and speakers, across the width of the stage if you get what I mean. So if we had sixteen speakers linked up then mine were scattered here and there and so were his. That was to try to balance the sound out across the arena. Three things were wrong with the theory. One, the crew said the best place to hear us was about three miles up the road. In the stadium, it was fucking crap. Second, I couldn't hear my bass sound as I was stood in front of Jimi's sound as well and obviously people were there to hear him, not me, so he was louder. I decided to start standing in front of the speaker stacks so I could pick up as much of my sound as possible to check if I was going out of tune or losing the tempo. You know what he was like, he'd go off on one and Mitch and I had to try to stabilise everything so he could get back into the body of the song once he'd done his 'fancy dan' stuff. The third problem didn't surface until the back end of the last tour after we'd done dozens of these stadiums. My guts were playing me up something chronic. Loose! You have no idea mate. I didn't trust the doctors over there so I waited until I got home. This GP asked me what I did for a living. When I told him he said standing in front of the speakers had done it. He said the amount of amplification we had had to use to fill these football stadiums when the bass speaker was thumping out the notes I was struggling to hear, my intestines were reverberating like the speakers themselves. Not really advisable, he said, bound to cause damage long term. Tell me about it I said. Still there's always a plus side. I'll never suffer from constipation.'

We left him with his Fat Mattress friends and drove home, a little down as the five years had aged him plenty.

We made a few visits to Salisbury City Hall, as I said, and the manager there was a character. He certainly had an eye for making money. We knew the way he booked his bands. He had local support bands from a network of contacts. Martin had obviously been over and told him what a marvellous new group he had uncovered. So that was how we ended up supporting Noel and the boys. For about a fiver I expect.

The top bands he booked through London agencies and he had a series of contracts for bands costing say fifty up to five hundred. He would then call in these contracts to suit the time of year. A cheap band if he reckoned he was going to get a small crowd due to some other big draw in the area. Then he'd see a band on the way up the charts and he'd call up to the agents to get them into his venue as soon as possible and he'd get a good crowd as the band were 'hot'.

When the Bee Gees came over to the UK from Australia, they signed up to a London agency and a contract came to this guy in Salisbury. Two hundred for a new band he'd never heard of? Into the drawer it went. When the first record 'New York Mining Disaster 1941' was released it was not a smash hit. Two hundred quid? He thought the agency was having a laugh.

199

Into '67 and Top of the Pops on a Thursday evening. 'Massachusetts' gave the Bee Gees their first UK No1. On the Friday morning he rings the agency.

'I want the Bee Gees here the Saturday after next for two hundred'. The agency said no way, they wanted a grand at least. Anyway, they were playing somewhere else.

'I've got a contract here,' he said, 'they had better honour that contract or I'll see you in court.'.

He had them by the balls. The contracts were water tight. The Bee Gees played The City Hall. They were turning them away at the door and there were hundreds outside, it was pandemonium! He made a small fortune that night, I doubt if that style of contract survived much after the mid-Sixties. A little bit costly if you get it wrong.

23. Comin' Home

I remember seeing Ozzy Osbourne on a chat show, probably 'Parky' and this story has always stayed with me. He had got back home after a gruelling tour of the States, single in marital terms but his head was in two bits. This was the guy who had grown up in the Midlands and was just a local boy with his roots in the Black Country, as well as the madman who was his alter ego that took any drug going, drank for England and ripped up a storm on every stage he appeared on. He had walked to the shed at the bottom of the garden, set it alight and just stood watching it burn to the ground. The little old lady who lived next door was putting her washing out on the line and looked over the hedge, calling him by his real first name, and said,

'Oh you're back then John. Just winding down are we?'

When you are working hard, playing hard day in day out, you need to let off steam. Then you need a place to go to where you feel normal, even if only for a few hours, before you have to get on that merry-go-round again. For me it was The George, a pub in the middle of town which was later turned into a trendy place for middle aged blokes to go in to get off with young girls.

The George was an updated version of the pub my Dad used to drink in on the corner, twenty yards away, before it got knocked down in the interests of progress. The new George was the place to be during the Sixties and although the licensing hours were significantly shorter than today, we never felt we were being short changed. We didn't have enough cash to stay out much longer anyway.

For three or four years, when we were playing many miles away from home most Friday, Saturday and Sunday evenings, I went into the George at lunchtime for as long as my timetable and wallet would permit. So even if I had only got home at three or four in the morning, I was in the pub by eleven o'clock on the Saturday. A pint of bitter with a dash to help with the recovery and to join the regulars. They were always sat by the juke box on the back wall, not because they were going to put any money in, but because they knew that as people had loaded it up the previous evening, they would get a free session for maybe an hour or so, perhaps even through until they upped sticks and wandered down to a local club for a couple after time.

There were always two I could rely on being there, Barry and Len. Others like John, Billy, Alan and a few more were in and out from time to time, but these two were my 'winding down' people. Barry was a few years younger than me, while Len was much older and married with a family. They both worked at the Avon in the tyre factory and they were as different from me as chalk and cheese. They didn't let me forget it either.

I'm not knocking the stereotype of the working man that they typified back then. It was just the way the world was. They worked all week and got paid on Thursday. Then the cycle began - Friday night, Saturday lunchtime. Saturday night Len would be back in, this time with the wife. Barry was out with the lads, although a year or so after these normalisation sessions ended he was going out with Len's daughter. Perhaps he'd had an eye on her all along. Who knows?

If I was home on Sunday I would be there on the step outside the pub a couple of minutes before twelve and Barry and Len would invariably be there too. We spent an hour chilling out with a couple of beers then I was home to Mother's Sunday lunch. They stayed on and presumably returned to The George or the club later in the evening, I can't say for certain as I was rarely if ever in the pub on a Sunday night. We were either playing or I was shattered from the previous forty eight hours and hit my bed early. On occasions like that as soon as my feet touched the pillow I was away.

Once the weekend was over, money was tight and from Monday to Thursday they stayed home. They were on the same merry-go-round as me but they didn't realise it. I saw their existence as normal, something I craved on those lunchtimes after a long lousy journey in the van, a dodgy venue the night before, lack of sleep and perhaps an even longer trip to look forward to in the afternoon.

But the reason I kept going back in was they kept me sane and kept my feet on the ground. They would read the paper, passing comments on football or racing. No politics, no rugby or cricket and the music from the juke box in the background playing last night's pick by a lad for his girlfriend covering the silences. I joined in from time to time but if it was football Barry would ask,

'Who was it you said you supported? Birmingham City? What you know about football could fit on the edge of this beer mat.'

Nothing too hurtful, just a gentle piss take and so it continued. Because I worked in an office during the day, what did I know about working for a living? Where were we last night anyway? Wherever we were near, or invariably far, they had something to say about it.

'Bath? Haven't they got fed up of hearing you yet? Ilfracombe? What a god forsaken place that is. Can't you find anywhere to play except a dump like that, particularly in February? Jesus, if you've got to go to Tenby for a few quid you ain't going to be making the big time anytime soon!'

They were quite a double act.

Over the period of time we drank together there were just a handful of Saturday nights when I was at a loose end and went into The George for the evening. Sometimes I had a young lady with me sometimes not. Len was in his usual seat, dressed up rather smartly on these occasions. Rather than his casual lunchtime attire, he wore a white shirt open at the neck (not to the waist, but a couple of buttons, always), dark blazer, flannels and black shined up shoes. Len had a comforting right hand round his pint glass while his wife had both her arms linked around his left arm. Sort of protective, you could say. Perhaps she was worried in case he wandered off, but she was always very quiet, at least when I was around.

The George was the only place I ever came into contact with Len, except in the factory on odd occasions, so I have no idea what she was like at home, or in company that she was comfortable with. I wish I could have seen her like that because she always gave me the impression that I was never going to be on her Christmas card list. She never spoke to me, she just sat and stared at me while I was talking to Len even though I was wary of staying any longer than a couple of minutes as I didn't want to intrude on their 'quality time' for too long.

If we were travelling back from a gig in the early hours, it was generally just me and our roadie Chris who were awake. Just as well he was, obviously, as he was driving. He liked me to stay awake to keep him company and shout if he nodded off. We woke everybody else up one night when we were passing RAF Kemble. It was

204

foggy as fuck and the visibility was down to twenty yards in places. If you were passing that way back then you might recall they had a Spitfire or some other World War Two fighter plane perched on a display stand just in front of the main gates. We came out of a particularly dense patch and I saw this plane at about fifteen feet off the ground heading straight for the windscreen. Instinctively, I ducked and yelled out "Fucking hell, watch out!" Chris laughed like a drain, the lads in the back moaned at me for disturbing their beauty sleep and I sat there the rest of the way home wishing I had a spare pair of kecks.

Anyway, I digress. It was on quiet times like this that I mulled over what I might have done to upset Len's missus. I was sure I hadn't sworn in front of her, positive I hadn't told a crude joke and absolutely certain I hadn't played fast and loose with any of her family. It was a mystery, one that was never solved.

Anyway, for those three or four years Barry and Len helped keep me sane, even if another family member gave me a few twitches. Every now and again, they would let the cool indifference slip. Perhaps I imagined it, they certainly would have said it was wishful thinking on my part, but just once in a while I felt they had a sneaking admiration for what we were doing. Whether we made the 'big time' or not we were clocking up the miles all around the country, visiting places they were unlikely to, rubbing shoulders with people they listened to on the jukebox in The George and were never going to meet in the flesh.

Of course, even if you could prove they weren't indifferent to our exploits, they would have said,

'We listen to the people you play with in the pub, yeah, but we don't very often pay for the privilege.'

They would have had the last word I reckon. They always did.

24. Good Times, Bad Times

I've told you the story about how we started working for Howard and his agency in Bristol. So far I may have done him a disservice by not telling you about all the great venues he sent us to on this side of the Severn Bridge. He did put me off going to the other side much in later years, thanks to his insistence on long weekends away in the Principality, but there were two stand-out venues this side that I can share with you.

The first was the Bamboo Club in St Paul's, Bristol. We arrived at about seven o'clock in the evening, on a cold winter's evening. The streets were deserted and the area around the club looked tired and dilapidated. 'This should be a barrel of laughs' Chris said as we started to unload the gear from the van. As we lugged it up the hall to the raised platform at the far end we got the feeling we were not quite what they had been expecting.

Merv was in charge of the contracts and had his copy from Howard on hand and was quite prepared to show whoever was in charge that we were booked to play there that night, but nothing more was said about it until the night was over. We set up the kit, did the sound check and went to the bar for a drink. As there was no sign of another pub in the vicinity, and it seemed uninviting anyway, we decided to stay put.

By now a healthy number of people were coming through the door - mostly blokes and quite a varied age range too, from eighteen to well not eighty, but getting there. They all had one thing in common. Apart from the fact that they were all black we seemed to be fascinating them as, after getting a drink or even while their mates went to do the honours, they almost without exception wandered up onto the stage, where we were sat around a couple of tables, and looked at us and our equipment, said nothing and moved away. Very odd.

The guy who had seemed in charge when we first arrived came up and gave us the nod to start playing. It was the usual stuff, an hour and a quarter on, half hour off, hour and a quarter to finish. So we got ready and began our set. We had done enough gigs with the line up to have it down pretty well, so it went okay. A mix of Wilson Pickett, Sam and Dave, Otis Redding, plus a few Tamla favourites and the odd, off the wall song that I had picked up from trawling around the record shops.

The first part of the set was like an 'In Concert' if you remember those programmes on TV. We played, the audience sat or stood and watched and at the end of each song there was polite applause. Gradually the females, who were thinner on the ground, got up to dance and they persuaded a few of the younger lads to join in. By the end of that first hour and a quarter we had achieved what we always set out to do, get the floor pretty full of people enjoying themselves and being ready to see us play again after the break.

In the interval we made our way to the bar and found we were not entirely alone. There were two fifty-plus peroxide blonde ladies at the bar, in earnest conversation with a couple of middle aged blokes. Nick pointed them out and said,

'We aren't the only white people in here after all.'

Dave the trumpeter told him to button it.

'Dickhead,' he said, 'they're brasses, can't you tell?'

We got our beers and made our way back to the front and were chatted to on our way by a few of the younger lads in the crowd who wanted to know where we were from, what we were going to play in the second half and did we know such and such a song. The usual stuff.

These days we are a much more multi-cultural nation but in the mid Sixties in West Wiltshire there were only a couple of dozen West Indian people in town. They worked in the local factories and it was extremely rare to see any more than two or three at a dance or a club. On the vast majority of gigs we played in the first couple of years we never saw a coloured face. Once we had graduated to colleges, universities, service bases and the bigger cities we came across them much more frequently, but in those venues they were making the attempt to integrate. Here it seemed there was no such attempt. That's when the little bells started ringing in my head. Why were the management surprised to see us? Why were we the subject of so much scrutiny by the audience as they came in early doors?

I didn't have long to wait for my answer. We played our second set to a packed dance floor. Boy they knew how to enjoy themselves. We kept the tempo up and they rocked the joint. We got a really warm round of applause at the end and slowly the club emptied. The guy in charge came up to pay Merv the money and Merv queried why there had been some confusion when we first arrived. They had approached the agency and had asked for the band they wanted by name. They had heard of them from clubs in and around London.

They had asked Howard if they could book this West Indian soul band Hearts and Souls. Whether he pulled a flanker on them by ignoring the slight difference in name and putting us in there or not, I don't know. As it happened, they asked us back again on a couple of occasions. Whether they managed to get the real thing I can't say.

209

It was a really good venue for us and we went back on a weekday evening once in a while to see the other bigger names they had booked in from time to time. Jimmy Smith the organist was there one night, so of course Merv just had to go to see him. Root and Jenny Jackson too, they were very good. Once we changed our style some time later we were destined to play other venues. Sadly The Bamboo Club was destroyed by fire some years later. But it was a terrific venue.

For a couple of months there was no comeback on our name confusion at the Bamboo Club and Heart 'n Soul kept slogging away across the West Country roads and over the Bridge. Then Howard phoned Merv and said he had been contacted by a London agency complaining about us. We hadn't worked for them on a buy and sell deal, so it was nothing we had done as such, it was our name. They represented 'Hearts and Souls' and as they were professional and longer established they wanted us to change our name. We thought Howard would stand up for us and tell them to take a hike, but he folded and said he was struggling to sell us lately because so many clubs and halls were caught up in the same name confusion. So we had to change our name again.

We came up with two or three fairly quickly and used each of them once at venues in and around Bath. We just happened to be playing in Bath on a Monday, Friday and Saturday in the same week, so we thought we could get some feedback from people and then make a decision. So on Monday night we were The Double Decker Donut Band. General opinion was that it was too lightweight and suggested we were a comedy act. On Friday night we were Oliver! And although this seemed more popular we wondered whether we would have problems using the name, complete with exclamation mark, as it may have been copyrighted by the stage show and film. Then on Saturday we were The Copperpot Band. Nick had been

210

shopping in Trowbridge and walked by a shop window. In the bottom left hand corner of the display window there it was, a copper pot. He thought it was an omen.

After the Saturday gig, The Copperpot Band it was. I don't think we did a straw poll of the audience to see if it was a popular choice or not. Merv and the two Daves liked it and nobody else came up with a better option so it was adopted by default basically. For the next two years or so we criss-crossed the country under that name and Howard was happy enough. He had solved his inter-agency headache and he'd also got a name that was fairly nondescript, so he could book us into a wider range of venues. If you had Soul in the band name it was a bit of a giveaway what music you were going to play. Copperpot meant nothing to the people booking us and the work we did for him increased. A win win situation I think they call it.

RNAS Yeovilton was the second cracking venue Howard booked us for quite a few times. We played at HMS Heron which was the social club for the Sergeants' mess. This was always a Wednesday night gig as I recall. We liked the midweek 'residencies' at places in town which filled in a couple of Wednesdays a month, but a trip an hour down the road every now and then was no problem, especially as it was a good gig. More often than not it was just us on our own playing to a room full of helicopter pilots for the best part of the evening. There were a few wives on camp, but not many. It didn't seem to matter though, we always had a good time. It was an opportunity for us to try out new numbers and routines after our usual practice night on Tuesday. If we cocked it up in that first set when we only had a handful in the audience it wasn't a disaster and if we had then sometimes we stuck it in again in the second half to polish it up a bit.

Every now and again we supported a group a bit further up the food chain. Generally it has to be said they were on the way down rather than on the way up. One I remember was the Downliner Sect who had a few minor hits, 'Little Egypt', 'Baby What's Wrong With You' and featured 'Love Potion No9' and 'Poison Ivy' in an act which was based on a fairly basic twelve bar philosophy. A bit dated I guess, but they were a good bunch of blokes and we got on with them okay.

We played with Peter Jay and the Jaywalkers one night and turned up expecting to see an eight piece band akin to Sounds Incorporated. Perhaps I got my wires crossed but the blurb in the music press gave me the impression that was their bag. Not by '66 it wasn't. They were a four piece and basically a backing group for a singer called Terry Reid who had a soul voice I would have given my eye teeth for. Evidently he started singing with Peter Jay when he was only fifteen and after eighteen months on the road he was already a pretty exceptional talent. We stood, listened and admired their set, although it was Terry who was the stand out musician. He never really got to be the household name you would have thought he was destined to be. He toured on a Stones trip Stateside to critical acclaim, but there was no breakthrough to the so called 'big time'.

The only other thing I remember vividly from RNAS Yeovilton gigs was a trip home after another enjoyable Wednesday evening in Somerset. It was a warm summer night as we drove through Trowbridge on our way home when the van coughed politely and slowed gracefully to a halt about four miles short of our intended destination.

'Bollocks. We're out of petrol.' said Phil who was driving on this occasion.

We were right across the road from the village pub car park. Did we want to push it up the slight slope and leave it there until we could retrieve it the following day?

'I'm not happy leaving it with all the kit in,' Merv said. 'Can't we push it up the next bit then we ought to be able to freewheel for a while. If we all push (there were seven of us on this trip) we can be home in an hour or so.'

Optimistic. We tried to push the van up the next incline and it was fucking slow going. Apart from anything else it was difficult to get six people across the back of the van to concentrate on pushing effectively, so it was two for the most part and four giving a token shove. We got about halfway then ground to a halt.

'Let the handbrake off Phil,' says I 'we'll turn the van round and push it down the slope to the pub and park it up well off the road.'

I was convinced this was a reasonable suggestion, but it was greeted with total apathy.

'Fuck that! We've got to walk home from here anyway. Just push it into this driveway and lock it up. Let's get walking.'

I think that was Nick or one of the Daves. They set off for home and those of us that remained did as we were told. Then it was a long walk home and up in the morning, off to work. About half past nine Merv rang.

'Why didn't you get the van right off the road?'

I told him Phil was pissed off with the others walking off so he left it where our first efforts at pushing the van had got to. Clearly it wasn't enough.

Merv went on, 'There were traffic jams half a mile either side of the van, so they contacted Martin at work. He had to get over there and move it. He's not happy. He's getting a six pounds fine. (I know, it doesn't seem a lot does it, but it was then.) Oh, by the way, the reason the police found out about it so quickly was because you parked the van in the driveway of the village police house. The local bobby couldn't get his car off the drive and phoned it in to his superiors. He's had to go out on his rounds on his pushbike. Didn't you see a blue light over the door?'

At one o'clock in the morning it wasn't on you prat, I thought, but he was obviously on a roll so I just let him get it off his chest. He was there too, for heaven's sake. I don't remember which camp he was in, pub car park or just dump it, but he might have spoken up last night. He was the one who was worried about leaving it in case someone nicked the kit. What safer place than in the driveway of a policeman's home? Six pounds well spent I thought. Anyway, that was Yeovilton for you.

25. Saturday Night's All Right For Fighting

I've mentioned the fight at Tetbury that seemed to be sparked off by a drum solo, so there were venues to be wary of trouble, as well as some that were downright dangerous, although not necessarily because of the chance of a punch up. In chronological order, as far as my memory serves, here are some instances for you.

When Martin was driving around looking for places that hadn't heard us play in the early days, so that he still had a chance of getting us a gig, he ventured as far as Midsomer Norton, a few miles from Bath. There was a ballroom right in the middle called the Savoy Rooms and it was a venue that most local bands played at some time or another. Naturally, it wasn't called by its proper name, everyone knew it as the Cabbage Patch.

In early '64 we were booked to appear as support band to a Bristol group that had been around for several years and were pretty popular in Midsomer Norton. This meant we were struggling right from the off. The audience were nowhere to be seen, either still in the local pubs, stood around the corridors and foyer of this large ballroom or watching us play our first set with a degree of indifference. We cleared off as soon as our scheduled time was up and the local favourites took centre stage. The crowd came in from outside and the hall was pretty much full while they did their stuff. Of course, when they finished it thinned out again, but a group of lads remained at the back of the hall, possibly ten or twelve of them, all greasers. The dance floor had around twenty people, mostly girls dancing around their handbags, so the second set was going a little better than the first.

After we had played four or five songs, one leather clad, greasy haired individual approached the stage and, as I was jingling my tambourine in an instrumental section, beckoned to me to stoop down so that he could talk to me.

'Play "Walkin' the Dog." he said.

Oh the naivety of youth!

'We played it in the first half mate, sorry.' I said.

He beckoned to me again.

'"Fucking play "Walkin' the Dog" unless you like hospital food.'

'We've had a request.' I said to Merv.

He wiped the sweat from his brow having just worn himself ragged on his instrumental piece.

'What did he want?'

'Well,' I said, 'would we mind playing "Walkin' the Dog" again as he and all his mates enjoyed it so much in the first half and would appreciate hearing it again.'

Merv didn't want to change the running order straight away so he stuck to the next one on our play list. The group of greasers began their slow inexorable walk down the hall to the front of the stage. There was a lot of hair, leather, brass and even a chain wrapped around a clenched hand, not an autograph book anywhere to be seen.

Merv took the hint and 'Lady Mac, dressed in black, silver buttons all down her back' it was then lads. What a change in their demeanour, they were nodding or shaking their heads, singing something close to the right lyrics. A couple of them even tried to keep the beat with their knuckle dustered hands on the wooden lip just across the footlights at the front of the stage. When the song was over, they whooped and hollered as if the Rolling Stones themselves had delivered their version. I waited anxiously for another request and hoped to fuck it was a song we knew, but it never came. Once the dog had been walked they stayed for the rest of the set and looked up at us with a vacant but strangely threatening expression.

Once we were back in the safety of the dressing room we were wondering if we might have to stay there for a while until they gave up and cleared off to pick a fight somewhere else in town. The other group were still about and had a chuckle when they heard us talking.

'Just as well you knew it lads. They frequently knock seven shades of shit out of any band that plays stuff other than rhythm and blues and think 'Walkin' the Dog' is beneath them. They don't bother us because we've been here so many times. They know we could play it if we needed to. It's the first timers they target. If you get a booking here in the future they'll probably leave you alone.'

I made a mental note to tell Martin there wasn't enough money in the whole of Somerset to convince me we should return to the Cabbage Patch but of course, we did and we played 'Walkin' the Dog' at the start of the second half on each occasion. Whether they were in the hall, beyond the footlights, who knows? They never came up with any requests ever again.

In Devizes the Corn Exchange was a frequent venue for us. We played there dozens of times in different guises when were young and innocent, in '63 and '64 especially, the town still had the barracks on the road out of town and, as luck would have it, the Black Watch were stationed there for a while. Joy of joys. In the summer of '64 we played a gig there on a Tuesday evening and then returned for the Friday evening into the bargain. The place was packed with squaddies and local lads and lasses and the inevitable happened. A load of young Scottish

217

squaddies were out on the town, drinking far more than was good for them and eyeing up the local talent and the local lads were taking umbrage. It was Waddies 6X or rough cider for them and it was kicking off big time in the hall. The bouncers were having a hard time trying to cope with the scattered skirmishes all over the floor, but one bloke stood out head and shoulders above the rest and he wasn't taking any prisoners.

I had heard stories when I was thirteen or fourteen about this guy called Spike. There was a milk bar in the middle of town and we went in there from time to time. A lot of the local hard men were regulars but if you kept out of their way they let you keep breathing - and this was during the daytime. I was too young to be allowed out on a Saturday night at nine o'clock and beyond so I only heard about the fights third hand. We always seemed to have problems with a gang from Bradford on Avon, a sleepy little town on the face of it but appearances can be deceptive, and even today it has its dark side. They would pile into a couple of cars and pop over on a Saturday night to get acquainted with the young people of Melksham. This normally ended up with visits to hospital and the police station, but they were determined to have a good time.

The milk bar had a public phone which worked. So when the Bradford lads were spotted a call was made to a Devizes café and Spike was asked if he was interested. He had an Oldsmobile, or some old American car which, with a following wind, could get down to Melksham in a handful of minutes with six or seven lads on board. He didn't have anything against the opposition personally you understand, it was just he fancied a ruck every now and then. Anyway, back to the Corn Exchange and the Black Watch.

The big unit was Spike, bleeding from a cut on the top of his head from a bottle, he was clearly angry. A fair fight was one thing but the Black Watch had started to play dirty so they had to leave, pronto, they were frog marched out into the warm night air, a couple at a time if necessary. Peace was restored and we were able to finish our set undisturbed. The atmosphere was still a bit tense at the end of the night as the crowd filed out through the doors at the end of the hall. The locals were wary of squaddies on a mission who may be waiting in the Market square outside. They needn't have worried. The Black Watch were nowhere to be seen.

We got our kit down and started carrying it through the side door to our van. After we had got about half the gear stowed away, down the slope came about six or seven squaddies. They had gone to get more liquid refreshment and were well beered up and spoiling for a fight. We were still only a five piece in those days, six if you included Glyn, who was driving, but we were no match for these kids hardened on the streets of Glasgow or some other godforsaken Scottish town. We thought were in for a good kicking or even worse as several of them were carrying bottles or glasses.

Spike appeared in the doorway, just checking we had got everything away and he could lock up that side of the building. He sussed the situation and walked out towards the advancing Black Watch.

'Go home boys,' he said calmly, 'There's not going to be any trouble tonight.'

It wasn't a question, just a statement. There was a moment or two when I thought we were still in trouble then slowly they backed off and wandered back up to the market square on their way back to barracks. A few insults and threats were aimed in our direction but we didn't react. We knew our place.

'Thanks Spike,' I said, the first time I'd ever spoken to him, but not the last.

He came to work at the factory where I was in the offices and for many years he stood on the door at dance halls and clubs and had less and less to do as the years rolled by. His reputation was made. He didn't need to prove himself to anybody and for the most part punters knew to leave well alone and behave. I still see him from time to time when he comes home from Turkey, where he retired to the sun, and he always has a warm word or two and I shake his hand still grateful for his coming to our rescue that night. Of course I have to get the wife to cut my meat up for me for a couple of days afterwards because his hands are the size of dinner plates and the crush factor is off the scale, even now when he's into his seventies, but it's worth it all the same.

The next two are a little hazy as regards which order they came in, certainly we were in Copperpot country, so were a seven piece soul band. We'll go to Stroud Subscription Rooms first, because it won't take long to tell. When people ask me which fight was the worst I ever saw, there is never any doubt, Stroud wins it by a mile. .

It wasn't a mass brawl. We'd played our first set and had a pleasant break in a local pub chatting to some of the local talent, hoping to get better acquainted later, and we were back on stage getting into our second set. There were a load of kids gathered in front of the stage and although the dance floor wasn't full, there were plenty of people around the edges. A blonde girl arrived at the front of the stage with a lad who was all over her like a rash. I was just idly watching these two canoodling when Nick nudged me and said,

'Watch it. Look at that girl coming down the hall.'

She had clearly spotted the two love birds at the front of the stage and she was not happy. A few words were exchanged between the new arrival and the lad, then she turned her attention to the blonde. As I watched the action unfold, while trying to sing the right words and notes of whatever song we were playing, the argument became a tad physical. The lad kept well away and let them get on with it. The ones at the front of the stage created an arena for the two girls as the crowd swelled. We did our best to play on, while keeping an eye on what was going on below us. It was the most violent fight I ever witnessed inside a dance hall, made all the more strange as it was two girls. They were pulling hair, scratching and biting and rolling around on the dance hall floor, for a couple of minutes.

The new arrival got the blond in a headlock and started punching her with her free hand. The bouncers had arrived on the outside of the ring of people watching this unfold and were in no rush to get amongst them to sort it out. It was a blood bath. The management were quick off the mark and had already called the police. Two young coppers arrived and approached the two women with due care and attention. When they eventually stepped in to break up the one sided fight, helmets went flying and the crowd cheered and then booed as the entertainment was finally brought to a close. An ambulance was summoned for the unfortunate blonde, while her assailant was forcibly removed still kicking and screaming. We just carried on playing, but I don't think anyone noticed What was going on in the bear pit at the front of the stage was far more entertaining.

We had a long weekend in Wales in front of us when we pitched up in the Brecon Beacons at a venue by the side of the main road but some way out of the nearest town. We were the only band that Friday night and there were seven of us on stage. We ran through our usual routine of sweet soul music in the first half and it went OK. The hall was about half full I guess and it was only a short walk to the bar on the premises, so no need to walk up the road for a pint this time. Sitting on the front of the stage chatting with Phil, I saw two locals looking as if they wanted to come over for a chat. Two girls of maybe eighteen summers, they were short, well built and reasonably good looking. Phil called them over and they trotted across and sat down. He had a way with women as I've mentioned on many occasions. Later that night I wished he hadn't.

They were regular visitors to the place and said it was always half empty in the first half. Once it got past ten o'clock the lads from the colliery would come off shift and come in to virtually double the numbers. Phil was getting on well with one of the girls, the better looking one, so I switched my attention to her mate. I noticed one thing about her in particular. She had a fine upstanding pair of headlamps. She caught me staring at her chest and didn't seem unduly worried. I had been looking for some time but I still hadn't seen them move. Not one quiver. Merv, Pete and the others were milling around us, sticking their noses in and wanting to get back on stage for the second half. So Phil and I took our leave but invited them to stick around until we'd finished playing.

So there they were, dancing away in front of us for ten minutes or so as, true to their word, the hall began to fill up as more and more blokes moved onto the dance floor via the bar. It was Pete's favourite song up next, 'Night Train', and once I had introduced it I jumped off the stage and started dancing with the two girls. Her mate made an excuse to go off to the bar or the loo and I was left alone. Merv followed up with 'I Put a Spell On You' the Alan Price version that we had enjoyed so much that night we caught the soul bug, and I started a slow dance combined with a deep snog with tongues, all going to plan so far. Initial investigations proved what the eye had perceived earlier, namely that they were big and firm and definitely all her own.

As we shuffled around the floor at the front of the stage, there was no warning of what happened next. As I came up for air from a lengthy snog I spotted a large shape about six inches from my head. As I struggled to identify what it was she screamed and put her arm up to partially parry the blow. Now I remember, I thought, it's a bloody big fist! Despite her intervention the left hand side of my face received a hefty blow and several teeth had a brief moment of panic, where they didn't know whether to abandon ship or stay in my mouth. She was holding this powerful looking dwarf back from doing me any more damage. I got back onto the stage and Merv, having finished his solo, tried to introduce the next song without pissing himself at my discomfort.

I managed to get through the remaining forty minutes or so without this bloke and his mates rushing the stage and, when we had finished, she came over and apologised for her brother. She was going out with his best mate who had just gone underground to start the night shift, which explained why he wasn't here with her. I decided not to pursue the question of why, if she was likely to see her brother, she cheated on his best mate in such a public way, but the blood I could still taste in my mouth and the ringing in my ears made me hold back. The brother had been dragged away by the rest of his mates and was at the bar. Not much chance of a nightcap tonight then?

We got the kit down and into the van. We drew lots and four lads stayed in the van overnight, while four of us got a bed in the hotel that the venue was attached to. There were two singles and a double available. More drawing of lots and Dave the guitarist and I drew the short straws. With Dave snoring and sleeping the sleep of the Just, I had a restless night, never able to get comfortable, whichever side I laid my head down. It was dawn before I dropped off and then knock, knock on the

223

door. In walked a middle aged female with a morning cup of tea. Her face was a picture when Dave's head stirred from under the covers. She avoided conversation. It would have been difficult for her to speak at all with her lips pursed so tightly together. The remainder of the weekend passed without further incident, except for the hours of ribbing I had to suffer of course. About the smack in the kisser not the night spent on either extreme edge of the double bed me and Dave spent you understand!

26. We've Gotta Get Outa This Place!

As I said earlier, there were places where you had to be wary of trouble, but one all nighter in Birmingham, now that really was scary. There was no aggro whatsoever; it was the venue that scared me shitless.

We were familiar with the concept of all nighters. The first we ever did was in Bath when three or four soul bands played right through to seven in the morning. We started at about half one and played for about an hour and a half. With a disco run by a maniac to thread it all together, it was OK but you were bloody knackered by the end of it unless you used artificial stimulants of course which we didn't.

The gig in question was when the band was pared down to a four piece and playing a far heavier brand of music. We arrived in the centre of Birmingham one Friday night in '69 or '70 and, after searching the streets for a brightly lit nightclub for maybe twenty minutes, had to ask for directions. The derelict factory site with boarded windows was not what we had anticipated and we began to wonder what our agent had let us in for. We found a small crowd outside a four storey building, who we thought were queuing up to get in. They were, but not how we imagined. An industrial type lift was in the far corner of what we thought was the entrance hall to the club. The steel doors clanked back and a twelve foot square floor area was revealed. Tickets were scrutinised and the next batch of revellers were taken up to the top floor.

The bouncers in charge of the lift nodded in our direction and, without saying anything, suggested we would be next up with our kit. Chris and Ralph unloaded the gear and we all pitched in once the lift returned to the ground floor. When we reached the club itself it was fairly spartan. Basically, all they'd done was clear out whatever machinery had been up there, paint the walls and strip the wooden floors. All the doors had been removed and once you had seen enough of the first section with its tables and chairs, you could go through to the next area where a small stage had been built in one corner. There was no furniture here at all, just some shelving around the walls for drinks in plastic cups and battered tin ashtrays.

When you moved on to the third and final section of the top floor you could see they'd spent some money, there was an extremely well equipped modern bar with subdued lighting and lots of chrome fittings. We decided to let the roadies sort out what the running order was and how many bands were sharing the total running time of what we reckoned would be about six hours. We sat down in the comfortable seats in the bar and had a quiet pint. Chris and Ralph joined us and looked a little troubled.

'What's up Chris?' asked Phil.

'There's only one other band. They've got top billing and you're doing three one hour spots each.' replied Chris.

Shit. We hadn't seen that one coming. I got up and went to find the bogs and, not seeing any obvious signs, I just wandered through a door in the far corner of the bar assuming there would be a corridor and bogs in there somewhere but there was nothing at all. Clearly the stairwell for pedestrian access to the other floors had been at that end when the factory building was in use but the problem was the double doors to the stairwell had a thumping great length of chain padlocked through and around the handles.

That's what I meant about a dangerous place to play. Try as I might I couldn't get the image of that door out of my head all night. Everyone on that floor was at the mercy of fate. An electrical fault or a burning cigarette could have meant maybe two hundred people trying to escape down four floors, with the only escape route being an ancient goods lift, which took about two dozen people at a time, maybe a few more at a pinch. But in the panic who knows what would have happened? It didn't bear thinking about. Unfortunately I'd seen the padlocked doors that would have been our only salvation, so I could think of little else.

We dragged our way through the three sets, so did the local heroes who were top of the bill and, at about half six in the morning, we were the last party into the lift, with our gear, to be carried back to terra firma. I know how the Pope felt when he kissed the ground after landing here for the first time. My sigh of relief must have sharpened up some of the others tired reflexes, because they asked me what was up.

'Claustrophobia I suppose,' I lied, 'glad to be out of that lift.'

We helped Chris and Ralph load the van and were soon on our way back south. They were all asleep except Chris and me, he needed me to check he was on the right road and wasn't nodding off. I couldn't have slept that morning anyway, I was just thinking how good it felt to be alive.

A couple of weeks ago, as I was walking off the bowls green to go into the clubhouse for tea, I glanced into the hall which had been prepared for a wedding reception that evening. (Did you hear me right then, the bowling green?! Rock 'n roll then bowls. How the mighty are fallen). Anyway the hall had been transformed into the

227

inside of a marquee by cleverly draping cream coloured material around the walls and from the ceiling. Together with all the other paraphernalia it looked superb. It almost made me want to get married again! While I was standing at the bar waiting to get served, a couple of places we played all those years ago came flooding back. They had absolutely no connection to wedding receptions, but just go to show how health and safety concerns were lower on people's priority list than they are today. Thank goodness too.

The first venue was a Sergeant's Mess for certain. I think it was an RAF base near Ludgershall in Wiltshire, right on the Hampshire border near Andover. We went there as the Copperpot Band on a Friday evening in the height of summer, so it was '67 or '68. The hall we were to play in was pretty spartan. No stage, we were to set up in the corner of the room. No comfortable seating to speak of. The room was furnished like a school dining room, large tables and very basic plastic chairs with tubular steel legs. In order to 'tart' it up for the occasion a couple of the squaddies had got hold of a few dozen parachute silks and slung them across the ceiling to try to give the impression of clouds. Artistic bunch in the RAF back in the '60s mind!

We started playing about eight o'clock and the hall filled up pretty quickly. There were all sorts there, blokes just out on the piss, husbands and wives out for a dance and a good night away from the kids. It was going really well. Dave the trumpeter was a Navy boy although he kept that information under his hat, but he was obviously a little edgy about something else. When we finished the first set we got a beer and sat on those bloody uncomfortable chairs having a natter while the audience tucked into a buffet that had been laid out on tables in the opposite corner.

'What's up Dave?' I asked.

'Have you thought what would happen if one of these parachutes catches fire?' he replied.

In those days, fire retardant materials were virtually unheard of. More people smoked than they do today and it was legal to smoke indoors too! Just looking around the bar and the rest of the hall you suddenly noticed how many men and women were smoking. Dave went on,

'In the first half I saw a bloke dancing with his missus. He still had a fag in his hand and was waving his hands above his head like a lunatic. The tip was about a foot beneath the nearest parachute. I was shitting myself. One spark and the lot would catch in seconds. Those floor length curtains on the big windows at the side are as dry and dusty as fuck. They'd go in no time flat. The burning silks would drop on to the people underneath and...'

We get the picture, cheers Dave. We've only got one more set to go. It'll certainly fly by now, thinking about being trapped in a blazing inferno, burnt to a crisp while singing James Carr's 'You're Pouring Water on a Drowning Man'!

We got out of there alive, but we did have a quiet word with the guys who were organising the thing and suggested either going for something different to decorate the room or at least 'no smoking' on the dance floor. They hadn't realised it was a problem but thanked us for our input. We never went back thank goodness.

Lymington was a venue one of our agent's sent us to on a couple of occasions. The first occasion was as 'Elijah & The Goat' and we had a good reception. The young guy who ran the gig and was the DJ asked us to come back about two months later. No problem, it was a decent trip down there. The town itself was pretty in the daytime and the pubs and restaurants were more than acceptable.

So we went back on the appointed Saturday afternoon and did a bit of sightseeing, eating and drinking, then rolled up to the hall to wait for the guy to turn up. When he pulled up in his car, he jumped out, clearly pleased to see us again. He was excited about how the venue was becoming more popular with the kids from town and places nearby. He had decided to give the place a new name for his Saturday night promotions. From tonight it was to be called 'Clouds' nightclub.

Dave the Trumpeter was long gone from the band by this time, but the other Dave, Pete, Phil and I had a quick glance at one another. As he unlocked the doors, still full of his new enterprise, our worst fears were realised. The whole of the hall area was covered in parachute silks, not just a few dotted about. Man it was cloudy! He had had the bright idea to let them come down in parts to not much more than six or seven feet off the floor. So as you walked or tried to dance around the room your head was literally 'in the clouds'! He thought it gave the place an 'ambience' and was keen to hear what we thought.

'We ain't playing in here,' said Chris as he stood at the doorway with a Marshall speaker cabinet in each hand.

He put them down and walked into the hall, prodding parachute silks as he made his way to where we were standing.

'Can't you take these down?' he asked.

The poor bloke was deflated to say the least and a bit panicky, thinking we were going to disappear leaving him with a hall full of people and no band. After some negotiation he agreed to tell each and every person paying on the door that it was 'no smoking' inside because of the parachutes. He had three or four lads who came along to help him run the place but no bouncers because there had never been any trouble. He said he would get them to patrol the dance floor and catch anyone who was smoking. We didn't have much option but to go with that plan because it wasn't practical to take the parachutes down before the gig. So we played for the second time in a couple of years with the threat of a fiery end hanging over us. Literally!

27. Ch- Ch- Ch- Changes

A lot of the time you were just happy to be playing at any old venue. The money came in handy for paying the hire purchase payments on the gear, putting petrol in the van to avoid spending cold nights in the van in the middle of nowhere or, worse still, walking home; tax and insurance plus the odd repair on the van. The night we were in London for Sybilla's and found ourselves in Farnborough doing the extra gig earlier in the evening was a rare double header for us.

Not long before the Copperpot Band ran its course and switched to another style of music, we found ourselves lumbered with having accepted two dates on the same night, without realising it until about a week before. It was too late to change anything so we hatched a cunning plan.

The two venues were in Frome and Bradford on Avon, only about ten miles apart. The Frome venue was what is now the 'Cheese and Grain', in its very early days. In recent years it has become one of the leading venues for various types of music in the West Country. In Bradford we were to headline at St Margaret's Hall, pretty much in the centre of town, somewhere we had played on several previous occasions.

Phil was going to do the talking once we arrived in Frome. His plan was to tell the organisers of the Frome gig that we had to leave early because we had a recording studio booked in London for a late night session when we intended laying down some tracks for our debut album. He had to convince the guy that we got this night time slot because it was a reduced rate and all we could afford. Then Phil came up with a running order that meant the disco run by the organiser would only cover the first fifteen minutes from when the entertainment was scheduled to start. We would then play until a quarter to nine, he would give us a fifteen minute break so we could get a couple of beers down, then we would go back on at nine for forty five minutes, leaving him to fill in the rest of the evening until half ten. Whether he swallowed Phil's hard luck story about the studio costs or whether he saw some mileage to be gained by being in the spotlight when the vast majority of his audience were likely to be there I don't know. But we were on!

Chris and Ralph were working that night and, as we needed to dump the gear in the van rather than place it strategically to allow five or six others to squeeze in, a couple of the sports cars were in the car park too. When the final chords of the last number had been struck and were wafting their way over the heads of the packed crowd in the hall, Chris and Ralph leapt into action. The brass section and the guitarists took their instruments and put them in their cases and went straight out into the car park past bemused lads and lasses who weren't in on the change in the standard running order. The cars pulled out onto the road out of town with a squeal of tyres and gravel spitting at the paintwork of anyone unfortunate enough to be parked nearby.

In the hall as the latest hit song was blasting out from the disco, Chris, Ralph and I were already getting amplifiers, drum kit and PA gear rolling across the floor towards the exit. A few willing hands were offered as we had left Merv's Hammond organ until last, and gratefully accepted they were too! In no time flat we were stashed away, if somewhat precariously, and off we went. We opted for a B road which, as the crow flew, gave the optimum trip. There was nothing on the road at all so we were able to floor it pretty much all the way, give or take the odd hairpin bend that these old roads seem to have in spades. We pulled into the car park by the Hall and the others were on hand to help us get the gear in. The other part of Phil's plan had been to get to Bradford with everyone bar me, the singer, tell the management we had van problems and our kit was likely to be delayed. We knew there were two support bands, so he was going to ask the others if we could plug in to amps, mike up our saxophone and trumpet, sit in on whichever drum kit was in place, and pray one of the bands had an organ of some sort. Then they would have been into an extended 'Night Train' and 'Green Onions' buying time until the rest of us arrived.

As it turned out, they arrived to find the gig had started late, the first band had overrun, and the second was off stage in about five minutes. We were still in with a shout! The hall had the benefit of a stage door at the side so we could get the gear on stage without disturbing either the audience or the band playing. As soon as they finished their final song the front curtain closed with a flourish and we sprang into action. Everyone had their appointed tasks and everything went like clockwork and we were ready to play; knackered but ready to play. We were introduced, the curtain went back and we ripped into the same few numbers we had started with in Frome not too long before. Fifty minutes later our contribution was at an end. Yessir, at eleven o'clock.

We had finished in Frome at nine forty five and started in Bradford at ten past ten, twenty five minutes stage to stage! Not something I would like to try too often. We kept our eye on the calendar a bit more closely after that I can assure you.

235

We had had some photos done for Howard's agency by a Bristol photographer who was keen on outside shots as well as studio ones. We went up on the Downs and got fucking soaked as it pissed down for about an hour until he gave it up as a bad job and we went back to his studio. We all looked like the cat had dragged us in, with our hair either unnaturally scraped back off our faces or just matted on our foreheads. Our stage gear which we had changed into before our trip to the Downs was still sticking to us in all the wrong places so the resulting photos were a disaster.

I knew we were going to be in trouble some time soon, because it was always a set of photos that signalled a group member deciding his future lay elsewhere, or we did. This time it was Merv who had decided enough was enough. He was training to be a solicitor's clerk or something like it and wanted to concentrate on his career. He was no longer convinced our big break lay just around the corner. He was probably right. The Soul train was chugging slowly onto a branch line which led nowhere. We had already started to add strange songs into our set to appease some murmurings from agents, people who hired us and even from within the band. They were more likely to feature Dave on guitar and some even dispensed with the brass section altogether.

The beginning of the end was nigh. Merv came around to see me personally to drop his bombshell. I hadn't seen it coming. He wasn't going to jump ship straight away and agreed to see us through those gigs we had booked over the next few weeks. Once we all got together to discuss how we would tackle this setback, Nick and Dave suddenly looked up and said they were disenchanted too. Gigs were drying up a bit from Howard. He was finding it difficult to get us work locally as we had been everywhere several times, and further afield it was the same money, which meant we turned some down because we weren't happy travelling three hundred miles for forty quid between the eight of us.

Losing our brass section and our keyboard player put us in a real bind. We played a few gigs without Nick and Dave, while Merv helped us out, but promoters were unhappy at paying for an eight piece, when only six showed up. Howard heard about that and turned up one night in Dursley or somewhere like that, we had a few words and that was the end of a beautiful friendship.

One of the last few scheduled gigs we were contracted to do for Howard was in Abergavenny. Although Dave was a no show, Nick and Merv were on board so we just about got away with it with the management. It was a good gig and we played well considering and the crowd's reaction was good too. It was a new venue for us so they weren't tired of us like some. As the gear was being put back in the van Chris came out with an amplifier under his arm and said

'Ted, get back upstairs to the manager's office mate, You've got some Performing Rights shit to fill in.'

Brilliant, just what I needed. I went dutifully up the stairs and the manager produced a PRS form and a pen and left me to it. Chris came up to find me struggling several minutes later.

'We're ready to go, come on.'

I explained I was trying to fill it in as close to the truth as possible, but I was never sure who had originally done some of the songs we were covering.

'Forget it. Make something up like you usually do.'

There were posters on the office wall for forthcoming events and a performance of 'Elijah' was upcoming. The last half dozen songs on our play list still left to be name-tagged were staring at me from the blank paper. For no reason that I have ever come up with since, I attributed them to Elijah and The Goat. Chris thought it was a hoot. We left the form on the manager's desk and trotted downstairs to the van. The usual moans and groans of "come on, get in" and we were on the road again.

Once Merv had played his last gig we got together to start thrashing out what brand of music we might move onto and the subject of our change of name came up. Chris said,

'That's easy. Ted's already come up with it.'

Had I? When was that then? Chris was becoming less a roadie and anyway more a manager and spokesman lately so the rest of the band listened to his insight into which direction we should be heading.

'Let's listen to this Taj Mahal album I bought. There's some good stuff on there. Keep the guitar based stuff that we recently added and look for other material along a heavier Blues based sound. Now you aren't tied to an agency you're going to have a few weeks to get a new playlist together while we look for an alternative source of work. If that's the sound we're agreed on what's wrong with 'Elijah and The Goat'?'

After a few chuckles from Pete, Phil and Dave the guitarist, they had a few minutes tinkering about with the old Stones song 'Paint It Black' and lengthened the middle section with an instrumental where Dave was given free rein. He got an Indian sitar feel to his guitar and improvised around that, ending up with eight minutes of song that was slotted into the second half of our proposed set.

'What do you reckon then?' asked Chris.

'I like it,' said Pete, 'it sort of tells you that we play progressive rock without giving the game away completely.'

Perhaps the longest sentence Pete uttered in all his time in the band. So it was agreed, Elijah and The Goat it was to be. In the following two or three weeks we learned songs by Fleetwood Mac, Steppenwolf, Taj Mahal, Joe Cocker and adapted a few other standards from bygone days to be able to get back on the road again.

I found myself having to get to grips with 'Good Times, Bad Times' and 'Communication Breakdown' from the first Led Zeppelin album rather than the Wilson Pickett, Sam and Dave and Otis Redding songs that were more suited to my vocal range. Somehow we managed to get 'Love Story' and 'My Sunday Feeling' from Jethro Tull to a standard that the lack of a flute in our line-up wasn't a problem. One practice night I took along an album by Taste called 'On the Boards' and we rated it big time. We did six or seven tracks off that album and 'What's Going On' will be the first song played at my funeral. Rory Gallacher was a genius. Typically underrated by the public, but if you know your music, you know he was the man.

28. Amen

I promised you another story about Amen Corner didn't I?

It was a Thursday evening (again!) and we had a gig in Cardiff at a Jewish Boy's Club. Howard's contract gave us an address but we had no idea where that particular part of the city was, so we left Melksham as soon as we were able after finishing work and prayed it was nearer to Newport than Swansea. Sod's law was proved once again as it turned out to be on the far side of Cardiff and we were pretty close to being late by the time we pulled up outside our destination.

We were fairly confident we were in the vicinity as about a dozen blokes between sixteen and sixty appeared from the red brick building in dark suits, with lots of hair and big hats. They were not keen on starting up a conversation so we wandered into the hallway of the place from whence they came and lo, before us, was a shining light. It was over a notice board with our name on it, indicating we were due to play there that very evening.

We found a caretaker who let us into the large room that passed itself off as a youth club. There was a low stage to the right of the door and a couple of trestle tables to the side with various soft drinks and assorted chocolate bars and crisps. Clearly we were in for a dry night if we stayed on the premises throughout. Nick was 'excused duties' as far as humping the kit in from the van was concerned and sent on a recce to find the nearest boozer.

Our late arrival meant we had virtually no time for a sound check and absolutely none for a run through of any of our new material. Young children started arriving within minutes and an alarming number of grown-ups percentage wise. I mentioned the age profile probably for the only time in the telling of these stories for good reason, which we'll get to later. One of the younger grown ups introduced himself as the youth leader and we sorted out running times and so on, then ran the two hundred yards to the nearest hostelry for a couple of swift pints. Welsh beers back then were an acquired taste and I don't remember whether it was Hancock's or Brain's or some other brand that's been lost in the midst of time and mergers but I do remember the journey back had to be negotiated at a reduced speed due to the unpalatable nature of the bitter I now had on board!

We changed into our stage gear and my white suit made one of its brief appearances. I had it made for thirty quid in Leslie's in Bath. He had a boutique in Northumberland Passage and the eponymous owner, who was in his fifties and batting for the other side, measured your inside leg even for a tie. Fair play he made a good job of it, the suit that is, and his hands were warm when he did the measuring as I recall. The big problem was the colour of course. It showed every mark, plus the ultra violet lights in several of the clubs we visited made me appear to glow. After about three months Mother had the bright idea of having it dyed bottle green and took it into the local cleaners. It was returned with an apology but no hard cash. The colour was uniform at least so I could still be seen in it, but bottle green it was not! Mother said it was lovat, (I had to look it up for the spelling) but I told her I didn't love it, but as I had laid out thirty notes for the bloody thing I wasn't going to chuck it out without a fight!

Anyway, back to the Jewish Boy's Club. The youth leader was getting anxious about us getting on with the playing side of things so we obliged. We rattled through the hour and a quarter scheduled for our first half and after bringing the volume down a tad early doors it went very well considering. There were plenty of Jewish teenagers in, based on their appearance, but the ratio of one grown-up for every half a dozen kids put a damper on proceedings. The boys were huddled in one corner, the girls in another and apart from a couple of the adults venturing onto the floor for a brief jive that was it.

A steady stream of customers made their way to the trestle tables and stocked up on fizzy pop and confectionery, so the people serving there were kept on their toes. Once we took our break we had a choice, risk the beer up the road or have a bottle of Coke and hope it didn't get back to our mates at home. I chose the latter.

The trestle tables were staffed by two matronly ladies of indeterminate age with their hair securely pinned on the top of the head and honest to God they had white aprons too. Very attractive look in the mid Sixties evidently. Just the 1860s not the 1960s!

As they were busier during the break they were ably assisted by a young girl with long raven black hair. She was obviously very shy and hid her face from view as much as possible by looking down and hiding behind her mane of hair. As I ordered my Coke and Mars Bar from one of the matrons I caught her sneaking a look at yours truly stood there in my white suit. Perhaps they had some subtle ultra violet somewhere and I was glowing. Perhaps she had a sort of St Bernadette moment and thought it was Himself come to show her the true path. Whatever. It was time to get back on stage for the

243

second set of forty five minutes and hope that Phil hadn't spotted her too!

As we gathered up our motley crew from around the room, the door opened and in walked two young men. Quite a few of the girls (and boys) squealed in recognition and rapidly crossed the floor to pin them to the wall just to the left of the stage. We had to get on with the business of knocking out a selection of sweet soul music, while trying to coax a few more onto the dance floor, plus try to put a name to the familiar faces to our left. Phil had the answer.

'That's Blue Weaver and one of the saxophone players from Amen Corner.'

'What the fuck are they doing here?' said Merv.

Checking out the competition perhaps or maybe they were members? They didn't look qualified somehow. Although maybe 'If Paradise Is Half as Nice' was a religious song but Radio One DJs never sussed it. By now we were at that point in the evening where Merv was due his instrumental showpiece so I let him have his moment in the sun and, happy days, there she was.

I asked her to dance and despite the dark looks from the grown-ups, the young Jewish lads and no doubt Phil, we took to the sparsely filled floor and proceeded to dance. Merv was far better than average as far as keyboard players went and it was obvious from the attention he was getting from the left hand side of the room, that Amen Corner's organist was realising he was up against it. Merv switched from keyboard to vocal dexterity as he ripped into 'I Put a Spell on You' and as the tempo slowed I risked a snog.

Now you know why I mentioned the age profile at the outset of this story! Once she lifted her head and that mane of hair parted to reveal her extremely attractive face I suddenly had doubts about how old she actually was!

Fortunately the couple of dozen chaperones were on hand to ensure nothing serious occurred and one tentative kiss later, her first without a doubt and I had convinced myself she was sixteen and not to worry. Then I got back on stage and we finished off the set. The guys from Amen Corner had made their excuses and left just before the end and we broke down the kit and loaded it into the van ready for the journey home.

Off we trundled through the streets of Cardiff on our weary way home when someone spotted a Chinese fish and chip shop still open!

'Let's get something now, rather than wait until the bridge,' said Nick.

We piled in and as there were seven or eight of us the waiters rushed to push a couple of tables together and shuffle chairs. We sat down and scanned the menu in a card holder on the table top. We all shouted our orders at once and a waiter nodded and smiled a lot without writing anything down. He disappeared into the kitchen.

A bloke in a suit who looked like he was the owner came over and asked where we had been and where we were going. He didn't need to ask if we were a group. The van was parked right outside his door. His English was reasonable and we had a brief conversation with him, then he asked if we wanted any drinks. Coffee? Tea? Coke? Our smiling, nodding waiter returned and we decided on coffees, five black two white. Still no writing.

Our food arrived. Every one of us had exactly what we ordered. Perfect. Nick was impressed.

'I never expected him to get that right did you? We were all talking across one another and how he got it sorted I'll never know!'

We tucked in and demolished the food in no time flat. Our waiter returned with the coffees. Five white two black.

29. From Mel To You

How did we manage to get gigs in the post Howard days? Well we still had access to the local residencies that we had built up since the early days, so that kept us ticking over. The gigs at the Corn Exchange in Devizes had been taken over by a different promoter and he was looking to expand his outfit. His name was Mel Bush and having booked us as support to some band or other, he had a chat about how we were coping since we had changed our name and style. We admitted we were struggling, so he offered to use us to 'buy and sell' groups that he wanted to put into local venues. As we had two venues in Melksham we could use our influence on, we continued to do one Wednesday in four, while he would 'buy' in bands from across the country to fill the other three. In return, he would 'sell' us to whatever region those bands' agencies covered, giving us six gigs every month, anywhere from the South of England to the Midlands and East Anglia. As he ran gigs in Devizes a couple of nights some weeks, we had those returned favours to pick up as well. Once we got out there showing what we could do, word of mouth provided some more interest and we were soon out and about almost as much as before, with the added bonus that, with the odd exception, we no longer had to go over that bloody Bridge.

So who did we play with, when we worked for Mel, particularly at the Corn Exchange? I can remember three that stick in the memory for different reasons.

On a Friday night, it was generally a chart name and we backed the Bonzo Dog Doo Dah Band when 'Urban Spaceman' was about number 10. They were a strange bunch, I only recall Neil Innes as being talkative. Viv Stanshall was on a different planet and the rest of the band just ignored us basically, even though we were sharing the same stage.

One Wednesday midweek gig we supported 'Eire Apparent', who rather pretentiously billed themselves as Jimi Hendrix's Eire Apparent, although I was never too sure of the provenance of that attribution. They were Irish, as you might have imagined, and as different as chalk and cheese compared to the Bonzos. They greeted us like long lost friends and we got on famously. Their brand of hard rock was pretty full on and the crowd loved the sound. We liked the slower, heavier version of the old Everly Brothers' 'Price of Love' they did and I persuaded the lads to give Bob Dylan's 'Highway 61 Revisited' a similar treatment a couple of months later. We played with them again at the Guildhall in Portsmouth and they appreciated the homage we had paid them.

Probably one of the biggest nights ever from those Corn Exchange days was a Friday night when we supported our old friends 'Amen Corner' (I told you they would cross our path again). They were at No1 with 'If Paradise Is Half As Nice' and as the place was packed with fourteen hundred, the majority of whom were screaming girls, Mel decided to use some pallets to construct a miniscule stage in the far corner of the hall, to the side of the normal stage, for us to play on. 'Amen Corner' were on a balcony that overlooked the dance floor. This was not normally in use and, quite frankly, the band would have been better served fighting the fans off at ground level because playing up there in the Gods played havoc with the acoustics and their sound was just

248

a blurred mess, and loud at that. Still, the punters were happy. Mel must have been happy with the takings too.

It was one of Mel's Friday gigs, when we were just watching rather than playing, when we dropped in to see 'Fat Mattress' and renew our friendship with Noel Redding.

People often say 'It's a small world," don't they? Well if we had the Wednesday night off when one of Mel's 'buys' was on in town, we would go down to see what he was buying, to gauge where we were in the pecking order, if you get what I mean. Clearly, he wasn't going to get a lot of joy if he approached some London agent and said, "have you got a hundred pound band I can have? Oh and here's a forty pound group you can take in return." So the bands we saw were on the same rung of the ladder as we were and, as with any musicians, you take a look, form an opinion and then either think they're crap compared to yourselves or how good you must be if two agencies rate you as equals.

So who did he trade in for us? In November '68 when we had only just started this buying and selling business we went to the Cons Club to see a blues band called 'Gethsemane'. They had a fairly standard line up with the guitarist suddenly switching to a flute for a couple of numbers late in the second half that made me take more notice of him. Up until then I had thought they were a fairly ordinary blues band but, because I watched him more closely, I recognised him immediately when he appeared on TV about a month later. Surprise, surprise, he had joined Jethro Tull. It was Martin Barre, the guy they brought in to replace Mick Abrahams. That did our self esteem no harm at all and Dave kept an eye out for anyone talent spotting a guitarist for several months.

Perhaps a year or so later, a band called 'The Blossoms' were in the Cons Club and, to be fair, they seemed to go through the motions a bit, they were good musicians and the lead singer/guitarist had a good rapport with the crowd. We went up and had a chat with them afterwards and I asked how things were going. The singer was non committal, but looked across at his mates and then said they wouldn't be playing as 'The Blossoms' for much longer. He left it at that and I assumed there were internal problems in the band. Christ, we knew about that. Then, on Friday week, Chris came round to pick me up in the van on the way to a gig somewhere and asked if I'd seen 'Top of the Pops' last night? I shook my head, they rarely had the bands we featured in our act on the poppy shows. I concentrated on 'The Old Grey Whistle Test' to find where the next act we should be covering stuff by was at.

Chris continued "It was that band we saw down the Cons last week, only they weren't called whatever it was, they were called 'Christie' and did some awful pop song they reckon will be number one." It was 'Yellow River' and Jeff Christie was the guy who told us they wouldn't be 'The Blossoms' much longer. A pity really because as 'The Blossoms' they could still have had some credibility. Although they were doing it by numbers the night we watched them play we recognised there was some real musicianship there, then they go and sell out for a hit record, with a crap song into the bargain. Ah well!

The relationship with Mel Bush was fairly short lived unfortunately. I've no doubt you know the name. He was described in an article as 'The Man Who Hired the World'. He'd been in a group himself back in the dim and distant past. They were 'The Four Specs' from Box, a village between Bath and Melksham. He was the drummer in the original line up, but he recognised he wasn't up to much so became their manager. A name change to 'The Gonks' ensued, associated with the cuddly toys that came onto the market in about '61 or '62, no doubt an early indication that Mel had that certain something, an eye for the main chance that sets the top entrepreneur apart from his contemporaries. You also don't want to be shy of trampling on a few people if you want to reach the top. Mel never had any problems on that score allegedly.

The time we spent working with him was beneficial to both parties. We travelled more widely than before and got some really interesting and prestigious gigs under our belt, thanks to his buying and selling policy. We did quite a few college and university venues.

I remember a Saturday night in Bristol for the Union where they had us supporting Shakin' Stevens at the Anson Rooms. Shaky was about eighteen then and just at the start of his career. When we finished our opening set 'The Sunsets' took to the stage. Shaky was nowhere to be seen. Listening from the side of the hall we wrote them off as old hat. Don't get me wrong, they played Rock 'n Roll as well as any band I've ever heard before or since. Someone in the audience had a pop at me when he saw me shaking my head and walking away from the stage.

'What's up mate, can't stand the competition? They really played that song brilliantly.'

'Of course they did,' I replied, 'they should do, they've played it for long enough.'

That was our gripe with a lot of older bands we played with. If you take 'The Sunsets' they had probably formed in what, 1958, and hadn't moved on at all. Virtually every song they did was from the Rock 'n Roll era, so after say eight to ten years practice they sounded tight and professional. We had always moved with what was in vogue and so the turnover in our play list was massive. We tried to add a couple of new numbers every week if we could get the time to practice. Inevitably, this meant we had a few rough edges on some songs when we tried them on an audience for the first time.

Meanwhile, back at the Anson Rooms, Shaky was introduced on stage. Boy did that change the atmosphere! He went on to play the young Elvis on stage in London some time later and from what I saw that night it was no contest. 'The Sunsets' backed him note perfect as you would expect, Shaky had all the moves, the women were standing at the front of the stage drooling. He was the dog's bollocks, credit where it's due, but I still didn't like the music.

How had we amended the stuff we were playing from those early post Copperpot days? We had ditched 'Dust My Broom', 'Statesboro Blues' and 'Diving Duck Blues' by 'Taj Mahal', a couple of numbers off the 'Taste' album had gone too. The second 'Led Zep' album had given us 'Whole Lotta Love' and 'Heartbreaker'. 'Black Sabbath' gave us 'Behind the Wall of Sleep' and 'Thank Christ for the Bomb' by 'The Groundhogs' had offered up some great tracks.

I think I heard Tony McPhee first on John Peel's programme, bought the album, looked at the sleeve and saw Ken Pustelnick. We had met in Bristol when he drummed with the 'Deep Six Blues Band'. Yet another recruit to a big name outfit from the same rung of the ladder as we were on. I took the album along to a practice night and we got four or five songs down before we went home. We held off using them until after the next practice and added them to our play list ready for our next trip around the college circuit.

While we were still in Mel's good books we were booked to play at Bath University, just the job for us as it was only down the road. It was a Friday night and as support band we were put on a tiny stage in the Small Hall. The full sized stage in the Large or Great Hall (or whatever it was called) was reserved for 'The

252

Groundhogs' and 'Shakin' Stevens and The Sunsets'. Exactly. You couldn't make it up could you?

We now had a slight problem. This was the first time we had played with a band whose material we covered. What should we do? Take five good new songs out of our repertoire and cobble back together the memories of songs we had discarded as past their sell by date? Or should we risk it and assume they wouldn't know since we were some distance away from the Hall they were due to play in? Bugger it, we decided to pick the three we considered we did the best and strung them together right in the middle of our set. 'Ship on the Ocean', 'Rich Man Poor Man' and 'Eccentric Man' and just introduced them as 'songs you may hear later from one of the best progressive outfits on the music scene today.' Fair play to them, if they did hear we'd ripped off their material they never said a word.

In case you were wondering, 'The Sunsets' did pretty much the same act as before. The only thing that made it different was that the students in charge of the stage lighting etc. overdosed on the dry ice and you could only see the group from the waist up. Shame really, because it took about ninety percent of Shaky's act out of sight. Some might say this was a blessing, I couldn't possibly comment.

I mentioned that our time working for Mel was brief. Well, I've got to hold my hands up and admit that was my fault. If you read any literature about the Mel Bush Organisation you soon realise that instead of some massive number of people beavering away for the main man, in fact it's pretty much always been him and his sister. We talked a lot on the phone when she rang with details of gigs and met many times at the Corn Exchange where she was generally on the door, taking the cash in the kiosk in the foyer.

Whether she knew that I fancied her I have no idea, I'm not even sure if Phil and the lads knew. So I wasn't too upset if she rang me at work, or if I had to ring up to see if there was any work in the offing. This was what the split with Mel was about in the end. Although we had some gigs through our local contacts and follow ups via the work we had got through him, there was a dry patch and we needed to be working more regularly. I phoned to chat to him, but either he wasn't there or he didn't want to speak to me. Instead of being my normal placid self, something had happened, perhaps a bad day at the office, and I ripped into his sister about the lack of work coming through. Inexcusable I know but what was done was done. The line went dead. Mel rang some time later and announced that we had reached the parting of the ways. I never got the chance to apologise to his sister and my chances, if slim to none before, had been kicked completely into touch.

Of course, in a way, that was the catalyst for his future success. In Mick Gold's 'The Man Who Hired the World' article he tells how Mel became disenchanted with groups and management.

The promotion side took over full time and by the mid Seventies you could see MBO at the top of lists of tour dates for Elkie Brooks, David Essex, Elton John, Mud and many others, an eclectic mix, let's face it. He's had Vanessa Mae and Myleen Klass under his wing since! In 1974 he hired Wembley Stadium for 'Crosby Stills Nash & Young', Joni Mitchell and The Band, you need some balls to bring those sorts of gigs off. A successful career, enough to have a few quid put by to buy your own football club if you wanted to, he bought Weymouth FC in case you wondered. (All the time I knew him I had no idea he liked football.) A way down the ladder from Chelsea or Man U but the potential on the South Coast has always been untapped. Who knows? The thing with

Mel is he knew a thing or two about promotion. (I can't believe I put that in. That was terrible.)

The lads were a bit pissed off with me for a while after that episode, but we couldn't feel sorry for ourselves for too long, we needed to work, write some of our own material and get some tracks down to hawk around the record companies. It was about this time we first met Al Read and his role in our search for the Holy Grail is documented later on.

30. Money, Money, Money

We had a fairly happy relationship for most of the time with our Bristol agency. In the end we upset Howard because we dropped from an eight piece soul band to a four piece heavy metal band, but circumstances dictated that. We had a few money issues of course. All bands had problems with agencies hanging on to their money for as long as possible! Merv had set up a bank account in his local Lloyd's to handle our incoming cash (meagre) and outgoing hire purchase commitments (substantial) but there were no overdraft facilities. On two or three occasions the manager, one Arthur Chapman, rang Merv at the solicitors where he worked and enquired whether any cash was available which would avoid him having to return a cheque marked 'insufficient funds'. We already stretched the patience of anyone receiving the cheque in the first place by post dating it, making sure the words and figures disagreed or failing to sign it. Sometimes all of the above.

On the first occasion, Merv was able to tell him that we were out that evening and a 'little something' would be deposited the following lunchtime. Happy days! When Arthur was on the blower again in a week or so, Merv explained that we had done three or four gigs in Wales and all of them had been the dreaded 'cheque to the agent'. Arthur was not too au fait with the pop music world and wanted some money paid in or the cheques he had would be bounced back from whence they came. Merv gave him Howard's number and suggested he rang and asked the same question we had asked every month for the past year or so.

Arthur made the call. Perhaps the three senior partners were out on business and a minion took the call from this well spoken elderly gentleman. A polite request for the transfer of funds from their establishment to Merv's home address at their earliest convenience. Whatever it was, it did the trick, and we were back in Arthur's good books and hadn't defaulted on an HP payment.

What probably proved to be one of the early 'black marks' against our name which finally led to the parting of the ways was the third occasion Arthur felt the urge to return a cheque due to the precarious nature of our bank balance. He didn't phone Merv to find out how we were fixed cash bookings wise in the coming days, but rang the agency and asked to speak to Howard direct. He felt he knew enough about the music business now to tell Howard in no uncertain terms what a cad he was, making us travel hundreds of miles, at all hours and in all weathers, then not recompensing us for our efforts for several weeks, even months. Arthur felt this was 'not cricket old bean'.

That went down like a lead balloon and in Bristol the following Saturday night when we were in Downend, we had a surprise visit from Howard. He handed Merv about eighty quid and said " I think this brings us pretty much up to date. Do me a favour, Keep that poxy banker off my back!"

We had a fairer selection of cash and cheque gigs for the next year or so, which was nice. Whether some agents kept their cash under the mattress away from the taxman and didn't want too many questions asked by the 'establishment', who knows?

This brings me back to our times working for the Kray's entertainment agency in and around London.

258

Work which Howard got for us in spades after our doing the gaffer a big favour on our first trip to the big city. We played at a large pub in Welwyn Garden City supporting a country and western outfit, who were good at what they did. We thought they were pants of course. Not what we called rock 'n roll.

The beer cellar doubled as a changing room and we piled in there to change out of our stage gear after the gig. We were joined by a bloke who was dressed in a dark suit, had a crew cut and was almost as wide as he was tall. And he was just shy of six feet! He had appeared from nowhere, as the pub manager had showed us where to set up our kit, where to change and what times we were on, so who was he we wondered. He asked to see our contract for the evening and Merv handed it over without a murmur. Not daft our Mervyn! He then put his hand into his inside jacket pocket and withdrew a wallet. He counted out the stated amount as per contract and Merv signed a receipt.

'Thanks lads. I'll tell the boss you done a good job again tonight.'

With that he was out the door and we were left to our thoughts. Nick and Dave were just beginning to get their breathing under control after thinking he was going to bring a shooter out of his inside pocket. Merv was wishing he'd signed his proper name on the receipt rather than 'John Champion' which was our standard signature for paperwork of that nature. We had a couple of beers to steady the nerves while we watched the other band's set, not to get through what they were playing without throwing up you understand, but to allay the thoughts which had you thinking about the type of business other members of the said boss's family had been involved in! As we drove back home that night, any motorway bridge we saw on the short stretch of

259

Motorway we had to travel seemed to be calling out our names!

In reality, it was one of the best relationships we ever had with an agency. We played in Ilford in a club on a Friday night, which was a bastard to get to because of the traffic and we were as close to being late as made no difference. Wynder K Frog was virtually resident there according to the posters, so we reckoned our soul sound would be spot on for the clientele. It was and we had a full house by the feel of it, but we were probably punching a little above our weight that night. The reception was condescending rather than warm I remember and the women, many of whom were little crackers, gave us all a wide berth, even Phil. Which made a change. Ah well, lose some, lose some more!

We didn't have a visit from 'The Management' chap that night, the DJ passed over the readies I think and we made our way home to Wiltshire in the early hours, somewhat chastened by the experience.

There are several reasons why the Lewisham Town Hall gig sticks in the memory. We had arranged to travel up early once again to get some shopping done in Carnaby Street and the King's Road. I bought some rather fetching dark glasses (to go with my by this stage lovat green suit) and a suede jacket that I wore until it practically fell off my back many years later.

By the time we had trolled around the boutiques and done some people watching, then fed our faces in a Wimpy (Oh please! No need to scoff, we weren't blessed with a fast food joint on every corner like today you know!) it was time to pile into the van and head off to the venue.

A very imposing building it was too. Naturally, the caretaker lived miles away and didn't fancy turning up until he had to, so we had time to kill before we could get the kit in and set up on the stage. We wandered up and down looking for a decent pub without much luck, then most of the group retired to the van to sit and wait in the warm, some having a fag.

I was determined not to go on without something to loosen up the old vocal chords. Even all those years ago, believe it or not, the roads were manic, especially around six to half past on an early Saturday evening. So I just kept heading on up the road, precariously crossing over various junctions until I spotted a pub down a side street. I chose the quiet saloon/snug rather than the public bar and ordered up a pint and whisky chaser, then sat down in the corner opposite the door.

Having demolished these before the barmaid had had time to check my money was genuine before committing it to the till, I went back for seconds. The public bar was busy and rowdy and as I stood looking over the barmaid's shoulder I saw several pairs of eyes staring menacingly in my direction. Time to make a swift exit on any normal occasion, but having started to order another couple of drinks I felt disinclined to leave before I'd finished them.

The outside door opened and some early evening customers entered. Two couples, early thirties perhaps, the women wearing lots of slap and cheap jewellery. The men suited and booted. Clearly regulars, they were welcomed with a warm smile from mine host, something I never realised she had and they remained at the bar, drinks in hand, engaged in conversation. I didn't need to earwig what they were saying because I was obviously the target. At the end of every comment one or more of the group would look over to where I was sat. Accompanied with a sneer from the males and a giggle from the females. I think I've got that the right way round!

The penny had dropped long ago that 'outsiders' weren't welcome in this part of town but I wasn't prepared to give up just yet. Firstly, my throat needed more lubrication. Secondly, my money was as good as anyone else's and if I chose to drink in their pub dressed in grey trousers with twenty four inch flares, a striped Ben Sherman in autumnal colours and newly purchased shades they could like it or lump it! So after a quick check of the clock over the bar to see if I needed to get back to the Town Hall I set about getting my two companions down my neck as soon as and returned to the bar to get some more in. Viewing time at the zoo was now over and I was allowed to get on with getting myself merry without interruption. Still never got the barmaid to crack a smile in my direction though.

When the clock ticked round to a quarter to eight I drank up and left, only attracting a glance or two as I made my way carefully across the room. I made it out of the door into the street without incident and breathed in the cool night air. Big mistake! I was some way down the road to being bollocksed!

Anxious faces greeted me when I arrived back at the venue. Some were the lads wondering where the fuck I'd been for so long, others from the large crowd that were now in the hall who doubted my ability to climb up onto the high stage let alone anything else! I was shown where our changing room was and somehow got my suit on. "Let's get it on!" I said.

Merv announced our arrival on stage with the opening bars of (you should know by now surely?) Otis Redding's 'I Can't Turn You Loose' and we were off and running. Much of the evening is a blur it has to be said but with hundreds of people dancing the night away it went surprisingly well. After the first set was over a DJ played some tracks and I sat in the changing room with a couple of the lads making sure I didn't slope off to the bar which was at the far end of the hall. The rest returned with their drinks, then Nick handed me a Seven

Up and asked for the few coppers back he had laid out for it. Terrific! Just the ticket!

During the second set I found time to check out the significant number of females in the audience and without a word to the group, leapt from the stage and disappeared towards a group of three lookers dancing on their own, handbags on the parquet, who looked like they needed a fourth to even up the numbers. I asked if I could dance with them and they blew me out pronto. Rather than slink back to the stage hoping no-one had noticed I headed across the hall and another group of three girls materialised, one of whom grabbed me by the arm and invited me to join them. Merv had kept things going with his usual contributions but I thought I ought to climb back up and do my bit. I was trying to tell my dance partners that I had to go but my words were snatched away on the 'Night Train' and when I got back on stage and turned around having retrieved my microphone I found three girls clambering onto the stage still keen to carry on dancing!

There were no bouncers to throw them back in those days so I was stuck with them! Rather than see me struggle to dance and sing at the same time, Merv introduced 'Green Onions' and another eight minute instrumental meant the crowd had to suffer me gyrating with a not unattractive female, plus her two companions Lanky and Dumpy who were bopping away on the other side of the stage in front of Merv's sizeable organ. His Hammond of course! What sort of show did you think this was?

After the song had ended I thanked our dancing trio and the crowd gave them a cheer as they climbed down to remain at the front of the stage for the rest of the performance. Clearly one of them wasn't going to let me get away so lightly! Once the set was over everyone was keen to crack on with getting the kit stowed away in the van and start our journey home.

The three girls were still hanging around. Lanky and Dumpy were soon aware there were no takers so they gathered up their coats and bags and pootled off. My dance partner was saying her goodbyes to them and I was stringing along, on the off chance. We were now outside the hall where Chris our roadie had moved the van while we were finishing our set, to make the loading up move a tad swifter. The side door was open! Happy days!

Needless to say I have no recollection of the full details of what happened thereafter. The booze taken on board earlier, the passage of time between then and now and the fact that these stories are more about 'the journey' for the various versions of the group than salacious items for your titillation. At any rate any serious goings on were curtailed after about ten minutes by Nick, Dave, Chris and probably a couple more banging on the side of the van and asking me to get a wiggle on.

'Hasn't she got a home to go to?'

So we emerged from the van, not to raucous applause, but to the sound of the back doors being flung open and kit being thrust purposefully into position. I said my farewells and off she went into the night. The journey home was uneventful, all of the band members in the seats in the back nodded off fairly quickly and I stayed awake and kept Chris company. We were in Hungerford before he made any comment.

'It's your own fault they were pissed off.'

'How come?' I asked.

'You should have persevered with the first three. They were quality. If you could have kept them interested until me and Ralph got there we would have all been in the back of the van and them buggers would have had to wait!'

So those were some of the gigs provided by the Kray agency. Hard to remember how long we got work off them. At least a year maybe longer. Contracts arrived. We travelled to the venues, mostly very good venues too, we played our sets and the management paid us the cash agreed. Every now and then either our friend from Welwyn Garden City or another muscle man arrived to slip into the changing room or wherever after the gig. As these were nights where contracts specified 'cheque to the agent' he was on hand to collect the dues from the venue, make sure we didn't convince the manager that it was indeed cash, but also to let us know that we were required to keep it 'honest'. As long as we played ball the work would be regular and reasonably rewarding.

None of these venues ever had any trouble. No fights on the premises. No drunken behaviour from the patrons. Groups we played with, either as top billing or support, always played sensible set lengths which always kept musicians happy. Nobody had a bad word to say about the agency. It begged the question whether the venues were paying for more than the groups being booked in, a little protection money perhaps. Who knows? From our point of view it was a 'win win' situation.

Why do these things never last? I don't recall the venue for what turned out to be the last gig we got from the Kray agency, but we were contracted to play for a couple of hours somewhere in the London area. It was a late call from Howard and we had to get there for the Friday evening, with gigs he had arranged in Wales on Saturday and Sunday. Because it was short notice there was no contract. Howard told us it was thirty, cheque to the agent. We were in need of some cash for the petrol and food required for the weekend and possibly a bed for the Saturday night for the chosen few to ease the cramped quarters in the back of the van! Bummer!

We did the gig and the manager came across and chatted about how much he'd enjoyed the music. "Who wants to come and sign for the money?" he asked. Phil was off like a rat up a drainpipe. When he returned he had the cash in his hand, but he said we had a problem.

'He paid me fifty!'

'Didn't you tell him it was only thirty?' asked Merv, adding that Howard had told him it was cheque tonight anyway.

'Don't be a prat,' said Phil, 'this will be a bonus for tomorrow and Sunday. We won't be chipping in ourselves for fuel and grub for a change.'

Nick was the only one who was concerned about the financial misunderstanding. He reckoned we should give twenty back to the bloke, saying he had been mistaken, in case the muscle men were despatched to break our legs, or worse, give us a 'home of our own' somewhere along the motorway system.

Merv and Dave the guitarist were more interested in whether Howard and/or the Kray agency had been pulling a fast one and booking us out for far more than we had been collecting. We didn't know whether the venues had the same contract as we get posted to us, we just assumed they were the same.

Whichever way round it was, we travelled home, did the Welsh trip and returned to Melksham tired and weary, late Monday morning. Merv had a call from an irate Howard before lunchtime giving him a bollocking about picking up cash, when he had told him it was cheque.

Merv suggested we may have been stiffed. Howard never got us any more gigs from the Kray agency. Whether he had been duped as well we never discovered. It was probably another of the little black marks that went against our name and finally led to us going our separate ways.

31. Homeward Bound

Some time ago I mentioned that we always seemed to bump into someone who was on his holidays or a few sandwiches short of a picnic, if we stopped to ask for directions after arriving in a town or city looking for the venue for that night's gig. Just like today you can never find a copper when you need one. Well just to reinforce the feeling that 'it's a small world', one evening I shall never forget was a trip to Swansea University. Not for Howard, this time, but either Mel Bush or Al Read. It was late Sixties, maybe even 1970.

We drove down in the late afternoon. It was a horrible grey, drizzly day and we were pootling along on a ring road that, according to the directions on the contract we had been given, should take us to the Main Hall but we saw no one for half a mile in either direction. Chris was getting twitchy as the appointed time for our arrival was getting close.

'Fuck me! This is a city for crying out loud. You'd think there were would be some bastard around we could ask!'

Then up ahead we saw a young chap in a duffel coat, hood up and head bowed against the strong wind and rain.

'That's got to be a student,' says I, winding down the window, letting the rain blow into the back of the van.

'Oi shut the fucking window you sod!' shouted Dave or Phil or both.

I was more intent on asking the student where the venue was than worrying whether their hair was getting blown about.

'Excuse me. Can you tell us where the Main Hall is please?'

The student turned towards the van window, smiling and said "Of course I can Ted. Hello lads. I'd have a lift with you, but it's there about twenty yards in front, on the other side of the road."

'Hello Hugh!' I managed. 'What the fuck are you doing here?'

Stupid question wasn't it. Obviously, he was at Uni. We travel bloody miles from home and the one bloke we bump into is a lad who, when he was about thirteen, used to come up to the youth club and watch us practice in the early days. In fact he was the next door neighbour of Brian the drummer who didn't quite make it before Malcolm joined.

He went on to say he'd seen the name 'Elijah & The Goat', had heard about our changes while at home during the holidays and thought he would come down to see what we were like these days. He'd told his mates to get down there tonight too as he assumed we were pretty good, based on what he had heard in the past.

We had no idea who we were playing with as the contract just specified where, when and for how long and that we were doing two forty five minute sets. Hugh informed us we were supporting an American band called 'Daddylonglegs'. We hadn't heard of them so we were keen to hear what they were like. I guess forgettable would best describe them, a country rock quartet who played for an hour and had less people watching them than we did. Honest. Of course, all Hugh's mates were there when we were on, so that made a difference.

You can never find a copper when you need one, did I say? The opposite of course is always the case. We'd had a few brushes with the law although nothing serious. Those long Welsh trips used to be knackering, especially if it was a weekend away and you were likely to get home on Monday morning just in time to be dropped off at the factory gate. That happened more than once, as an old boss of mine recalled when I bumped into him last winter. He had his son with him and told him that I sat glassy eyed at my desk all morning, wearing the same clothes as I had had on all weekend, unshaven, and worse than useless on the work front. Lunchtime would come around and I was off home for a clean up and a change of clothes. Sleep would have to wait until later, usually about three o'clock in the afternoon. Happy days!

One Monday morning we were on the approach road just on the Welsh side of the bridge. Phil was driving but was struggling to stay awake and Nick was sitting on the engine cover (it must have been the old J2) and shouted at him when he strayed over into the fast lane.

'Take over Nick,' said Phil.

'I'm bushed.'

So, still doing fifty or fifty five mph they tried to swap places and naturally the van was not keeping in a straight line. There were no other vehicles stupid enough to be on the road at such a god forsaken hour so there was little danger. Nevertheless, we heard the brief noise of the siren and then the cop car overtook us. They flashed at us to stop and we pulled on to the hard shoulder. We'd practised the routine before, but this was the first time we'd put it into action. As our drivers had always had a few bevvies we worked out that if we all piled out of the van on the nearside, with seven or eight of us confronting them, they might have difficulty identifying who was actually at the wheel. We had all seen the US cop shows, so we had a plan. We would then

271

'assume the position', that is legs apart, hands outstretched above our heads, strung out along the side of the van. Childish, of course it was, but it was a laugh, so why not?

The two Welsh patrol men approached us.

'Hello boys. Having fun are we? We followed you for a mile or so and you were weaving all over the road. '

'Yeah, we saw you in the mirrors and thought you looked lonely out here with nothing much to do.' said Merv.

They checked the van out, then gave up the identity of the driver as a lost cause. They declined our invitation to follow us over the Bridge and have breakfast, so we all piled back in and Nick drove us on our way.

Being two up in a jam jar was probably okay, if your mate was a decent sort, but alone no wonder they got lonely. The reason I mention that is because of two coppers we met on separate occasions, when they were working on their own at night. One was a village bobby somewhere between Swansea and Cardiff, the other was a motorcycle cop just outside Minehead. The first was on another night of wind and rain in Wales, a miserable night to be out and about, whether in the van as we were, or on foot as this poor old sod was. I remember we had been playing in London the previous weekend and had dropped into Carnaby St and the King's Road in the afternoon to do a bit of browsing, maybe buying too, and I had picked up a psychedelic pink card with really fancy script that invited whoever read it to 'Piss Off'.

I thought it would look just the ticket attached to one of our speaker cabinets and so that's where it was, on a speaker cabinet in the back of the van. Without realising it, or so he swore afterwards, Chris had stacked it so the card was slap bang in the middle of the back window. So there we were, minding our own business on the way back from Tenby or Haverford West, bombing along towards Cardiff, dreaming of being at home in bed, rather than stuck in this van with the rain crashing against the windscreen virtually all the way back when, as we drove through this small village with terraced housing right on the road's edge on either side, doing more than the legal limit without a doubt, suddenly a figure appears from an alleyway and signals with a torch beam straight in Chris's face that he would rather like us to stop.

A screech of brakes and a groan of protest from those in the back, rudely awoken by the sudden movement, and we were stopped by the side of the road. An elderly policeman, who must have been only a few days away from his pension, approached the passenger side of the van. When I wound down the window, he shone the torch into the back, then along the three of us in the front seat and asked,

'Where have you been tonight then lads?'

We told him our itinerary for the past three nights spent in his wonderful country and he was most impressed. He then wanted to know,

'Where are you going back to then?'

We told him the other side of Bath, thinking he was unlikely to know where we lived, even if we had told him.

He was in no hurry to let us on our way and, thankfully, the rain eased off for a while so when he wandered off around the front of the van checking our tax disc and that our headlights etc were in order, Dave and Nick in the back wanted to get out to stretch their legs. So we all got out onto the pavement and wandered towards the back of the van, to meet up with chummy when he had finished chatting to Chris and checking licence and insurance details. We arrived just as he had turned his attention to the back window of the van.

'You've got a lot of equipment boys, haven't you?'

Then his torch beam moved to the left hand side of the van and we saw the card on the speaker cabinet revealed in all its glory at the same time as the policeman. The beam moved on briefly and then returned to the card.

'Not very nice that boys is it?' he chuckled. 'Have a safe journey home then.'

With that he wandered back to his hideaway in the alley and prepared to resume his lonely vigil as the rain started to come back down again with some purpose. We got back into the van, gave a final wave to the village bobby and, keeping within the speed limit, drove on through the streets and on towards the Bridge.

'Why the fuck did he stop us?" chuntered Phil. 'He couldn't prove we were speeding, our van was OK and our documents. What sort of an offence was displaying a card that read 'Piss Off' anyway? Whose idea was it to have it in the friggin' window?'

I sat in the front keeping my head down as the flak was flying back and forth. I reckoned he stopped us because he was bored shitless stood there in the rain, no trouble on his deserted streets, no traffic for ages probably. We came along and he thought it would kill a bit more time of his shift, so as much as anything he stopped us for someone to talk to.

The second bloke was a different kettle of fish, far too clever to be riding around on a bike. He laid out his bait and trailed it along under our noses daring us to take a bite and then he got us hook, line and sinker. We had just pulled up the long drag out of Minehead after playing in a hall in the middle of town. When we were doing a weekend in the West Country we had stayed overnight in there more than once. The caretaker came back about nine on the Sunday morning to lock up after us. This time we were going straight home. We passed a lay-by on the top of the hill on the other side of the road and he was sat on his bike, facing away from us, apparently looking out over the valley, back towards the lights of the town.

Chris spotted him and said,

'Copper'.

We were struggling up the hill in second so there was no danger of being done for speeding.

'Why worry?' I said, "he's going the other way.'

Chris reminded me that he had three pints during the evening and kept an eye on his rear view mirror.

'Bollocks! Here he comes.'

Chris slowed down as matey swept past and indicated we should pull over. He parked up his bike and walked slowly back to the van. He took his big gloves off and undid the breast pocket of his jacket. We waited for the note book to be taken out but he just ambled up to Chris' window. Chris wound down the window and rested his arm on the glass, with his right hand across his mouth to try to block any alcohol fumes from reaching Easy Rider's nose.

After the usual preliminaries of licence and insurance he looked into the van, past Chris' conveniently placed hand and saw four faces staring back passively.

'Where have you been playing tonight then lads?' he asked.

A bit of a pointless exercise really, since we had just come up the Minehead road and there weren't many options in town apart from where we had been playing and Butlins. We told him where we'd been.

'Oh yes. I know it. Many in tonight?' he continued.

There was a chorus of voices all with around about the same estimate of how many there had been in the audience. It averaged out at the best part of a few.

The conversation was a little more friendly in nature now and he suggested that, being in a group, we had the pick of all the young girls, especially the pretty ones. Phil was the first to jump in with both feet and agree, saying there had been several stunners there tonight and very friendly they had been too. A couple of others chipped in with complimentary comments about the local groupies. He seemed eager to pursue this angle and said,

'I guess you get a lot of young girls throwing themselves at you in your line of work? It must be difficult to tell how old they are sometimes, when they're all dressed up too?'

Someone said, 'If they're big enough, they're old enough.'

That got a laugh all round, on the inside of the van that is. The motorcycle copper started to turn away from the window and then looking back over his shoulder he said,

'My fifteen year old daughter said she was going to the dance in town tonight. She's big for her age. I hope you didn't take advantage, for your sakes.'

It all went quiet inside the van. Chris started her up and we drove on up the road towards Bridgwater. The biker had turned around and headed back towards Minehead.

'She was that big girl in the white dress,' said Phil.

Well that was a relief, I'd clocked her too as she walked across in front of the stage. She was statuesque if you were being kind, or built like a brick shithouse if you weren't. If she was only fifteen, she was the same in years as she was in stones or thereabouts. She was never at risk, her dad needn't have worried.

32. Sex, Drugs & Rock n' Roll

Everyone's heard that phrase I guess and I've no doubt there are some pervs flicking through the pages looking for a detailed description of all the women that came my way over the years. Well you'll get no cheap thrills here pal. For one thing I've been married for nigh on forty years and I ain't going to own up to a load of 'previous' to be taken into consideration. For another, the close on one hundred and fifty girls involved never did me any harm and if I don't dish the dirt on them, then hopefully I'll avoid reading about myself in the Sunday rags. Ivan the bass player with the 'Argonauts' was right though when he said,

'One thing about being in a band, you never go short.'

What about the drugs then? Well I've never even smoked a fag, let alone any weed. We came across people who did smoke dope, some who popped pills and some who were obviously abusing chemicals on a daily basis, but I never felt the inclination. A few beers and the buzz of performing to an audience were all the things I needed to feel I was having a good time. We were all pretty much the same, any of the various band members. One guy had a joint now and then, no names mind, but apart from driving his car into a ditch on the way home from a gig one night and us catching up with him in the van, to find him sat there giggling unharmed, he seemed to be able to take it or leave it.

How on earth did we avoid all the pitfalls that await the young band members of today? They were there, no doubt about that. Perhaps what has changed since those days is that us 'hicks from the sticks' were sheltered from the worst excesses. Today, the drugs are everywhere, not just the big cities. We would get back home from big bad old London, where you were on your toes all the time looking for a potential problem, and we would be in a rural setting that hadn't changed a lot since the war. It had changed some, but only slowly.

The next twenty years saw communities fragment, the family unit start to be eroded and all those venues, on virtually every corner, were gone. There was nowhere for the band I managed in the mid Eighties to play, not without travelling miles. Then they were straight into 'bandit country', no chance to learn the ropes with six or seven venues in town, to audiences that knew you. If you get put under pressure to hack it in a hostile environment, or to keep up with your mates, then bang! 'Try this, it will make you feel great and play better.' Bollocks, too many casualties mate. I'll have a beer with you though just to show there's no hard feelings.

On a lot of gigs we didn't get a contract, certainly not the local ones, or the residencies, but it was normal for Howard to send through a sheath of them to Merv for the gigs we did for him in Wales and the West Country. It was useful to take along, for details like the actual name of the venue, the location, how long we were due to play and more importantly, whether it was cash on the night or cheque to the agent.

When we were moving further afield and he was involving a second agency, the contracts didn't always turn up in time for us to get hold of a copy. There were a couple of problems caused by this right at the end of our time with Howard and because of our habit of 'making a day of it' we were blissfully unaware of them.

Some bands had a reputation for being unreliable. Even with our track record on vans we could not be accused of that. We rarely, if ever, let anyone down by not arriving at all. We may have been late a few times it's true but it was on the way home we broke down. Sod's law. Agencies in and around London had obviously had some real bad experiences with 'no shows' so they devised a 'cunning plan'.

The first gig we realised something was going on was the Wirrina Ballroom in Peterborough. Phil was keen to leave at about one in the afternoon so we could get there by six at the latest. We had been told seven was the time when the hall would be open to get the kit in but, as usual, he wanted to practice and thought we might be able to find the caretaker and get him to let us in early. So we drove up via Northampton and arrived in plenty of time. The caretaker was about doing some chores, so we unloaded the van and set the kit up. We had a quick run through of a couple of numbers and Phil was the only one who wanted to carry on. The rest of us wanted to have a wander down into town, find a pub, then get a bite to eat.

With Chris and Ralph on roadie duty that night, there were nine of us altogether as we walked into town. There was a really nice pub a couple of hundred yards down the road so we all piled into the bar. There were more of us than there were already in the boozer, but the landlord took one look at our clothes, hair and how many of us were still under the age of twenty five and said,

'Sorry lads, we don't want you in here.' Charming!

When we were back outside on the pavement, Ralph suddenly took a wedge out of his pocket. He'd been paid at lunchtime just before Chris had picked him up. When he wasn't humping our kit about he was grafting and it was a tidy sum.

'We'll have a bit of fun with this bastard. See how he likes this.'

He swung the bar door open again and strode in waving the notes in the general direction of the landlord.

'Just because they're young and you don't like the way they look, you think their money ain't good enough. Well, these boys spend big and this is what you turned down. No problem, we'll go somewhere else and they'll have their best takings of the year!'

That took the smile off his face. Ralph came outside and we found another pub and had a couple of beers which we paid for ourselves, Ralph's money had to last all week, so the vast majority went back into his jacket pocket.

When we walked back up to the ballroom, there were two vans parked outside, alongside ours.

'Bloody hell,' said Chris, 'they must have some kit if they need two vans'.

As we walked through the foyer to the bar we saw a bunch of lads in heated discussion with someone who looked as if he was the manager. We didn't take a lot of notice, it wasn't any of our business. We just got a beer and headed to the dressing room to get ready for our first set.

When we came back out again a couple of minutes before we were due on, a band was just finishing setting up their kit. We said hello, had a quick chat and then we were on for an hour or so. We didn't get to talk to them again until the very end of the evening. Chris asked what the fuss had been about earlier and their lead singer said it was a mix up, according to the manager. Another band had turned up saying they were booked to appear here tonight, but the bloke told them,

'Sorry lads, you must be mistaken, I've got the two bands I need. Have you got a contract, something in writing to say this is where you're playing tonight?'

They hadn't so he'd sent them packing.

The penny didn't drop that night and because we kept turning up early on these longer trips we were okay for a while. After a Friday night in Wales, we had a long slog to Gillingham in Kent. I don't know if we left later that afternoon, but it was the Grand Prix weekend at Brands Hatch that did for us. The traffic was horrendous and it was only a practice day for crying out loud. We were a good forty minutes late getting to the gig. A burly bouncer on the door was letting the punters in when we walked up the steps to find out where to unload the van.

'Can't be here tonight lads,' the bouncer shrugged, 'both our bands are here. Where does it say you're here? You got a contract? See a poster with your name on can you?'

We swore it wouldn't happen to us again but it did. Some agents had got fed up with bands letting them down. So they booked three for the big venues and it was the first two to show that played, the third went home. We arrived as early as we could from then on, but it was a shitty system loaded in the agents' and venues' favour.

33. True Colours

When we started out we had a fairly limited range of material, confined to Chuck and Bo and the British bands we liked, who cut their teeth on the same music. So Stones, Kinks, Yardbirds, Animals numbers were the bread and butter on 'The Krowat's' menu. When we got bitten by the Soul bug these songs were confined to the bin and new heroes took their place. When we played at the County Hotel in Taunton one Wednesday night in 1967 we found we were on the same stage as 'Savoy Brown' and 'The Pretty Things' were topping the bill.

We'd covered a couple of their minor hits, which we felt never really caught the mood of what they must have been like 'live' back in the early Sixties, so we were looking forward to hearing them play. When we got our kit set up on the stage we recognised Dick Taylor and Phil May from the early pictures we had seen in various pop publications. We never got the chance to chat to them particularly, apart from brief hellos and nods, as we fitted bits of kit in between theirs. They were obviously pretty pally with 'Savoy Brown' and the two pro bands mingled together, leaving us to get on with it.

One bloke stood out from the crowd of musicians. He was about 6ft tall and very thin. His legs, in skin tight blue jeans and cowboy boots, looked like pipe cleaners. He wore a T-shirt and one of those fringed cowboy jackets. On his head, over his long blonde hair which was half way down his back, he had a stetson with a feather in the brim.

In the centre of the dance floor, immediately in front of the stage, was some scaffolding, perhaps ten feet high. We wandered over to the bar, having done our sound checks, and got a beer. The management had given us the times of our two sets; start the evening off for an hour, get out of the way so 'Savoy Brown' and 'The Pretty Things' can do their thing, then close the evening off with a further forty five minute set. We stood at the back of the hall and chatted about the bands we were supporting and tried to work out why there was this scaffolding in the middle of the room. Were they decorating the place and couldn't be arsed to move it? Were there going to be TV cameras in tonight? We didn't come up with any reasonable answers.

After we had played our set 'Savoy Brown' were next up and they were a really tight unit, playing older style Rhythm and Blues. We stood and watched them pretty much all the way through their set. I spotted the tall thin guy wandering over to the scaffolding and carrying some equipment and nudged Merv in the ribs.

'What the fuck do you reckon that guy's doing?' I asked him.

Merv was convinced he was a photographer. The bloke had climbed to the top carrying some kit, which wasn't easy in those high heeled boots, but he got there eventually. Whatever he was doing up there wasn't visible from floor level, so we were none the wiser when he clambered back down the rather rickety structure.

In the interval, while 'The Pretty Things' were getting the stage ready for their act, thin guy was back, looking as if he'd either had a few, or taken a short cut to getting where he was at, with some artificial substances. This time it took even longer to get up to the top of the scaffolding. We got to the side of the hall to get as good a view as we could of both the stage and our mysterious friend and saw he was sitting cross legged in front of the bits of equipment he had taken up. 'The Pretty Things' began to play but he was off in a world of his own and never lifted his head to look in their direction. The penny dropped as the opening chords of the first number had hit our ears. When I dragged my eyes away from trying to fathom out what he was doing up there, the light show that bathed the stage in psychedelia had begun its magic.

We'd heard about them but never played with a band that used one before. I think what confused us initially, was that this was 'The Pretty Things'! We had always associated them with R&B, with being the wild men of rock, particularly since the Stones had gone all commercial on us. Having said that, it was sensational. The light show lifted the overall effect of their performance, for me at least. A memorable set, and if the bloke in the feathered stetson had been coherent when he eventually came down from on high, I would have told him so too. Sadly he was off with the fairies and I had to get back on stage to finish off the night with some Otis Redding, William Bell and Eddie Floyd numbers.

Considering the number of gigs we played over the years, it was surprising that the only other band we backed who had a light show were the Scottish group 'Tear Gas', who we played with at the YMCA in Bath in '69 or '70. A totally different type of show theirs was, with lots of cartoon characters and World War I tanks. Whether it had anything to do with the songs they were playing, I never found out, as their accents were so strong I couldn't make out a word they were saying.

34. Didn't We Almost Make It This Time?

If you asked me which of the top names we played with was the most ignorant, it would be a toss up between Georgie Fame and Ginger Baker. It's been well documented why that may have been the case at various times in their respective careers but' as my old Mum used to say' it doesn't cost anything to be civil'.

I've already told you of the night we played with Georgie Fame at Ross on Wye. The gig with Ginger Baker was in Weston Super Mare at the Winter Gardens. It was after the days of 'Cream' and when he had his 'Air Force' on the road with Graham Bond and a couple of girl singers, but people like Steve Winwood and Rick Grech had moved on by the time we played with him. They had probably worked out it was going down the tubes and they were right. I've always told people that 'Zoot Money' was on keyboards that night, but it may be the memory was playing tricks on me. Speedy was there again on drums and he was still smiling and chatty as before.

The other bands on the bill were 'Van der Graf Generator' and 'Juicy Lucy'. The former were a progressive rock band similar to ourselves and we traded punches (in the musical sense you understand) to establish who was actually bottom of the bill. It was a close run thing on the night. I thought we edged it but they lasted a bit longer than we did in the harsh light of day. As for 'Juicy Lucy', I felt their agent should have told them to change their name if they wanted credibility, the same as ours had when we had suggested the 'Double Decker Donut Band' as an alternative to 'Heart 'n Soul'. Musically, they were OK but I couldn't see a concept album coming out from a band with such a jokey name. We played with them in Bristol, supporting 'The Groundhogs' at another college gig and, much the same as on that night, they stayed in the dressing room drinking and smoking, refusing to talk to anyone else, whether it was the support band or the top of the bill. 'Big time Charlies' was what Nick called them, and he was a pretty fair judge I thought.

When it was time for Ginger Baker to take to the stage, there was a lengthy delay as kit was moved around. His drum kit was only about half set up while we had all been playing. More gongs and cymbals were put in place and eventually he appeared at the back of the stage, looking like death warmed up as usual. He led his assortment of musicians on and had a quick bash and crash to get warmed up. Considering what gods we had thought him Eric and Jack had been, what followed was a shambles. Musically it lacked direction and purpose for me. On the drums Ginger was superb. Despite whatever havoc he had wreaked on his mind and body, his drumming was still brilliant but the songs they played were instantly forgettable, only showing brief glimpses of the musicianship that the band members obviously had in bundles.

After they had finished playing and filed off to luke-warm applause from what, admittedly, hadn't been a large audience at any time during the evening, we waited at the back of the stage, to get a word with the great man. We didn't wait long. A leggy blonde, about half his age, and a cracker to boot, put his leather jacket around his shoulders and they walked straight towards the back door of the building straight past Dave and Phil who were paying him handsome compliments, more than for any other musician we ever played with. What a pair of brown nosers they turned out to be! He never acknowledged them or gave them a sideways glance. He was out the door, into his Jensen Interceptor and had driven off back to London before you could say 'bastard'.

Not all of them were like that. Some of them were like your best mate within a couple of hours of meeting them. Most were just ordinary blokes with an extraordinary talent for singing or playing a musical instrument.

When you spend the majority of your time on the road with a handful of people, you don't have the luxury of a circle of friends, like normal people. You keep different hours for a start and you can't commit to playing a sport, as Malc discovered. Relationships are the next thing to suffer, because you need someone special to put up with you being unavailable four or five nights a week, when you are up to a couple of hundred miles away from home in some cases. Do they believe you when you say it was a quiet night, and no I didn't get off with any of the women there, do they buggery. If you take them along then the other lads get pissy, because they feel their hands are tied. If they have a sudden urge, or it's offered to them on a plate, they can't do anything because your missus will dish the dirt as soon as she gets back. We did take our ladies along to local gigs on many occasions, the more the merrier, but you could bet your bottom dollar they would want to get home early or something to just take the edge off the night.

One thing was guaranteed. If you had your ladies with you, there was more available crumpet than you saw at that venue before or after. Bearing that in mind, the next time you went back, you made sure they didn't come along and, you've guessed it, it was a bird free zone. It happened every time without fail.

Starting up when we did, it was Germany that was the Mecca for new groups to aspire to, for obvious reasons. The Beatles had gone there and it hadn't done their careers any harm. Of course, once we had heard the truth about what a shit-hole most of the venues were and how mind numbingly boring the days were while you weren't playing, the attraction wasn't quite so great. Dave and the rest of 'The Argonauts' put us off making that journey - even if we'd been asked, which we weren't.

We did get one invitation, very early on in our days with Howard's agency, to go to Belgium or Holland for a weekend festival. If it had been a beer festival we would have gone regardless of the money, but it was a music festival. Negotiations over our fee were protracted for some reason or other, and from Merv telling us it was a 'definite' booking over an Easter weekend, as the days and weeks dragged by in February and March, it became a 'definite maybe' an 'almost certain' then a 'possibility' and eventually 'what booking?' I remember him turning up late to a practice evening, to break the news grudgingly. I was livid. I kicked out at the nearest piece of furniture, a chair, which skidded across the floor and thudded into the legs of the sister of a mate of mine. Gary had a clothes shop, where I bought loads of stage gear and they'd dropped in for a natter before we got stuck in for our practice session, and left pretty smartish, with the sister being another who crossed me off her Christmas list. Shame too, because she was a looker, and although she was out of my league, I still hoped I was in with a shout. Fat chance after that.

If you remember Rich and the Vick incident from the New Forest well, he had a mate who worked on the QE2, as a purser or something. He lived locally and, like Rich, he too had an MG Midget. So while we were bombing about the country to gigs and sundry social engagements in the assorted sports cars in and around the group, this guy tagged along during one summer, probably '68, and hung around into the back end of the year too.

Our roadie Chris always had an eye for an opportunity and one night suggested our switch to progressive rock had opened up a brand new market. He was convinced British bands were going to go down a storm in the States, playing the sort of material we did. As we were in a relatively quiet period after finishing with Howard, and Mel Bush was only just starting to get us work, we had no real obstacle to prevent us looking in another direction.

One night when we were hanging out in a country pub, chilling over a pint in their beer garden, Chris asked this guy if he would suss out the possibilities of us getting gigs in the States, when he was in New York on his next stopover. At this embryonic stage of our rebirth as a four piece band we had no demo tapes and thankfully no publicity shots, so I think that although he agreed to give it a go, our new chum was thinking this idea of Chris's might be a trifle tricky. Little did we know that after he jacked in his roving life on the ocean waves, he would start his own business, making a small fortune into the bargain, when he discovered he had the sort of talent in sales that enables people to sell sand to the Arabs.

We were picking up more work from our local contacts, plus some from Mel Bush, so we didn't see the guy until a month or so later with an update on his progress. He came to a gig one night with Rich and said he hadn't had much luck on his first stopover. How many nights he was in New York I don't know, but he just trawled around a few bars and made enquiries, asking barmen and customers whether there were any clubs with live bands in the area, without a lot of success. So on that trip he gave it up as a bad job and just had a few beers instead.

This last trip, however, had ended up with him and a few mates going a bit further afield in a taxi to find a bar away from the bright lights. What they hoped to find he didn't elaborate on, but one barman they talked to was into the music scene and gave him directions to a club where rock groups played virtually every night of the week. All local bands, nobody top flight but a regular crowd in to watch their act.

He persuaded his mates to go down the block with him to find this club, paid to get in and watched some pretty dire rock band for a while. He asked for the manager and, using the skills that later made him a millionaire by the time he was thirty, talked us up as the next 'big thing' to come out of England. By the time he left the club, we were booked for one night at eight hundred dollars, the date to be agreed in a couple of weeks time when he was next in New York. Not only that, but the manager agreed to put him in touch with other venues in the city and provide him with contact numbers for the college and university circuit. Our guy could get representatives to come to the club on the night we played and see whether they wanted to sign us up and give us work.

Why this club manager was bending over backwards to help us, who knows? We never found out who he was. We had a snap decision to make. Get our gear and ourselves out to New York for this one gig. If the contacts came good, we might be on the road in the States for the next couple of years and who knows what could have happened from there? A couple of us were up for jacking in our jobs and taking the risk. The others were either married or getting there and were less inclined to take the leap of faith. So in the end we thanked Rich's mate for his efforts and told him to tell the club manager thanks but no thanks. We never saw him much again after that, perhaps he was miffed. Perhaps we missed our one 'big' chance. We'll never know now will we?

35. You Can Call Me Al

I've trawled through the early years with Martin, our first manager and mentor, for some anecdotes that might be of interest and recounted the hectic schedule that Howard set for us as we criss-crossed the map looking for soul venues to visit and the all too brief period with the 'man who hired the world' Mel Bush, who helped us make the transition from soul to hard rock less painful. Which leaves us with only one guy whose influence shaped our lives during the late 60s and early 70s. That was Al Read.

We had a lot of work on the college or Uni scene in '68 and '69, where it all came from I can't remember. Some would have been during the last rites with Howard, some with Mel and no doubt we had a few we fixed up via personal contacts we had made at gigs originally booked through the agents. Whichever it was, we were playing at a Bristol college and a chap called Mike Tobin approached us to book us to appear at The Granary Club.

The Old Granary was in Welshback and was originally a jazz club. Monday nights were a bit quiet so Mike and a few mates had started to hire the venue to promote Rock music at the end of '68 and had built a reputation for the place. It went on to become a major venue on the national club circuit. Loads of top name bands played there. After our first gig, Mike introduced us to one of his colleagues in the enterprise, Al Read.

After almost a year promoting the Granary gigs, they had progressed from being a group of lads interested in music, light shows, art work and anything creative into the 'Plastic Dog Agency'. They were an irreverent bunch of long haired hippies who drifted into something which appealed to us after suffering the mainstream, old style agencies. They were young like us, not middle aged or ancient like most agents, and seemed to have access to exactly the type of venue that our music was suited to. The Granary was right up our street and we loved playing there. Whether it was Mike or Al who first put the idea forward, I don't know but we were in and out of there on one Monday night a month for the next year or so. We liked to think of it as another residency.

Our first gig there in December '69 was with 'Tea and Symphony'. When we arrived there were a few technicians from the BBC mooching about and it was obvious they had been recording a jazz session for some programme or other. When we found what passed for a dressing room, we came across an elderly guy with a trumpet. He said 'Hi' and carried on putting his gear away, just chatting to Dave and Phil in what sounded like an American or Canadian accent. It suddenly dawned on me it was Maynard Ferguson. I was too late to stop Phil putting his size ten's in it, by asking the guy if he was a session musician. Frosty? You could say that.

We set up our gear on the small stage and wandered along to the Old Duke for a couple of beers. This was our local on Granary nights, nothing wrong with the beer in the club itself but the ambience in the Duke was better. When we got back to the Granary, we filed in the front door, past a long string of kids queuing up the stairs to get in for the night's entertainment. The long bar on your right as you went in was filling up and was bathed in light. The hall itself was dark and dotted with small tables for the punters to rest their glasses. Not too many seats around. On a balcony at the entrance end of the club, immediately opposite the stage, was the DJ and the light show. The atmosphere was building. We played an hour of our brand of hard rock to an appreciative crowd. 'Tea and Symphony' followed us with their individual brand of musical theatre, they were a motley crew.

We thought we dressed 'out there' but these guys were out there and then some. The crowd filled out in the hall as they took to the stage, leaving the bar mostly empty. This meant we could avoid the dash to the Old Duke for a refill or two, so we got a beer and went up on the balcony to watch their set and also have a natter with the DJ, Ed Newsom. He had introduced us onto the stage from his lofty perch and as he hadn't seen us play he was a little uncertain what to expect. Once he had heard us and was aware Mike and Al were looking to get us on board on a regular basis, he wanted to come up with something specific to bring us on to. While we were trying to make out what it was 'Tea and Symphony' were about, Ed and Phil had their heads together, deep in conversation about possible intros.

We left Ed with a few ideas and he got things ready for the interval. Once 'Tea and Symphony' had closed their theatre down for the evening, we were back on for about forty minutes to finish off the evening. True to form, as the main band departed so did a lot of the kids and we played out the last few songs to a rapidly emptying club. Even the bar staff were putting the cloths on the taps. What happened to last orders? Just one more pint please? Oh how times have changed. It was still only just after half past ten. Still it made for an early night. Back home by midnight if we were lucky. Stop in Bath on the way back for a pee and pray the chippy was still open. After we had got the kit down and ready to lug down the back stairs to the van, Mike and Al came over for a chat.

It had gone well, they were happy. We were happy. We looked forward to returning in the New Year.

What I remember about our next visit can be written on a postage stamp. It was in the middle of January and we supported 'Marsupilami'. They had a rather elegant flute player. Her I do remember. There was a lot of impact to their sound with hard rock, this disembodied flute and even some poetry thrown in. They were very much a 'student' band for me. Probably got loads of work in colleges and universities where style scored over content. I couldn't see them doing Working Men's Clubs somehow. We would play anywhere. This stamp is bigger than I thought. My memories of those early days in '70 are sketchy on where we played other than at the club. I had started seeing a new young lady on New Year's Day and she was prepared to put up with the 'I can only see you this Tuesday and next Thursday' routine, so it was obviously destined to be an important relationship. Reader, I married her!

One midweek gig she came to, probably the first, was at a club just outside Bath, right on the river. This was the end of January I guess and the winter rains had caused flooding all around the area. The flood waters had gone down about a week or so before, but the smell lingered, so did the marks half way up the walls where the water had reached. All the carpeting was in a large soggy pile in the car park. It was a club we frequented a lot while we were working for Howard in the mid Sixties. They had a basic menu in the small restaurant area to enable them to serve alcohol later than normal pubs and clubs, which made it a good place to join. If we were playing in or around Bristol on a Saturday night we would drive back through Bath and drop into the club for a late drink and a dance with the bevy of beautiful females that sort of establishment attracted. It made the night a bit longer, but what the hell.

Strangely enough I don't ever remember actually playing there before. This occasion may have been because it was their first night open after the flooding and we were available and prepared to work cheap. Who knows?

We also did a college gig in Bristol around this time, maybe March, where we were backed by a band made up of students. Presumably, from the wild applause that greeted every number, they were supposed to be studying at that particular college. They were not that great to be honest, but they did have a rather attractive young girl playing sitar. Not too many of them in bands, even in the late Sixties, early Seventies, sitar players I mean, not attractive young ladies. As I was backstage chatting to her, while she nervously waited in the wings for her stage debut, Pete reminded me once again of his maxim 'True to one, Mister, true to one.' Fair enough. I wished her luck and went to the bar with Pete to have a couple of beers.

We went back to the Granary in April with Liverpool Scene. Andy Roberts the guitarist was the standout performer for me. I've never been impressed by Roger McGough but at least he was someone I had heard of. Being a cultural philistine I had never heard of Adrien Henri and after his performance that night I doubted I ever would again. In May it was 'Warm Dust', who we'd supported before. In fact Mel had booked them into one of our residencies in town so we were nodding acquaintances. The singer was in the group 'Ace' later, then 'Mike and The Mechanics'.

It was about this time that Pete decided he wanted to play drums in a band that did more commercial numbers. (I saw him about five years ago still doing 'Thin Lizzy' and 'Status Quo' covers. Not for me thank you).

They say that lightning doesn't strike twice, don't they? Bollocks. We had our first lot of colour photos done in town about six weeks before Pete came out with this bombshell. None of us saw it coming. I can still get a giggle out of those publicity shots when I show them to my kids. I was wearing a maroon hat, had extremely long black hair and a beard! I was wearing an orange grandad vest and dinky little dark red waistcoat over bright orange crushed velvet flares. I had bought these in Carnaby St some months before and I was so taken with them I wore them on stage at every opportunity. The other three lads were similarly hirsute and sartorially challenged, but we were in a band so it was expected, alright?

We didn't have far to look for a replacement for Pete. A drummer from a Trowbridge band called 'The Profiles', who had packed up some time previously, was ready, willing and able to come in virtually straight away. Pete had been a pretty good drummer, whether on the Soul music or the heavier stuff, but Paul's style was as close to Keith Moon's as anything you would be likely to see, so he added something extra.

'Plastic Dog' were unsure 'Elijah and The Goat' was a winning name, so they asked us to consider a name change to coincide with a change in line-up. We had started writing our own material by now. We were covering more 'Led Zeppelin' and 'Black Sabbath' numbers which, when mingled in with the 'Rory Gallagher' and 'Groundhogs' tunes we were already featuring, gave us a strong play list. Particularly for the type of venue Al was booking us into. While I was raiding mother's literary collection for inspiration on lyrics, I came across a piece by Byron called 'Childe Harold'. Convinced it was the answer to a maiden's prayer, I offered it up to the lads for comment at our next practice night. Not impressed. Nobody else was coming

300

up with anything, so I returned to scan the novels, poetry and reference books most of which start at 'A' so soon I was on Alexander the Great. His horse was called Bucephalus. If they didn't like 'Childe Harold' what chance did that have I thought.

The next time we got together, in the van on our way to a gig, I suggested Bucephalus as a suitable name for a progressive heavy rock band. It didn't take long for Syphilis to be mooted as an alternative that our detractors might come up with, but it was a definite maybe. In fact by the time we were on the way back we had decided it was the dog's bollocks, even if we had to explain it every gig for the next six months. 'It was the name of Alexander the Great's warhorse you know'.

Thinking back, that gig was in Lymington, a place we had played a couple of times before. We were sat in the pub up the road at half time and Chris, Dave and I were still discussing the name change. We were fantasising on the name of our first album, should it ever materialise and I thought 'Horse Power' was a good title. Dave agreed wholeheartedly and could see the front cover with this huge white horse rearing up on its back legs.

'Does it have wings, Dave?' I asked.

Dave asked why.

'That was Pegasus you prick, this is Bucephalus. It may not have been white anyway.'

Whatever colour it was, Chris was impressed and there was no going back. Bucephalus it was, a new front skin for the bass drum was prepared and after one misspelled attempt, we were reborn (again).

I don't know about you, but band names generally, were fairly tame in the early days, peaked in the early Seventies and have gone downhill ever since. We all know the blockbuster names like 'The Beatles', 'The Who', 'The Rolling Stones' and so on from the Sixties. In the Eighties and onwards we've had 'The Clash', 'The

Stranglers', 'Bananarama', 'All Saints', 'Boyzone', 'Take That', 'The Killers', 'The White Stripes'. All very ordinary don't you think?

Where's your imagination fellas? What about matching some of these names? 'Principal Edwards Magic Theatre', 'Burning Red Ivanhoe', 'Barclay James Harvest' and even our old friends 'Van der Graf Generator'. I'll leave you to think of your own contributions for a while. I'm sure you can think of more outrageous ones than I have.

We'd been back to the Granary Club during summer and early autumn of 1970, picking up more fans to our particular style of music. There were two groups of lads that came to the Club most weeks, one from Iron Acton, the other from Wotton-under-Edge. The former were a bunch of hard rocking maniacs, the latter loved the music but were a little more reserved. They both wanted us to play at venues in their home towns and we obliged on several occasions. Wotten-under-Edge was somewhere we had been for Howard, but Iron Acton was a new one on us. When we went there for the first time, the reception was incredible. Whether they didn't get a lot of live music out there in bandit country or not I don't know, but our fans from the club were well away even before we arrived. What they were on I don't know. Together with the local talent that seemed to have gone without for a considerable time and were all over us like a rash, it made for a busy evening.

We played on a very low stage, which meant the manic dancers (all males) were falling into the kit and us at regular intervals and Chris was pulling his hair out trying to keep things under control. The women were gathered in packs around the stage and as we finished our first set, it didn't matter which way we tried to leave the hall to escape to the relative sanity of the pub up the road, we were intercepted by females who couldn't keep their hands to themselves. Very nice too under normal circumstances, where were you when we needed you girls? All four of us in the band were either married (Dave definitely and Phil sort of), or engaged (Paul and me). I told you that back in January I'd found someone prepared to put up with the odd evening per week, well her birthday was in July, the rest is history and even Chris was courting strong. We had to leave the Iron Acton ladies wanting I'm afraid.

In October we went back to the Granary to support possibly the biggest band we had had to back there so far. It was 'Mott the Hoople'. They were returning to the Club with a couple of albums and singles behind them. Their latest song was 'Roll Away the Stone' which did OK, but there was another year before 'All the Young Dudes' and pop immortality. Now this is one of those 'war' stories that you may or may not believe, it's up to you,. I know what happened on the night, because I was there. It started out as an ordinary Granary evening. We turned up, set up to play our usual opening set, ready to clear away for Mott the Hoople to take centre stage and we would then be prepared to return for thirty minutes or so after their set, when people traditionally drifted off in to the Bristol night air, leaving us to finish with a handful of the more enthusiastic drinkers.

Our friends from Wotton and Iron Acton were in the crowd and Ed the DJ had finalised his selection of a number with which to introduce us. We listened to the strains of 'Also Sprach Zarathustra' more commonly known as the theme music to '2001 A Space Odyssey'. Ed invited 'Bucephalus' to take the stage, so on we went to an unusually highly charged reception. Ian Hunter and one other band member were watching alongside Chris our roadie at the side of the stage. We were going down a bomb and Dave's guitar work was probably as good as I'd ever heard it. Paul was in inspired form on

303

the drums and Phil and I managed to avoid cocking anything up and spoil what looked like turning out to be one of our best performances ever. Ralph was about somewhere in the hall, probably checking sound levels so that he could tell Chris if my mike level needed to go up because the other three were drowning me out. That was par for the course. Before he came back to tell Chris what needed to be done, if anything, he decided to pop in the gent's for a quick slash.

When he did get back he told Chris the rest of the band members were deep in conversation in the bogs. They didn't know Ralph was working with us so they weren't too careful about what they said. The drummer was now 'suffering from a virus' and someone was going to have to tell the management that Mott would not be appearing. After we finished our first set, we were going to pop up to the Old Duke for a couple as usual, but we were waylaid. Ed filled in for an extended break and after some discussion and financial negotiation we went back on and played the rest of the evening. We ran out of material with about twenty minutes to go and had to reprise several songs from the opening session. Something like that night you don't forget. Naturally, we have always told people that we blew them away and the drummer suddenly succumbing to a virus was a cunning ploy to avoid failing to match our performance and therefore avoiding embarrassment. Well we would say that wouldn't we? With the absence of a doctor's note I'm not about to change my opinion. So there you are, 'you pays your money and you takes your choice.' That's war stories for you.

In the November we had the pleasure of backing 'Mogul Thrash', another of the more interesting names. We had seen them as the 'James Litherland Brotherhood' on our travels and there were several good musicians in their line-up who went on to bigger and sometimes better things. We headlined the 'Plastic Dog Christmas Party' as well a couple of days before Christmas. It must have been a great night because evidently there were two support bands. I don't remember seeing or hearing either of them.

36. Exodus

As we moved into '71 we were feverishly writing more material and moving from practice hall to practice hall. It was the two hundred watt Marshall stacks, the wild drummer and the drowned out singer with the heavy rock songs that put the neighbours off. Heaven knows why. We had been in a youth club hall in a local village for a year or so when an elderly gentleman tottered in one evening to complain. He was a retired professor, maybe in his seventies, and said he was having difficulty hearing his television because the racket we were making was coming loud and clear through his front window. It was the middle of summer so Phil asked him if he had his windows open. Once he confirmed that indeed he did have windows open, Phil suggested he closed them and then turned his telly up. This didn't appear to be an option. Apparently, the professor was concerned about our well being, since the volumes at which we were playing were in his expert opinion 'beyond the threshold of pain'. Terrific! Just the sort of line 'Spinal Tap' could have done with to explain why eleven was on their amps.

Unluckily for us, this old guy was on the board of governors or whatever, of the village hall and we soon got our marching orders. We ended up in Trowbridge for a couple of months in an old mill building. The ground floor was the venue for another youth club and the youth leader worked at the same place Phil and I did so we got a small room on the top floor for nothing, provided we did a free gig for him on a Saturday night at some point. I know we did the gig, but why we had to leave the practice room in a hurry I don't remember, it must have been complaints from the neighbours again. Our last port of call was another village hall out towards Devizes. It was about a hundred yards from the main road and seemed perfect. The nearest houses were on the other side of a sports pitch. Surely we'd be alright here? Well possibly, but Al wanted some publicity photographs done to go with the name change. I stalled for as long as I could but we ended up in the Cumberland Basin on a cold, wet Sunday afternoon for some mean, moody and none too flattering black and white snaps, which adorned posters for our gigs promoted by Plastic Dog for a short while. But that's another story.

Back in 2003 Al Read produced a book chronicling the Granary years between '69 and '88. I bought a copy for old time's sake and later that summer the Granary website published the result of a survey, where people who visited the Club frequently over the twenty years were asked to vote on the best night of the lot. The winner was the 22nd February 1971, the only occasion that 'Genesis' appeared at the Granary. Fame soon took them beyond the club's financial limits. Just to give you some idea of where they were on the ladder of success at that time, if you took 'Mott the Hoople', they were a one hundred pounds band, 'Savoy Brown' were half as much again and the 'Groundhogs' twice as much. 'Genesis' commanded half the money that 'Mott the Hoople' did. This made us feel we had a lot in common with them, maybe one rung lower, because although our 'residency' came with a bargain price due to the frequency at which we visited the place, Plastic Dog were asking twenty five to thirty quid for us when they booked us out to colleges and universities and the like. Mel Bush was asking much the same and the bands he exchanged us with, such as 'Gethsemane' and 'Blossom' were on that level as well.

'Genesis' had just released their second album 'Trespass' and their van was already outside the back door when Chris drove our van up to the building. We got the kit in and the band was already on the stage, set up and going through their sound checks. When these were completed, Chris chatted to their roadie and started to sort out where our kit could fit in on the small stage. As the jigsaw puzzle was being put together, the drummer came down from the stage and started to talk to us. Just general chit chat about who we were, what sort of stuff we played, what the crowd were like and so on. Dave, Phil and Paul disappeared up onto the stage to sort their kit out and have a quick run through. This left us in the middle of the hall on our own. A brief lull in the conversation followed, then he said,

'I'm Phil, by the way.'

We shook hands and I introduced myself. We chatted for ages as if we'd known each other for years. He had a wicked sense of humour (still has) and we talked about anything and everything. Suddenly, there was some commotion on stage and the singer reappeared from the dressing room to remonstrate with the roadie about a bass drum. I did wonder why there was a drum right at the front of the stage totally unconnected with Phil's drum kit. Evidently Peter Gabriel was keen on adding a few extra thumps on the drum at times he thought apt during a couple of the numbers they were doing.

Phil looked at me and raised his eyebrows, shrugged and was clearly unimpressed. Once all the sound checks and drum alignments were sorted out, we went our separate ways to prepare for the night to come. We had a couple of wives and girlfriends in tow that night, including my future wife, because 'Genesis' was one of the bands tipped to be on the way to the top. When we all got back from the Old Duke it was time for us to get on stage and the girls to stand in the bar area to watch.

Ed the DJ introduced us in time honoured fashion and our set was greeted with warm applause from one of the bigger crowds we had seen in the Club. We stayed in the bar during that night and watched 'Genesis' play rather than shooting off up the road to the pub. You didn't have to be a genius to tell they had something different from the vast majority of bands around. Peter Gabriel was wearing a white outfit that looked a bit like the one Mick Jagger wore in Hyde Park. His face was obscured by a carnival type mask and as well as standing at his mike singing and using his foot pedal on that lonely bass drum, he sat on the side of the stage on a stool reciting poetry. It takes all sorts I suppose. He's not of this Earth, you know Doctor. Phil Collins proved to be an excellent drummer, much appreciated by Paul. Tony Banks, Steve Hackett and Mike Rutherford were equally blessed in the musicianship department, but just got on quietly with the playing and left the theatricals to Gabriel.

Their performance came to an end all too quickly and the crowd were so chuffed they hung around longer than normal and listened to us play out the final half hour or so to end the show. Once the hall was emptied we all gathered on the stage, except Peter Gabriel who was probably removing make-up or something, and chatted as kit was broken down and segregated into theirs and ours and removed down the back stairs to the waiting vans. My girlfriend and I chatted to Phil about our autumn wedding and our proposed honeymoon in London. He said (like you do but don't really mean it) if we could tear ourselves away for an hour or so, he usually had a beer on Monday lunchtime in a pub on the Bayswater Rd. The pub was a couple of hundred yards up the road from the hotel we were booked into.

'Come on down and we'll have a beer to celebrate your nuptials.'

October came and on the Monday lunchtime, after a morning shopping in the King's Road and Carnaby St, we arrived at the pub to find Phil and Mike enjoying the late autumn sun stood outside on the cobbles in front of the pub. Other lunchtime drinkers stood around barrels being used to hold ash trays, beer glasses and the usual assortment of empty packets of crisps and nuts. Introductions and congratulations were exchanged and orders placed for refreshers for the two lads plus a well earned drink for yours truly and his new wife. The rest of the early afternoon was passed comparing what was happening with our respective bands and although they were making progress they were blissfully unaware just how big they were later going to become. We were recording demos and trawling around looking for someone to discover us. In February we had thought we were one rung on the ladder below them. We hadn't realised that we were actually holding the ladder. They were climbing it.

We said our goodbyes and Phil and Mike went their separate ways to pack a bag, ready to be picked up later in the afternoon to go off to Germany for a few gigs. My wife and I went back to our honeymoon. We were going to go up to the top of the Post Office Tower in the afternoon, but it was closed for some reason.

Meanwhile, back at the Granary in March we had supported 'Gentle Giant'. Not a bad name, certainly better than 'Simon Dupree and the Big Sound', a former incarnation. This version was textually inspired by the philosophy of Rabelais, which marked them down as avant-garde. Despite this I thought they were pretty good.

And so to April and another name from the past crops up. We supported Da Da at the Granary and my old

311

singing partner Elkie Brooks, plus Robert Palmer, who we had seen before with the Alan Bown Set at a college gig in Bristol, where we supported them. Five years on from that Carnival gig where we had backed her, in the absence of anyone else being prepared to do it, The Elk now looked very different. Long unkempt hair and a moth-eaten fur coat replaced the mod haircut and pink jacket and mini skirt of the '65 vintage. She remembered the night in question as being one she would rather forget and attempted to do so. The dressing rooms at the Granary were basic at best and we were all in the room together, Robert Palmer a little less communicative than Elkie and Pete Gage. For some reason, high up on the wall was a water cistern apparently totally unconnected to anything in the room, which was making some horrible bubbling noises and the whiff was strong enough to overpower the smell of dodgy cigarettes. Eventually, this thing bubbled furiously enough rather like one of those natural geysers and we were showered with what smelled like boiling hot piss and we all exited the dressing room sharpish. Something else had changed from the demure Elkie I had met in '65 too, her language was the worst I've heard from a woman before or since. Happy days!

We were up first. Chris informed me just as I was getting up on stage that their roadie had suggested we needn't bother putting up our PA equipment, I could share Robert Palmer's megawatt Marshall system. Oh I suppose it will be alright I thought. With the man himself standing by Chris at the side of the stage, we started with 'Ship on the Ocean' by 'Groundhogs'. After the introduction I was glad I had taken the trouble to learn the lyrics because for the first (and only) time, I could hear myself singing. The great man soon realised he had nothing to worry about but hung around for at least half that first set. Fair play I thought, I'll return the compliment when you're on. Chris managed to work out which knob to twiddle to reduce my volume to acceptable proportions and we got through the rest of the set without any serious hitches.

As with 'Vinegar Joe' which they went on to form together, the main appeal of Da Da was The Elk and her animal magnetism, plus that powerful voice, and Robert Palmer who was just class. While with Alan Bown he had been learning his craft but he was so much better now and of course, he improved even more over the coming years. As for Elkie Brooks, I had her down as a potential casualty of the Rock n' Roll existence. Seeing her as a kid in '65, then as she was in mid '71 it was difficult to envisage the recovery she made by the Eighties and 'Pearl's a Singer' era. Just goes to show you can't beat 'paying your dues'. She certainly deserved all the fame she eventually got, even if it took her twenty years to achieve it.

The times they were a-changing. Back at the end of March, Plastic Dog had booked us to support 'Fairweather' at the Neeld Hall in Chippenham, together with a Bristol band called 'Birth'. Naturally, we bumped into the singer of 'Fairweather' and renewed acquaintances yet again. Andy Fairweather Low of 'Amen Corner' was on his last legs by this time and, as a headline band, they weren't a lot better than 'Birth' or us, to be honest. The young girls liked Andy more than anyone else on the stage that night, but we got our knickers in a twist over the billing, because 'Birth' seemed to be in Al's good books and we were no longer his first choice when he was looking to fill a spot at the gig he was promoting.

A few words were exchanged and although we appeared in April with Da Da, that was the last Granary gig for Bucephalus. How we managed for work over the next nine months or so I'm buggered if I know. I remember we did some work for a Swindon bloke whose wife had permed Phil's hair when he fancied an Afro. His hair fell out not long after and he wore a long black wig on stage for a while. This bloke was a chancer and never lived up to his promises. So a few gigs in and around Swindon and that was it.

Wherever the work came from it was regular enough. We played most weeks and although it was nothing like the madness of the Howard days, we were writing songs and recording demos and trawling the record companies so it didn't seem to matter. In August we had a visit from a guy in his mid thirties, Steve somebody, who lived up by Devizes and worked in London for what had been Warner Bros, but were now called the Kinney Corporation. He said he was an A&R man. He listened to us practising, took a copy of our recordings away and said he would do what he could. As I listened to him in the pub, where Chris and I slipped off to while the lads were working on a new song or two, I thought of the bloke in Swindon and what a fine pair they made.

It was fast approaching October and I was getting married. Some of my hair had to be lopped off. Ouch! We have never had any of our wedding photos on display in any of our houses because even after a trim it was pretty long and with a moustache as well, my missus worried it might frighten the children. Naturally, the band members were all on the guest list, plus their ladies. Fair's fair. We'd been invited to their weddings too. Because Steve had become a vital ingredient in our quest for stardom, I was persuaded by Chris and Phil mostly, to invite him and his wife to the reception. I don't think they made it to the church. We were expecting the 'good' news any day and even on that Saturday in October he could have been coming to tell us what we had wanted to hear for years. Was he? Was he fuck!

After we got back from our few days in London, where we had met up with Phil and Mike, there was still no news from Steve. We did the occasional gig and then one Friday we played in Bristol, yet another college, and he told us someone from the record company would be down there to see us. We never saw hide or hair of anybody. They were there though.

Do you remember the photographs we had done in the Cumberland Basin in Bristol around the February '71? It was a bit longer in coming this time than on previous occasions but it arrived eventually. Chris rang me at work and asked if I fancied a drink later that evening. He picked me up in the van, but he was on his own. Perhaps the lads were going to be in the pub when we got there. After all, the flat my missus and I rented was a couple of miles out of town. I wondered whether Steve was going to be there as well. Chris was quiet most of the time, so it didn't seem strange that he didn't say a lot on the way into town. When we walked into the lounge bar of the pub, it was empty.

Chris wasn't looking forward to saying what he'd been asked to say. The rest couldn't face me themselves. Guys like Phil, who I'd known for ten years, Dave and Paul who had known me for less time, but knew how much I had put into the band, both physically, emotionally and financially. A contract was on offer from a recording company but they wanted to add a keyboard player and change the vocalist. Chris said the rest of the band were offering me the chance to leave, so the new band could go pro, or stay so that we remained semi pro for the immediate future until another record company came along with a more discerning ear for vocals.

It wasn't much of a choice. There was no guarantee another record company would step in with an offer that had my name on it. Can you imagine hanging on and forcing them to stay semi pro ad infinitum? We wouldn't have lasted another six months. So I left. Chris ran me home and I got out of the band wagon for the last time. Christ, I'll have you in tears in a minute! Don't worry I shed enough that night for both of us. Going on eleven years and hundreds and hundreds of gigs and then someone decides you ain't gonna make it as a singer. Why didn't Martin say something back in the beginning, I could have learned to play the drums.

And so 'Now' were born, a more commercial name and repertoire, but who the new singer and keyboard player were I don't know and never bothered to find out. Eighteen months later after making about one pound fifty per week each on average they split up, as did the marriages of two of the band members. Phil moved to Southern Ireland to run an organic farm, after running a furniture making business near Trowbridge. What he was growing on this farm I don't know. I've never seen him since the last time the band were together before Chris gave me the news that I was not wanted on the journey. Dave and Paul stayed local and have kept playing on and off to this day.

We got together in the mid Eighties to bury the hatchet and tried to think of a bass player we could use if we got together again to do a couple of charity gigs for old time's sake. Something always cropped up. Dave's job took him to the States for three or four years, so that kicked that into touch. Time passed and although we still chat from time to time, we haven't yet finalised the dates and venues of our farewell tour.

I never sang again after 'Bucephalus'. I did some DJ work, promoted bands and cabaret acts in and around town in the Seventies. I managed a young band in the Eighties, which prompted the initial getting back together with Dave and Paul, but I never really fancied joining another band. I had invested so much of myself in the ones I'd been associated with that I didn't have

316

anything left. Was I bitter? You bet I was for several years. It wasn't just missing the singing, missing that buzz when an audience show they like you, it was the camaraderie I missed. The in jokes, the humour that all bands develop, the close friendships that are within the band, that prevent you from forming long lasting friendships and making commitments to people and for occasions outside the band.

All of a sudden I was on my own, with a new wife, with no real friends, only acquaintances, most of whom I had turned my back on over the past decade, not because I didn't want to know them anymore, but I was either in the van travelling to a gig, playing or coming back. I was either practising or going out for a drink with Chris, Ralph and the lads. I had to start from scratch. So I did. We moved onto an estate with loads of married couples, mostly without kids to start with, and we made new friends. But it wasn't the same. You can't beat being on the road.